Be All In

Be All In

Raising Kids for Success in Sports and Life.

Christie Pearce Rampone and Dr. Kristine Keane

Foreword by Abby Wambach

GCP

GRAND CENTRAL
PUBLISHING

NEW YORK   BOSTON

Grand Central Publishing
Hachette Book Group
1290 Avenue of the Americas, New York, NY 10104
grandcentralpublishing.com
twitter.com/grandcentralpub

First Edition: August 2020

Grand Central Publishing is a division of Hachette Book Group, Inc. The Grand Central Publishing name and logo is a trademark of Hachette Book Group, Inc.

The publisher is not responsible for websites (or their content) that are not owned by the publisher.

The Hachette Speakers Bureau provides a wide range of authors for speaking events. To find out more, go to www.hachettespeakersbureau.com or call (866) 376-6591.

Library of Congress Control Number: 2020933517

ISBNs: 978-1-5387-5173-2 (hardcover), 978-1-5387-5171-8 (ebook)

Printed in the United States of America

LSC-C

10 9 8 7 6 5 4 3 2 1

Dedicated with love to our favorite athletes
Rylie and Reece,
Christian, Cameryn, and Sebastian
Who taught us more than anyone that success is about being happy

Contents

Authors' Note xi

Foreword by Abby Wambach xv

Introduction: Christie's Story xvii

Chapter 1: Giving the Sports Back to the Kids 1

Chapter 2: Communication 15

Chapter 3: Get Your Head in the Game 37

Chapter 4: Accountability 52

Chapter 5: Mental Toughness 70

Chapter 6: Authenticity 94

Chapter 7: The Car Ride Home 111

Chapter 8: Confidence 132

Chapter 9: Beating Performance Anxiety 154

Chapter 10: Concussion and Sports Injury 177

Chapter 11: Slow Down to Speed Up 201

Chapter 12: The Reality of Early Specialization in Sports 213

Chapter 13: Little Sky Blue 227

Appendix A: My Coaching Philosophy 241

Appendix B: Concussion in the Classroom 247

Contents

Notes   249

Acknowledgments   261

About the Authors   267

We cannot always build the future for our youth, but we can build our youth for the future.

> —*Franklin D. Roosevelt, address at the University*
> *of Pennsylvania, September 20, 1940*

Authors' Note

Is your kid an athlete? Maybe you played sports growing up. For so many of us parents, athletics have played an important role in our lives—from teaching us to stay fit to introducing us to lifelong friends. We want our kids to love being active, engaged team players. We want them to perform well, to be winners, and to feel proud of their accomplishments. And it can be hard to know how to make the right decisions to serve our kids along the way.

We composed this book in light of our professional and personal experiences over the past two decades, playing and working with athletes, coaches, parents, and educators. Christie Pearce Rampone, America's most decorated professional soccer player, is a two-time FIFA World Cup champion, a three-time Olympic gold medalist, a professional and youth sports coach, and a sports commentator, and Dr. Kristine Keane, a neuropsychologist, clinical director of two multispecialty neuropsychology practices, and clinical director of a neuroscience concussion program, has been working with professional and youth athletes for the past twenty years. We met when we were contracted by a hospital to speak to parents, athletes, physicians, and coaches on concussion and sports-related topics. Working together, we quickly learned that we were both passionate and concerned about the anxiety-provoking and high-pressure mind-set that is so prevalent in modern youth sports. Our work led to countless discussions about family pressures, parental sideline behaviors, the increase in elite teams and training, and the stressors that often accompany youth sports.

Be All In was born from myriad hours of research; airing our gripes, fears, and disappointments as well as our triumphs about our own children; and countless conversations and interviews with parents, coaches, and elite athletes. Our book was written as a gift to our multisport children, to their teammates, and to all the kids who play sports around the world. It is also our gift to their parents and families, who do all the heavy lifting, transporting, working, worrying, and caring so much.

The *be all in* approach is about being fully present in everything you do, on and off the field, in all spheres of your life. It is an alternative to the familiar sports mind-set that is focused solely on achievements and wins; being all in means knowing what your goals are, having confidence in your training, and being fully engaged in what's happening around you. Martin Luther King Jr. said that in order to succeed, we do not have to see the whole staircase; we only need to see each step. When Christie was a child, she never played on elite or academy soccer teams. Her family could not afford the fees or the travel requirements. Instead, she played on local travel and school soccer and basketball teams, often coached by her father. She did not attend collegiate showcase camps and never created career highlight films. She accepted her first offer to play Division I basketball for Monmouth University in New Jersey, and she was later welcomed to the soccer team as a walk-on. The US Women's National Soccer Team invited her to practice via a letter she received when she was boarding a bus on the way to a college basketball game. She wasn't planning it. She wasn't pressured into it. She earned it each step of the way.

It is our hope that our readers learn alternate perspectives about how to create realistic expectations for kids, set them up for success in all aspects of their life, improve game-day performance, and reduce the stress of dealing with coaches, parents, and losses. We wrote this book because we really listened and wanted to make a difference. We are thrilled to invite you and your family to *be all in* with us on the journey.

Foreword by Abby Wambach

Since I played forward on Christie's team for fifteen years, I certainly *hoped* to be the first pick to write this brilliant book's foreword. Now that she has chosen me, I can finally relax and try to put into words what Christie Pearce Rampone has meant to me as a player, leader, and parent.

Christie and I were teammates for fifteen years, bus seatmates for a decade, and co-captains of the United States Women's National Soccer Team. Now we are more like sisters than friends. Our daughters are BFFs, and we celebrate each other's lives post-soccer just as fiercely as we ever celebrated each other on the field.

Everything I teach my kids about how to use sports to build character, I learned from Christie Pearce Rampone. I know that Christie is the correct person to write this book because every lesson and strategy between these covers was first tested on me and our national team. We were her first students and the first recipients of her brilliance.

During halftime of every game that we played for team USA, Christie and I would find each other in the locker room. I would give her my breakdown of the first half and my ideas for the second half. She would listen carefully, even repeating what I'd said back to me. Next, she would walk around and repeat this process with every other starter on our team. I'd watch her quietly absorb everything she was told. Finally, in our team huddle, right before we'd step onto the field for the second half, she would deliver our plan of attack. Every single time I was amazed, not just by her perfect game plan, but by the process she used to create it. She was—and still is—an expert at observing, synthesizing, and creating an effective plan of attack.

In her post-soccer life, it's no surprise to me that Christie would team up with sports neuropsychologist Dr. Kristine Keane to write this book. For as long as I have known her, Christie has always wanted to give back. Christie and Dr. Keane have observed and documented some critical information about youth sports. Dr. Keane provides valuable clinical insights and the scientific underpinnings of the why and how parents can help their youth athletes. They have noticed that we seem to be forgetting some of the most important things about sports: mental toughness, accountability, fun, friendship, and becoming team players. It seems that many of us are so focused on "top of the mountain" dreams like championships, scholarships, and going pro that we have lost sight of the beauty and the wisdom that comes from the climb. Because of this, we're no longer creating climbers—just dreamers.

I am so grateful that Christie and Dr. Keane have put all of their hard-earned wisdom into these pages, because now when my kids ask me, "How do I become great like you?" I can just hand them *Be All In* and say, "Here's how."

Introduction

Christie's Story

When it comes to sports, a lot of people focus on the end result. In professional sports in particular, people talk about the end results—who won, who underperformed, who pulled an incredible play out of nowhere. But what is often lost is any acknowledgment of all the hard work it takes to get to that moment. Those of us who play or have played at the elite level make it look easy. But there are countless hours of behind-the-scenes practice, tears, physical injuries, performance fears, embarrassment, and triumphs that occur every day. We celebrate the World Cup win, not the practice outside the trailer on a field in the middle of nowhere in New Jersey.

I have trophies, medals, and wins, but the most meaningful things to me are all the moments in between. I focus on the space between where I am and where I want to be. I let it inspire me. When you remain focused on your journey, the outcome you desire follows naturally.

I have had the time of my life playing soccer. I not only earned a spot on the US Women's National Team; I won a World Cup gold medals in 1999 and 2015, a World Cup silver medal in 2011, and two World Cup bronze medals in 2003 and 2007. I won a three Olympic gold medals in 2004, 2008, and 2012, as well as an Olympic silver medal in 2000. In all these world events from 1999 to 2015, our team never finished outside the top three teams. I not only played on Olympic medal–winning teams, but I was eventually asked to be captain. I played in three professional soccer leagues including the Women's Professional Soccer league, the National Women's

Soccer League, and the Women's United Soccer Association, of which I was a founding member. I have two amazing children, and now that I have retired, I share my experiences with others through speaking engagements.

In the rare event when I was not on the soccer field—when I was injured, pregnant, or caring for my newborns—I've been fortunate to return to the game at the elite level. From the outside, it might look like someone was holding my spot, but that's only illusion that comes from focusing on the outcome. When I left to have a child, and when I tore my ACL, nobody was sitting around waiting for me to come back. On the contrary, there were at least five women lined up to take my position. But each time, I fought and I trained and I exceeded every goal I set because I trained with a be all in *mentality. For me, a* be all in *mentality is about understanding the big picture of what I want to accomplish. Of course I go into competition wanting to win, but over the years I have learned that winning is the wrong goal: especially when it comes to team sports, I can't control a win on my own—there are too many other people and other factors involved. What I can control, though, is what I bring to the field. When I use practices to hone my skills, when I am confident about the team strategy, when I am focused on who I want to be on the field rather than just what I want to see on the scoreboard—that's when I do my best. That's when I leave the field proud of the results I've contributed to the team and the game.*

Now, I need to be clear on this. I want the winning outcome as much as any competitor does. Maybe I want it more. So while I have always felt strongly about fully appreciating my journey rather than just the outcome, I was, and remain, fiercely competitive. It is simply who I am. Even if you and I are having a beanbag toss in your backyard, I am all strategy. And I am planning to beat you. It's just my nature. But I have a different perspective on how to get there. My focus is always on my process, and my intention is to win.

Young athletes today are under so much pressure, and too often it's being applied in the wrong places. Kids don't need parents coaching them from the sidelines in the middle of a play; they need parents who can help them set their intentions on the car ride to the competition. Kids don't need parents who speak for them; they need parents to teach them to advocate for themselves and manage their priorities. But those skills don't come if a kid is taught that the only thing that matters is the final score. My greatest hope is that reading this book gives you the tools you need to help the athletes in your life thrive.

I have always thought that sports are a powerful place for kids to develop the skills needed for success in their adult lives—things like leadership, organization, focus, and drive. Those are just some of the skills that I know I've gained over my years playing professional soccer, and those lessons started from when I was a very young player (back when basketball was my main sport!). So before you dive into the chapters of the book that explain how to foster the skills that young athletes need to thrive, I want to show you what it looks like when those tools get tested.

In July 2009 I was pregnant with my second child. At the time, I was training with the US Women's National Team and also finishing my first season with Sky Blue FC, the women's professional soccer team based in New Jersey. I carefully timed my pregnancy so I could give birth with more than enough time to recuperate before competing for a spot to play in the World Cup. I knew the recovery would be tough, but I had succeeded before, and knew I could do it again. I would much rather recover from having a baby than from a torn ACL!

I kept my pregnancy secret from my teammates with the exception of Abby Wambach and Shannon Boxx, two of my favorite people in the world. I was medically cleared to play, but I didn't want anyone to coddle me or treat me differently. I also didn't want to hear any negative opinions about playing soccer while pregnant. My plan was moving along beautifully. My health was intact, and my playing was unaffected. Life was good.

Until I got to Rochester, New York.

A strong, stabbing pelvic pain came on all of a sudden, in the middle of a scrimmage with my national teammates. It stopped me dead in my tracks.

"I think something is wrong. Take it easy on me," I whispered to Abby, *national team forward, two-time Olympic gold medalist, FIFA World Cup champion, and no stranger to pain.*

"I got you," Abby whispered back.

During a water break in the middle of practice, I quietly excused myself to go to the bathroom. Normally, I never leave practice for any reason. But this time I felt like I had a good reason: I needed to check for bleeding. If I had seen any, that would have changed everything—players must pay attention to what their bodies are telling them, and if an honest self-assessment says that you're going to do long-term damage if you keep playing, you have to sit out. If I had been bleeding, I would have gone straight to the hospital. But I wasn't bleeding. And because I had had enough experience playing pregnant before, I knew that what I was experiencing wasn't critical. It wasn't great, but I could carry on until practice was over. This was something I always did. I always held myself accountable to my team, no matter what.

It sure wasn't fun. I could barely walk by the time Coach Pia (Pia Sundhage, the coach of the national team) called it quits that day—almost quits. Pia liked to end practices with some kind of team-building exercise, and on that day she chose the crossbar challenge, in which players chip the ball from the top of the eighteen-yard line and try to hit the crossbar. Miss and you're out; hit it and you stay in. It is a fun skill-set game. As my teammates took shots like rapid fire, in an attempt to be the first one to hit the crossbar, I took the opportunity to slowly slip away, hoping to remain unnoticed, and get to the bus. I needed to sit down. I loved the crossbar challenge, but for the first time in my life I couldn't kick a ball.

When practice officially ended, Abby sat down next to me. She leaned into me carefully, which made me bristle. No coddling.

"Are you okay?"

I closed my eyes and focused on the mantras I always used to make it through pain.

Mind over matter.

Pain is weakness leaving the body.

The pain you feel today will be the strength you feel tomorrow. Pain is temporary. Quitting lasts forever.

That evening, I tried to sleep off the pain in my hotel room. By the middle of the night, my pain was driving me to insanity. My usual narrative of fighting, ignoring, and triumphing over pain was no longer working, to put it mildly. I felt myself moving in and out of consciousness.

All night I pushed my body to fight the pain. To ignore it. That is what I was trained to do. But I knew it was finally time to listen. Greg, our team trainer, drove me to a nearby hospital.

After hours of waiting around, I was told I would need an emergency hysterectomy. In shock, I signed the papers put in front of me and was wheeled into surgery within the hour. I wasn't entirely sure what was happening, but I was so worn down from the pain, I could hardly respond. I was put under anesthesia and the last thing I remember thinking was that I would be okay with whatever came next.

When I woke up, I was alone. I sat in my hospital bed for what felt like hours, wondering if I would ever be able to have a child again. I had no access to my phone. My anesthesia hangover was wearing off and I could feel the morphine numbing my senses. But it did not dull my feelings. I felt an overwhelming sense of emptiness. My thoughts ran wild. Rylie would never have a little sister or brother. The surgery would negatively affect my athletic performance. I might never play on the national team again. I was shattered.

When the nurse finally came to my room, she casually said the surgery was a success and talked about hormone replacements and medicine. The nurse said the surgeon had repaired a ruptured ovarian cyst and said my pregnancy was completely normal . . . my pregnancy was intact! I couldn't hear a word she said after she told me that my baby was okay.

I had my baby. I could play.

I was flooded with relief.

I couldn't have been more grateful.

Two Weeks Later

Once I recovered from surgery, I returned home to play for my professional club team in New Jersey, Sky Blue FC. The team was having a difficult season, with a record of six wins, seven ties, and five losses, and was in fifth place with two games left. Even though I'd gotten the green light—my pregnancy was healthy—I still kept it hidden from my teammates. This wasn't going to be about me. They were my home team, and they were like family. I wanted them to succeed and not be distracted or worried about me.

When I played for the national team, I was provided with comfortable travel accommodations, hotels, and lodging around the world. We were given three meals a day, all tailored to our individual needs. We were provided with medical care and massage therapy. Even our hydration was looked after regularly. All I had to do was focus on playing soccer. It was my living dream.

Sky Blue FC did not enjoy the same resources. Housing was scarce. My teammates lived in an extended-stay hotel to save money. There were no showers or treatment rooms in our locker areas. At one point we even had to use a trailer as a locker room. Our practice fields were also poorly kept. Most of our health-care providers volunteered their time for the love of the team.

As the captain of Sky Blue, I made it my mission to make sure my teammates had everything they needed even if it meant doing it all myself. I didn't want them distracted by better-funded teams. Success is about being focused, executing a plan, and trusting one another enough to evolve when the action gets intense. Sure, having cushy housing and a huge staff can make it easier to give all your attention to the game, but it can also coddle you. I wanted to teach my teammates how to focus on the game no matter how grim the circumstances.

I became the team mom for Sky Blue. I washed all my teammates' game-day jerseys in my own home. I regularly held dinners for my teammates. I listened to their stories and often gave advice about their personal relationships (when they asked!) and how they might improve their playing. I took my role to heart. I knew the team saw me not only as their trainer and captain, but also as protector and caretaker.

The day I returned to the team after my surgery, my general manager asked me to deliver the bad news: our head coach had been unexpectedly asked to leave his position one month ago after an issue with a player, and our assistant coach was leaving as well. Given my role on the team, the general manager thought this news would be best coming from me. When I told my teammates, I saw defeat and fear in every one of their eyes. We were already having a losing season. Now our coaching staff had completely disintegrated in a matter of a few months.

After practice, the general manager asked me if I would consider coaching the team for the remainder of the season. He knew I was recovering from surgery, but he had no idea I was pregnant. I had just been cleared to return to personal training two times a day and was already working more than forty-five hours a week with my schedule of meetings, interviews, events. It was a grueling schedule, and I had to check in with myself to see if I was up for it. But after careful consideration, I knew I had to step up. My team needed a leader, and I had the skills to set a good example, motivate the players, and set goals that would inspire everyone to do her best work. What was good for my team would be good for me.

I said yes. I would continue to play on the team as their center defender and coach my teammates simultaneously. Two weeks after surgery. While pregnant. No problem. I didn't even ask for a contract.

When I agreed to take on my dispirited team at the end of a losing season, I wasn't taking on these women just to get them to the end of the season with a coach. I fully intended to turn the season around. We didn't necessarily have the league's best individual players, but I knew we could be the best team collectively. And great teams win championships.

My first order of business was to ask my personal trainer, Mike Lyons, to be my assistant coach. We had very similar perspectives on coaching and communicating. Good communication was going to be critical to making sure that everybody was on board with our mission. The fastest way to derail a team is to confuse the mission: when people don't understand the goals, don't know the strategies, or haven't bought into the process, they go rogue. This leads to chaos—and chaos leads to failure. Once Mike accepted, I set out to create a plan for each game leading up to the playoffs. My focus was to address the games one at a time—every game was going to be different, and we needed to assess the skills of every team we were going to play in order to develop a strategy that would help us win. I did my homework, plotted carefully, and considered each of the opposing teams' unique history, players, and previous playing styles and tactics. Coach Lyons then implemented my plans from the sidelines. We created multiple formations and possible scenarios, and we communicated with each other and the team to make necessary adjustments during game time.

My second order of business was to restore morale. I implemented a zero-negativity policy for the team. There would be no discussions about the past—or the future, for that matter. Their focus was to be on the present state of the team and on each game. I didn't want to dwell on our past losses or ponder the possibility of a win. I didn't want them to be thinking about their personal stats. I wanted them to trust that I had a winning plan for everything that we were going to encounter, and they needed to focus on the plan in order to succeed. We might not have fielded the best players, but we could be unstoppable if we worked together and worked smart. I knew our genuine connection on and off the field meant we would have the confidence and the wisdom to rely on one another. If only my team could believe in themselves again.

My third and most important goal was to bring back our passion for the game. Many coaches would approach training a team like Sky Blue by imposing long hours and repetitive drills, especially given their losing season. But I knew my teammates would view that as punishment. I needed to bring the fun back into their game. Fitness and drills are important, but scrimmaging and challenging teammates are what we live for. With that in mind, I began practice with four-versus-four scrimmages. I wanted to bring back not just their playing awareness but also their love for the game. I knew this would bring back the competitive edge we had been missing all season.

I was forthcoming right off the bat about my own limitations as a coach—I had no idea how to create film for the team to review, and I didn't have the time to learn how. Instead, I asked my teammates to independently watch clips of their games and bring any questions to me and Coach Lyons. There were two major benefits to this: I learned how each player saw herself individually and relative to her teammates on the field, and my players began to cultivate more self-awareness. By making the players responsible for their own review, I was giving them the opportunity to develop their self-assessment skills. Watching film gave the athletes the opportunity to review the moments when they were successful, as well as where they needed to improve. The film provided time for the players to see their options on the field and how to handle those situations next time. I was holding them accountable while building their confidence in their individual games.

My plan worked. To my utter delight, Sky Blue won the first game I coached, and soon after, we made it to the national playoffs! The team was excited. We were having fun again, and we were playing with passion.

The Playoffs

We would have to win all three of our games over the next eight days to win the national championship. We would have to travel four hundred miles, over three different time zones, and would have to practice and recover while on the road. I continued to remind the team to stay in the present: "We are going to take one game at a time, just like we've been doing. No need to look ahead to the championship. We are going to enjoy this journey. We have nothing to lose!"

In the first game of the playoffs, we faced an incredible Washington, DC, team led by Abby Wambach. We had recently lost to Washington, 3–1, in *the last game of the season, only to play them as our first-round playoff game. I knew I would need to concentrate on our mental preparation more than our physical preparation. I spoke to the team about focusing on the game plan and letting go of any negative mental blocks they had acquired in the last game against Abby and her team.*

Our game plan was simple: we needed to force the DC team to play their game down the middle in order to shut Abby down. We executed our plan flawlessly. Abby was forced to play the game differently than she was accustomed to, and we gave her very little opportunity to do what she does best: finishing crosses. Thanks to our intense focus, we won the game with a tight score of 2–1. We gained an immense amount of confidence that day.

The next playoff game was held in St. Louis. This team was led by Jorge Barcellos, a highly accomplished Brazilian national team coach, and the US Women's National Team goalkeeper coach. Mental preparation would again be paramount. I didn't want anyone intimated by the stakes of the game or the reputations of the opposing coaches and players. I immediately set out to reframe their nerves. I wanted to shift their fear of defeat to the thrill of the game. I told them I played some of my best games against the toughest, most difficult-to-beat athletes. I taught them that anxiety before a game is fuel.

The idea of coaching this game excited me. I'm always up for a challenge, especially a challenge of Barcellos's caliber. I instructed my team to force everything wide, because unlike DC, St. Louis's strengths were within their middle. The St. Louis roster also possessed one of the most amazing goalies in the national league, Hope Solo, the two-time Olympic gold medalist and World Cup champion. Scoring against Hope didn't happen very often, but when it did, it felt amazing. To add to the excitement, Coach Barcellos had recently traded one of his players to Sky Blue. I made sure she would start in the game against her former teammates.

Once the game commenced, however, I took an alternative approach to coaching. I instructed two of my Brazilian forwards to simply do their thing. I allowed them to express themselves through their creativity on the field. Individual players are best when they are allowed to let their training take over and can truly be in the flow during competition. I told the rest of my team to defend around them to give them more freedom to play creatively. I gave no direct instruction on using specific tactics as I had done previously; I trusted that their mental focus would result in innovative playmaking.

The teams played evenly throughout the game, and the score remained 0–0 at halftime, in part due to Hope Solo's big-time saves. My forwards were frustrated but remained determined. In the second half, to everyone's surprise including my own, my center defender scored her first goal of the season, making the final score 1–0. Her goal was a result of our team fully trusting one another and creatively adapting to our opponents.

With that win, Sky Blue FC made it to the national championship!

We were flooded with joy.

Our final game would be held in Los Angeles and we were going in as the underdogs. On paper, the LA team was much more developed. They had a superstar in every position. In fact, they were so confident, they had begun celebrating the win the night before our game. Their locker room was already stocked with champagne, dresses, and heels for the after party. I reminded my team not to buy into another team's stardom. It wasn't about individual star power; it was about how those individuals worked together. I asked them to talk about the feelings about getting to the championship game. We talked about how we had nothing to lose. I created a relaxed and safe environment so my teammates could play freely, with no added pressures, like they had when they were kids.

Personally, and as much as I hated to admit it, I was fatigued. I was three months pregnant, and I was feeling it. I hadn't ever planned for such a long season, but I knew I had at least ninety more minutes left in me. I was determined to play and coach one more game.

LA didn't make it easy. For the entirety of the first half, forward Marta Vieira Da Silva, one of the best soccer players in the world, relentlessly battled me and the other defenders. I knew my defense relied on my leadership on the back line. So I toughed it out.

Then, in the sixteenth minute, New Jersey native Heather O'Reilly scored our first goal. Game on!

O'Reilly's goal increased the tension. Marta upped her game, and I kept up with her. I was shutting her down. Then, during the forty-third minute of the game, the unthinkable happened. Marta pushed me, and I fell face forward, hitting my belly square on the ball. The referees stopped the game and waited to see what I would do.

I was flooded with panicked thoughts.

What if I hurt my baby?

What if it's not safe to play anymore?

I can't stop playing without letting my teammates down.

I should have told everyone I was pregnant.

I took a deep breath and checked in with my body, making sure to be fully present to its needs and vowing to stop if I had to. For those few seconds, I mentally removed myself from the game, checked in with my pain, and decided I was good. I slowly rose to my feet, waved a hand at the referee, and gave my team a reassuring grin. I was fine. I knew in my heart my baby was too. I was totally focused, back in the zone, and ready to go. As I jogged back to my position, I smiled inwardly, knowing my determination would fuel my teammates.

Our defense remained strong during the second half. Not a single goal got past us the remainder of the game. We shocked the league and won the championship that day. We didn't have the best eleven individual players, but we were the best team of eleven. I could not have been prouder.

Our locker room was bare when we blasted through the doors at the end of the game. There were no banners, no balloons, and absolutely nothing prepared in case our team won the title. We managed to muster up only one lousy bottle of tequila.

My red Solo cup was empty when I raised it to toast my teammates.

"I would love to take this shot with you, but I am three months pregnant!"

The locker room exploded in cheers. We laughed, we hugged, and we cried. We relished our amazing accomplishment. We hadn't won because we were hungry for a championship title. We won because we were able to find our passion for the game again. We won because we played as a team and we played for one another. Most important, we won because we stayed present and focused on what made the game so special to us in the first place. We remained focused on the journey. We were all in.

Following the national team championship in 2009 and the birth of her second daughter in 2010, as captain of the US Women's National Team, Christie won a silver medal in the 2011 World Cup, an Olympic gold medal in 2012, and another gold in the 2015 World Cup.

Be All In

CHAPTER 1

Giving the Sports Back to the Kids

When Christie's daughter plays basketball, Christie's father is very excited. He never misses a game. A former coach himself, he is frequently found on the sidelines talking about the intricacies of the game to other knowing parents. He is particularly excited when Rylie plays because she reminds him of how Christie and her sister used to play.

My father is generally a quiet man and usually offers his opinion only when asked. But in the sports arena my father is an entirely different guy. He's comfortable there, being vocal with the referees or calling out plays. It's like he feels that he has a green light to sideline coach or talk with the refs, since it was not so long ago that he was actually the coach. Don't get me wrong. My father isn't nasty with the refs. He just says what he thinks and makes his opinion very well known. No name-calling. But he is definitely calling the plays like he did when he coached.

Dad knows my philosophy. He knows I feel that yelling at the referees turns things negative pretty quickly. I think it's important to remember that referees are human, and they make mistakes too! I don't always agree with their calls, but I always make a point of calming myself down before starting a conversation about a call if I feel emotional about it.

Sometimes, though, when my dad—Poppy now, to my daughters—gets on the refs, I get pretty bad anxiety. He can be pretty vocal in a small gymnasium where there is little chance of getting out of earshot. During one basketball game my daughter Rylie committed two early fouls. One of the fouls she clearly deserved, and the second one was questionable. There was a lot of fouling and pushing and shoving on both sides, but it seemed that the referees were favoring the other team. It was hard to watch.

The second foul got Rylie benched for the latter part of the second quarter, and then it was even harder to watch. My father turned his attention toward the refs, yelling, "Ah, you missed that one!" or "C'mon, that wasn't a foul!" or "Let them play!" He would even shout, "Great defense!" when one of Rylie's teammates was given a foul, to send the loud-and-clear message to the refs that he didn't believe she deserved the foul.

When halftime came, he and I shared a long and awkward silence. It was a tie game, and it was clear that the girls who were not getting the calls they deserved left the court feeling sorry for themselves. I felt like my dad had a part in that. I just gave him an eye, and I knew he understood what I meant. He knew I thought his behavior was outside my comfort zone.

I saw my father relax in his seat a bit as the third quarter started. He watched silently, and continued to grunt here and there, when he really wanted to say something. Then, to my surprise, my father stood up for the fourth quarter. With a sudden renewed energy, he was up on his feet, pacing, as loud and vocal as he was when the game started. Only this time, he didn't call out anything at the refs. He directed all his words toward the girls on the team. He was loud, but he wasn't angry.

Dad said, "Great teamwork!" "Way to pass!" "Great hustle!"

My dad spoke only words of encouragement, and the girls heard him loud and clear. The momentum of the game shifted. Before, the game had been tense. Girls were upset at their mistakes. They were playing with their heads down, not looking for one another, concerned only about making baskets and winning. But after my dad started calling things like "Great pass!" the girls really started looking for one another, playing with one another.

Rylie in particular thrives on support. She loves to make her grandpa proud, especially when she is playing basketball. She looks for his signature thumbs-up after plays. Once he began encouraging the players, Rylie couldn't stop smiling.

I think my dad realized that when he shouted, he was actually distracting the team and may have been encouraging them to think the referee was biased against them. Rylie and her teammates looked like they were worried about what they were doing wrong and concentrated less on the game. He saw that his yelling at the referees wouldn't change the outcomes of their calls; he could make a bigger impact by supporting the team. The girls were thriving off his positive feedback.

I loved that my dad was able to shift gears during that game. His actions spoke loudly—not only about how we can all make a shift from questioning and abusing referees to trusting, good, bad, or indifferent, but also about how our behavior toward the referees ultimately affects the athletes on the court.

Giving the Sports Back to the Kids

Recently, the *New York Times* featured an article about why parents behave so badly at sporting events.[1] The author noted that youth sports organizations are reporting increases in parents who yell, fight, and threaten and harass coaches, referees, other parents, and even the players. The author told this story:

In New Mexico, a crowd stormed onto a football field to protest a penalty. One member of the crowd grabbed a referee from behind and body-slammed him on the ground.

The assailant was the father of one of the thirteen-year-old players; he stood, horrified, at what his father had just done.

All the parents were required to sign a parent code of conduct, which included promises to remain in control of emotions and to remember that the game is for the kids, not the adults. The New Mexico Young American Football League banned the entire team of thirteen-year-olds for the remainder of the year.

We have had countless discussions, together and with other parents, about parents behaving badly. When people hear about the content of this book, the overwhelming response is, "I know *so many* people who *need* to read that book."

Every person reading this book could offer at least one horrific anecdote of a parent behaving badly at a sporting event. A parent harassing a referee, yelling at another child, or bullying a youth opponent. A parent being asked to leave the field by a referee. A coach being carded and thrown out of the game.

We often joke that the people who *need* to read this book won't, and the ones who will are the choir already preaching the same thing. Given the impact that all parents have on the sporting experience (well-meaning, bullying, ill intentioned, asleep at the wheel, or otherwise), we believe it is less efficacious to place "blame" on particular parents and more beneficial to understand and educate those involved in youth sports on the cultural and environmental aspects that may be more deserving of the "fault" here, or perhaps more likely responsible for the influence.

Researchers Travis Dorsch, Alan Smith, Steven Wilson, and Meghan McDonough found that most parents cited fun and enjoyment as primary motivations for involving their children in sports.[2] However, over time, parents' goals tended to change in concert with the sporting environment, and the results of those changes ultimately showed up on the sidelines. Their research showed that parents' sporting behaviors are often tied to the culture of the team environment. Regardless of the parents' initial intentions, their behavior ultimately reflects the attitude and expectations embedded within the team culture. When teams are deemed "elite" or held up as more competitive, parents become increasingly focused on their child's playing time, scoring, and winning of tournaments.

Depending on the team, participation in the CP3 Elite Soccer Academy can cost about three to four thousand dollars a year. Many of the CP3 Elite youth teams compete within their home state; older children on advanced teams play all over the United States. The academy is sought out by parents because its teams often advance to high rankings due to its children receiving training from elite trainers from soccer-centric countries like Brazil and England.

The CP3 Elite Stallions, for instance, comprise ten-year-old boys who compete regionally and throughout their state. The team culture values winning; individual youth development is considered a by-product of the championships. If you are succeeding against better teams and ultimately winning championships, you must be growing and developing. Right?

Here is the not-so-uncommon team-culture scenario. CP3 Elite Stallion parents often coach from the sidelines, become frustrated with losses and mistakes, and doubt the coach's treatment of their children, be it about assigned positions, playing time, or both. The parents are ultimately happy when they are winning and dissatisfied with losses. The CP3 Elite name, cost, and team success impact parent expectations of the team—and of their children.

In comes ten-year-old Brandon, who joined the CP3 Elite Stallions after moving from California. His parents, who served as team parents on his former soccer team, were excited when Brandon made the elite team, and they were eager to get involved. When the season started, Brandon's parents created a large wooden sign that read, CP3 ELITE STALLIONS, BOYS U11 TEAM, GOOD LUCK TO YOU! They painted a stallion on the sign, and the players' names and numbers were scrawled all over the board. It was beautiful! Brandon was so proud.

When Brandon's parents presented the sign to the coach, a young man from England, they were told that the sign could not be staked behind the boys during game time because it was against "regulations." When his parents presented the sign to the team parents, the team mom thanked them and told them they could stake it wherever they thought it best, on the parents' sideline, at each game.

The sign was not well received by the team and Brandon's parents felt it. None of the parents thanked them for making the sign, and, worse, most of the parents did not even acknowledge it was there. The truth was the parents saw the sign as a show of weakness to other teams. It was too babyish. The CP3 Elite Stallion parents wanted their kids to show up looking like a professional team. The uniforms, the personalized bags, the equipment, the gear; these things really look amazing. That's how the Stallions show up.

During Brandon's first season, his parents brought the sign to every game. By his second season, the sign made only a few appearances before disappearing altogether. Come season three, Brandon's mother became a team mom. Instead of peeling oranges, creating encouraging signs, and hosting pizza parties, Brandon's parents found themselves organizing additional team trainings with elite soccer coaches and arranging travel details for games around the state. Brandon's parents were all in. Brandon was happy, made many friends on the team, and was winning championships. His parents still cheered for him from the sidelines; however, they also became frustrated—obviously and vocally—about their son's mistakes. Games, tournaments, and rankings became the center of Brandon's family life. This was elite soccer. Or was it a loss of Brandon's childhood?

Individuals in groups can be easily influenced. Signs, gear, schedules, all are reflections of how people see themselves or want to be seen by others. Being on a team of parents whose culture condones aggressive behavior in sports might actually cause a parent to believe that the behavior is inherently acceptable. While each parent is accountable for his or her individual behavior, the real solution to an aggressive youth sporting environment and the possible loss of childhood is cultural climate change: reformulating, rethinking, and rewriting youth sports culture within the community.

Being a sports parent is hard work. It can be stressful to watch your child in high-pressure situations. It can be painful to see them fail, disappoint their teammates, play badly, or even be responsible for a team loss. Have you ever seen a sign at a tournament that had rules about parental behavior? Have you ever been asked to sign a pledge about parent and player conduct? These are some of the most important pieces of paper involved in your child's time as an athlete.

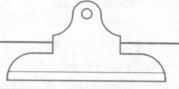

Signs Parents Encounter
Your child's success or lack of success in sports does not indicate what kind of parent you are.
But having an athlete that is coachable, respectful, a great teammate, mentally tough, resilient, and trying their best IS a direct reflection of your parenting.
Please remember: These are kids. This is a game. Coaches are volunteers. Umpires are humans. You do not play for the Yankees.
Reminders from your child: I am a kid. It is just a game. The officials are human beings. Parents should cheer everyone. No college scholarships will be handed out today.
Remember! This league is for the children. Please leave your ego at home.
Parent Pledge. I will teach all children to play fair and do their best. I will positively support all managers, coaches, and parents. I will respect the decisions of the umpire. I will praise a good effort despite the outcome of the game.

Hopefully, something of this kind has crossed your path as a sport parent. That said, it's increasingly likely that most parents, after being confronted with a sign like this, think something like, *It's not me. It doesn't apply to me. Not my kid. Not our team. We are different. We are playing at an* elite *level.*

There is clearly no one-size-fits-all answer to giving the game back to the kids. Parental behavior, from inappropriate and aggressive to excited and positive, depends on many variables. While many organizations have adopted parent codes of conduct and similar "good behavior" agreements and signs like the ones just noted, there is little evidence that these preseason agreements and in-season reminders actually engender any meaningful positive changes in youth sports.

The solution is not about targeting individuals. It comes from the community. Remember, it takes a village. And while we are teaching our children teamwork, we need to take a few suggestions from that same playbook.

Abby Wambach's *Wolfpack* proposes that if we band together as women, we can achieve great things.[3] It highlights the idea that we can get more done in groups, with support instead of competition, and with education. We propose that sports parents also band together in a similar vein. To change the culture of a team, the parents and coaching staff can interactively create a team mission statement. We propose a mutually agreed-upon statement that is reviewed at every parent meeting, before the season begins, during the season, and after the season is over. Such a statement would keep families, athletes, and coaches on the same page.

A team mission statement for parents, athletes, and coaches can foster the sense of community that most parents are looking for in a team. It can allay parents' fears of watching their children being cut from the team by teaching parents how to communicate effectively and appropriately with coaches. It can hold parents accountable for their behavior and provide alternative behaviors, such as taking a walk, breathing mindfully, or sitting alone during games. It can wake people up to their unintentional bad habits during game time.

Parents spend so much time, money, and resources training their kids and regularly competing, it only makes sense to dedicate at least forty-five minutes during the preseason to a mission that would enhance athletic performance and enjoyment. Further, parents can take ten minutes after a game to review how their mission statement is holding up. The time it takes to develop a mission statement is very little compared to the hours of hardship, burnout, disappointment, and energy on negativity.

Be All In Mission Statement

A mission statement is a written statement that reflects the goals, values, and purpose of an organization. For the statement to be effective, all stakeholders need to be involved in its creation and agree to its values. In the case of youth sports, the mission statement should reflect the intentions, rules, roles, and values of all stakeholders, including parents, coaches, managers, and administrators. In all cases the mission statement should be taken seriously. The mission statement should reflect everyone's vested interests.[4]

We suggest that one parent (the parent captain) be designated to assist in creating the statement and to follow up in meetings during the preseason, midseason, and postseason. The parent captain should be the parent who commands a sense of respect and community among parents on the team. The parent captain needs to enforce the mission statement and revisit it regularly with the team's parents. It should be used flexibly and revised as needed: as the community grows and develops, as children grow up, and as new interests and difficulties arise.

A youth parent mission statement could sound something like this:

We are a proactive, respectful group of parents who value skill and team development over winning and trophies. We understand that one game will not make or break one of our players. We focus on the whole team, with positive encouragement and praise, rather than solely on the welfare and achievements of our own child. We value organization, problem solving with intelligence, and technique over physicality. We think before we speak. We are accountable for our actions. We model passion for the game, team cohesion, and respect for teammates, parents, coaches, and officials. Our motto is "attitude and effort" over "medals and trophies." When parents, coaches, and all involved are all in physically, behaviorally, and emotionally, we inspire our children to be the best versions of themselves. We are all in this together.

A mission statement should clearly indicate the parents' vision for their children and the values of the team. Team values may include cooperation, support, clear communication, optimism, respect, motivation, trust, and honesty, to name a few. The mission statement should espouse positivity and include why parents put their children on sports teams in the first place. Every team mission statement will have its own unique feel, depending on the children's ages and the existing culture of the community. Above all, the team mission statement is meant to inspire, with sayings like "Play like a champion," "Make history," "You have to believe it before you see it," and "Courage is doing what you are afraid to do."

The team mission statement for parents should also be

accompanied by a set of actions or behaviors that are agreed upon by the stakeholders. By operationally defining the behaviors that accompany the team values, the mission statement leaves no ambiguity regarding expectations. Without the inclusion of a clear set of agreed-upon behaviors, it is difficult to assess whether the mission statement is being followed or is even effective. Here are some examples of mission statement actions:

- Parents agree to check their emotions about the game regardless of whether they are upset about an unfair call, playing time, or a mistake their child or another child made.
- Parents agree to let the coaches coach and the officials officiate. We will not yell at referees or coaches. We will not coach children from the sidelines unless we are designated as a coach. We will speak to referees, calmly, and only about safety issues, if necessary.
- Parents agree to let other teams do their thing. We will not verbally react to other parents' behavior or antagonize other teams.
- Parents are encouraged to use positive and supportive cheers during a game, such as "Good game!" "Keep it up!" "Keep competing!" and "Nice teamwork!"
- Parents agree to discuss disagreements, perceived problems, or grievances with the parent captain or the coach no fewer than twenty-four hours after the sporting event, rather than trying to communicate their feelings during the game.
- Parents agree to a nonjudgmental, nonshaming group atmosphere. Emotions run high during games. We are all fallible humans. When a parent violates the mission, parents agree to openly communicate with one another about the behavior. The mission is not to make anyone feel bad about themselves, but rather to help the parent community grow and develop.

On the same note, parents agree to maintain accountability for themselves and one another.

■ We agree to teach our children to take responsibility for their mistakes. We teach kids not to make excuses, not to blame teammates. We teach our kids not to compare themselves to their teammates, and to look for what their teammates bring to the game instead.

■ Parents will create a sense of community by planning and participating in off-the-field team events when schedules permit.

In addition, the mission statement set of actions should include an agreed-upon set of consequences for stakeholders who violate the mission. Some examples include:

■ Adult time-out chair
■ Yellow cards/red cards for parents
■ Loss of playing time for the athlete of the culpable parent
■ Removal of the child from the field
■ Sending the child over to the parent during the game

In Norway, the majority of children participate in competitive skiing. Children pay a nominal fee to join a ski league, and if their parents can't afford to pay, or simply forget, the children are still permitted to participate. All the coaches are volunteers, and there are no specialized trainers. The Norway skiing league enjoys very large numbers of youth participants year after year.

The league does not keep score or monitor times for any of the races, for any of the children—regardless of their level of talent or development. If you were to sit on the sidelines, while you would notice a wide range of variability in skill, all the children compete and learn together. The number one thing you would notice is that all the children, parents, and volunteers are having fun, laughing and smiling, confident and happy. It is hard to even imagine an aggressive Norwegian ski parent. And in all this bliss, Norway boasts an extremely competitive Olympic ski program that trumps those of most other countries.

Here is the mission: to transition from a highly competitive, FOMO-centric, specialized, and aggressive youth sporting environment to a youth sports culture focused on fun, individual development, and skill acquisition.

Good sportsmanship is a quality that helps kids thrive in all areas of their lives, and well beyond their athletic careers. In this book, we drill down into the qualities, characteristics, attitudes, and practices that will allow kids to excel at whatever sport they pursue—not just in their ability to compete, but also in their ability to learn new skills, become leaders, develop their hustle, and understand how to support everyone around them. Excelling in sports isn't always about trophies or MVP status; it's also about learning how to learn, focusing on a goal, having self-confidence in the face of challenges, and working well with others. Parents are critical partners for children to get the most out of their athletic experiences, and we've written this book to teach you how to give your kids everything they need to be champions—on and off the field.

Christie's first official travel soccer team was called the Point Pleasant Power, and her sister's team was the Point Pleasant Settas. She recalls that both squads displayed team signs that were displayed at every game and tournament. Proudly. Her team's sign featured a large lightning bolt, and her sister's sign a giant red poinsettia, front and center. The signs were handmade by team moms, and each player had a hand in painting them. They were proud of their team signs and never played a game without them.

We had those signs from age ten all the way through high school. Back in the day, we didn't have all the paraphernalia we have now. I can't imagine an elite youth team for ten-year-olds showing up with a handmade sign these days. But it would be fun to see. None of it had anything to do with the success that we found in soccer. The sign didn't reflect anything but togetherness and happiness.

CHAPTER 2

Communication

Good communication—between members of a team, between families and coaches, and one-on-one—is one of the most critical components for success. Children develop and grow based on effective communication. Parents play an integral part in ensuring that kids understand the basics of good communication: maintaining eye contact, taking turns while speaking, not interrupting, and, above all, knowing how to listen. The communication skills taught at home help children develop the ability and confidence to communicate with adults, authority figures, peers, and teammates throughout their life.

Amid the overwhelming schedule of school, sports, work, family, and life, purposefully teaching kids how to communicate can get lost in the shuffle. In sports, the ability to communicate to coaches and to teammates is vital regardless of the game or event.

Christie recalls one of her soccer players who struggled with communicating to her teammates:

Meghan, an athlete whom I have been coaching for the past several years, has shown herself capable of being very impactful. The majority of the time she is, hands down, one of the best players that I have come across. Her soccer IQ is high. She is committed and coachable. She is everything you could ask for in a player. The only thing that is missing is her ability to communicate.

Meghan is normally shy and introverted, but on game days she speaks through her play on the field. She gets the job done in terms of completing passes, being in the right position, and winning her one-v.-one battles, but her game breaks down when it comes to linking up with players and communicating. She does a lot of her teammates' work for them because she won't open up to them. When it comes to playing higher-level teams, Meghan actually becomes a disadvantage to her own team because her teammates have become accustomed to relinquishing their responsibilities and they become less efficient.

For example, Meghan needs to warn her teammates when a player is coming through or when there is a defender on. She should be using her voice to help her teammates know when they have time, if they are able to turn, or where there is an open teammate. While Meghan understands what to say, she has not yet developed the confidence to say the words. She is more comfortable just doing it herself. Instead of vocally assisting teammates, she physically takes care of other players' roles on the field.

For that reason, Meghan doesn't get noticed as she should on the field. She isn't giving herself a chance to shine. Because she is continually taking care of other players' responsibilities, she lacks the wow factor. I think a lot of coaches overlook her because they miss her true talent due to her silence. Without a voice, she easily blends in.

If Meghan learned to open up her voice, she could reach her full potential and become a very special soccer player. If she communicated to her teammates, Meghan would be even more efficient because she would not need to take care of everything. In order to delegate, she must speak!

Learning to assert oneself as an athlete is like learning how to participate in a conversation. Without the ability to communicate, an athlete might get lost and thus risks going unnoticed. It is like sitting at the kitchen table and not saying a word during dinner. It's awkward. It doesn't feel like you want to be there. It affects everyone around you. If you are not sharing your thought process, no one knows what you are thinking—and they don't know if you're committed to, or even invested in, the rest of the team. It's okay to be quiet, but it's another thing not to speak up at all. It's our job as coaches and as parents to help kids learn how to use their voice to participate.

Pay Attention: 93 Percent of This Is Body Language

The role of body language is critical on and off the field. Ask any kid who was on the receiving end of another kid sticking their tongue out at them. The receiving child knows full well the intended message. Psychologists often refer to the 55/38/7 formula, created by researcher Albert Mehrabian.[1] He posited that communication is 55 percent nonverbal, 38 percent tone of voice, and 7 percent verbal. His formula depends on variables such as person and context; however, it is generally agreed that 93 percent of communication is nonverbal—93 percent!

Be aware of your child's natural body language. What physical movements are repetitive? When do they occur and why? When you understand the natural body language of your child, you can teach them to understand the messages their body language conveys. Most important, once children learn that their movements mean something, they can express more conscious, intentional messages to their coaches and teammates.

You can foul out and pout from the bench, or you can cheer on your teammates. You can sulk and slouch on the bench, your head down or with a towel over your head, or you can lean forward eagerly, elbows on knees. Body language leads to a change in energy. We can teach kids that even when a game isn't going their way, they can still make an impact by changing their body language.

Many athletes do not realize how they are communicating their emotions. Some aspects of a sporting event can get an athlete understandably upset—an unfair call or a missed foul. But dwelling on negativity will affect the rest of the game. A change in body language can transform an unfortunate moment into a positive one. Awareness leads to change. Dr. Keane helps parents understand body language to better understand and help their kids.

One of my patients was concerned about her daughter, Abigail: she wasn't excelling in soccer and seemed disinterested, but also complained about insufficient playing time. I asked Abigail's mom about Abigail's body language on the field—her posture when sitting on the bench, standing in a huddle, or talking with her coach and her peers.

After our conversation, Abigail's mom noticed that Abigail dragged her feet across the field, avoided eye contact when walking past teammates, stood outside the huddles, shrugged her shoulders and even lowered her head when talking with coaches. Meanwhile, her mother said she talked ceaselessly about her love for soccer and how much she wanted to play. She got very upset, crying when she sat on the bench for the majority of the game, yet seemed to make no effort to change and thus earn more playing time. Abigail's mom was perplexed. If Abigail wasn't trying, how could she truly love the game?

I asked Abigail's mom to talk to her about body language and about her feelings. I asked that she propose to Abigail that she stop playing soccer for a while, while making it clear that that decision would be okay. That conversation and some further prompting worked wonders. It turned out that Abigail had been putting enormous pressure on herself; you see, her mother had been a decorated college soccer player. Abigail hadn't wanted to disappoint her mom. She complained about playing time as a mechanism; of course she wasn't getting playing time. She never put in the effort. She didn't know how else to tell her mother she didn't want to play anymore.

Abigail's body language had been telling her mother everything she needed to know and her mother was shocked once she saw it. She had no idea her daughter was feeling such pressure. After their conversation, she told Abigail that it was always her choice—not Mom's—whether she continued playing. Mom would be proud regardless of which activities Abigail chose. Abigail had lacked the self-awareness and the words to express her real feelings to her mother.

The body never lies; body language tells you everything. Abigail had been showing her disinterest to her mother, but she'd been contradicting that message verbally. Abigail couldn't articulate what her body language had been saying all along.

Christie teaches young athletes that standing with their hands on their hips conveys fatigue, even weakness. That throwing up their hands in the face of adversity signifies blaming, frustration, and anger. She also instructs them that a simple high five or hug can show someone you care. Teammates have enormous power over one another by way of body language. The body can be used to hurt a teammate's feelings or to comfort them. She teaches her athletes to be responsible for their emotions on the field, and that 93 percent of said emotions will be expressed through their physical movement.

No matter how you feel, when you're playing, your shoulders should be back and your head should be up. You play the game until the final whistle blows. Your emotions are for the locker room.

Most coaches watch film of the games: game plays, player interactions, and what athletes are doing when they are not directly involved in a play. When evaluating players, coaches are typically already aware of a given athlete's level of talent. They're often looking for other cues and traits. Off the field, coaches observe an athlete's behavior in the huddle and on the bench—how they interact with teammates. These subtle, often overlooked behaviors usually indicate a player's ability to lead, handle adversity, and interact effectively with teammates. Body language offers coaches the unsaid, unintended, but highly revealing truth about a player's integrity and character.

The Emotions Behind the Body Language	
Body Language	**Emotion**
Throwing hands up	Frustration
Head down	Annoyance
Stopping running or moving, or not making a run	Frustration with another player
Eye rolling	Anger
Hands on hips	Fatigue, weakness
Hands on knees	Breathlessness
Standing tall	Confidence, feeling engaged and focused on the game
Breathing through the pain	Strength
Victory stance with arms up in a V	Feeling like a champion

Parents can recognize their children's body language and how it affects their game. Parents should encourage open communication with a child to make them aware of their reactions to both negative and positive aspects of the game. You can teach kids that body language is very much a part of a game, a way to communicate to their coaches and teammates as well as to opponents. In terms of communication, parents must also be aware of how their own conduct can be perceived and impact their child.

Communication with the Coach

Mary's son Noah played varsity lacrosse as a sophomore. It was his first year on varsity, and he was having a very successful season. Noah was no stranger to athletic success, already a standout on his travel lacrosse team. That he earned not only varsity status but also became a starter on defense came as little surprise. Within a few games, Noah had proven himself one of the team's most valuable players. His teammates loved him, and spectators recognized his ability and importance.

But not everything was perfect. A new coach had recently taken over the varsity team, and the players were adjusting to his style of play. As a result, Noah made several mistakes that were frowned upon by the coach, earning him a seat on the bench. During one game, an error by Noah led to a goal for the opposing team, and he was benched for the remainder of the game. Until that point in his youth sports career, Noah had played at least half of any game, in any sport.

"Even on Noah's worst day, he is not playing as badly as some of the kids the coach puts in his place!" As Noah's playing time suffered, Mary's ire grew with each game. Mary also learned that the coach had been training some of the students at an outside lacrosse program, a program to which Noah didn't belong. This fueled her belief that Noah was being treated unfairly.

Other parents tried to console Mary by pointing out that many of the regular starters had had their playing time cut. But when Noah came off the field disappointed or angry, Mary was beside herself. Noah complained to his mother that he didn't know what he was doing wrong. In one close game against a particularly competitive opponent, Noah sat out the final twenty minutes. Other parents expressed their frustration at Noah's absence. They blamed the loss of the game on the coaching. Mary considered intervening. Noah had several discussions with his coach about playing time and, each time, came away confused. Mary was stumped.

"I want to ask his coach what the problem is, but I am not sure how to approach him. My husband disagrees with me and thinks I shouldn't say anything. He says I am going to make things worse for Noah. We even got into a fight at the game! It's causing our family to fight over lacrosse, a sport we have always loved!" Mary was in tears. "What should I do?"

Let your child try to problem solve on their own. First, discuss your child's concerns about their conflict with their coach. Then, teach your child how to communicate their concerns with their coach before you intervene. Coaches want to hear from their athletes and appreciate open communication. Remember, the coach, parent, and athlete each have their own agendas. The coach is concerned about the success of the team; the athlete is concerned about their individual success; the parent is concerned about their child's well-being. Sometimes these agendas can appear to conflict; in reality, a lack of communication might be obscuring one party's needs from another.

Mary's case was a bit complicated. Noah had already initiated several, ultimately unhelpful conversations with his coach. Mary was concerned that Noah was losing interest in lacrosse because he left each game disappointed and feeling helpless.

Coaches often say that 90 percent of parent meetings are about playing time. Parents are happy when their child is playing most of the game and ornery when they are not. Discussing playing time may or may not be appropriate, depending on the boundaries a coach has set up prior to the season. Coaches are often much more willing to discuss playing time with athletes than with parents.

Parents have every right to express their concerns. Indeed, we advocate that parents and coaches get on the same page. However, we also believe that parents should avoid discussing playing time with coaches. Parents should also avoid discussing other athletes, game-time strategy, and plays. We believe that if a parent knows their child has talked to the coach and was unable to problem solve independent of them, a parent meeting with the coach is absolutely appropriate.

First and foremost, a parent's job is to listen to their kids: listen to them vent; listen to them worry; listen to them discuss disappointments and fear and frustrations. Then ask them questions about what they want to see happen, what a best-case scenario would look like, what would make things better. Then help them figure out how to articulate these goals, whom to talk to, *and how.* They can encourage their children to facilitate that conversation.

A parent-coach meeting should focus on the athlete's mental health, physical well-being, and long-term developmental plans. Meetings should focus on topics such as how a parent might help their child improve or how they might assist them in managing their attitude or behavior. A coach might suggest additional technical skills training, physical fitness, or mental health practices. Promoting healthy communication between yourself as a parent and your child's coach can help create a feedback loop to ensure that everyone is on the same page. Forming a constructive partnership can often help avoid unexpected disappointments.[2]

But, again, don't always expect perfect resolution. Teams are ecosystems, with moving, even conflicting parts. Sometimes, one person (or family) must be called upon—even unfairly—to be the bigger person(s) to maintain team stability. Convey that to your child, and don't let your frustration as a parent bleed into your child's perception. Also, prepare for the possibility that the meeting might not go as planned—and even *that* might not be a bad thing.

When Mary asked to meet with the coach, he was hesitant to set it up. Instead, he suggested that Mary first meet with his assistant coach, which fueled her fire.

Mary and her husband set up a meeting to discuss not Noah's playing time but rather the coach's opinion of Noah's abilities and how they might help their son improve his game. They were surprised by his response: "Your son is a very special player. He is both talented and technical, and I very much enjoy working with him. His attitude is great. His teammates love him. I know he gets down from time to time when I don't play him, but I am harder on him because I know his potential. I see sophomore year as a time that I can use to groom his talent. I am working on your son's mental toughness this year. I have big plans for him."

Armed with this information, Noah's parents encouraged their son to trust the coach's approach rather than fight it. Mary was able to talk to Noah about using his playing time as teaching moments with purpose, rather than just random and unfair.

Because conversations like this can be tricky, there are some important things to understand when setting up a meeting with a coach. Noah's parent meeting was scheduled by email and did not occur immediately before or after a sporting event. Coaches rarely like to be approached by parents during that time. Some coaches set up a chain of communication prior to the beginning of the season: for example, beginning with the assistant coach, then, if further discussion is needed, continuing with the head coach, and lastly the athletic director. A clear chain of command is important for both coaches and parents to avoid misinterpretation and miscommunication. Mary used this chain to ask for the meeting that she needed.

Mary's meeting was well thought out and focused on her son's playing *ability* rather than strategy or playing time. She intentionally held the meeting to discuss things that she and her husband could assist her son with, instead of criticizing or questioning the coach's integrity or skill.

Many coach and parent interactions do not run as ideally and smoothly as Mary's did. Once again, don't always expect perfect resolution. Many parent-coach meetings occur spontaneously and are born of high emotions such as anger or fear. Many parents aren't thinking about their intentions or agenda before they set up a meeting. In fact, a good many of these meetings would never be set up if their child was getting playing time.

On a team Christie helps coach, one of the parents suddenly became angry and verbally aggressive to the head coach. Jim, the father to a girl who had played on the team for years, yelled, "Why are you making the girls play like this? You only have three defenders back there? What kind of formation is this, Coach? C'mon! Give these girls a chance to win out here!"

Jim continued to yell until the head coach pulled Jim's daughter Lucy off the field. The coach instructed Lucy to tell her father that she will be benched every time he yelled like that from the sidelines. This anecdote reiterates the impact of parental behavior on child psyche, even social standing. Remember also that everything today is on camera. Don't be that parent.

Other team parents were upset and confused by Jim's behavior. He didn't normally behave that way. On the other hand, they didn't like his calling out the coaches during a game. Their daughters were playing too. His behavior was aggressive and inappropriate.

The next day, the coach emailed Jim to set up a meeting. The coach, livid, told Jim that he wanted to discuss the things Jim had said during the game. Jim replied, "Just forget what I said. I didn't mean it. I was just angry. I shouldn't have yelled."

The head coach considered letting Jim off the hook. His colleagues told him the guy was a hothead and should be suspended from the next game. The assistant coach thought the right move would be to kick Jim out the next time he behaved inappropriately. But the head coach insisted on a meeting. "If you are going to yell things like that at me during one of my games, we are going to have to discuss it," he wrote back.

Jim and the coach met later that week.

The coach began the meeting with a question. "I would like to try to understand your perspective. Can you tell me why you think that the formation I arranged for the girls put them at a disadvantage?"

Jim didn't know.

"Can you tell me why you think I changed the formation?"

Jim had no answer.

"Do you have suggestions on other formations I should use that are better than the one I put them in?"

Jim had no suggestions.

"I changed up the formation because I was trying to teach the girls a new tactic. I wasn't worried about how they played because it was new to them. I just wanted them to try it out during this game. The opposition's formation presented us with a great opportunity to try something new and allow the girls to be challenged. Are you aware of that? Did Lucy tell you that?"

Jim's answer was no. But then he blurted out, "I am just so afraid for Lucy now that new girls have joined the team. You are going to cut her one of these days, aren't you? We are just afraid you are going to cut her."

Suddenly, the head coach saw Jim in an entirely different light. Instead of a hothead or obnoxious parent, he saw a father afraid for his child. Deep down, this is true of most parents. Their behaviors often do not reflect their true motivation, which is to protect their child. Sometimes, ugly sideline behaviors are actually rooted in love.

Communicating with Coaches

Not all coaches are going to be as psychologically minded, tolerant, or open to communicating with parents as are other coaches. As parents, the rule of thumb in communicating with coaches is as follows:

- Set up meetings outside of game day.
- Observe the twenty-four-hour rule: no discussion of the game with the coach within twenty-four hours before or after a game.
- Let your child initiate discussions with their coach before you intervene.
- Avoid discussions about other players or playing time.
- Discuss concerns about your child and what you can do to assist the coach.
- Give yourself the twenty-four-hour rule as well. The way you see the game may look entirely different the following day.
- Try not to be defensive with a coach: be secure in who you are, stop retaliating, and generally listen and stick to "I" statements to prevent unfair statements.
- Don't talk about other parents or kids.
- Be sure to attend all preseason and midseason meetings called by your coach to be able to understand, respect, and follow through with team rules and expectations.

When a parent needs to get involved:

- If you think your child is in danger
- If you feel your child is losing interest in the sport
- If you see a personality change
- If your child tells you they feel uncomfortable
- If coaches are degrading them, humiliating them, or comparing them to other players

Communication Isn't Everything; It's the Only Thing

Abby Wambach and Christie Pearce Rampone played together on a club that was arguably the world's best collection of soccer talent. The players were handpicked by the owner because each had achieved status as a leading athlete in the world of women's soccer. The athletes were all treated accordingly, and Christie and Abby were chosen as team captains.

The owner made sure that the women were looked after like consummate professionals and endowed with a lavish lifestyle. Players were housed in upscale West Palm apartments and provided with stellar health care and regular massage and were wined and dined at the finest restaurants. They were, appropriately, given the lifestyle of world-class professional athletes.

The club was a dream team, boasting awe-inspiring players, exceptional leadership, and an owner who truly believed in them. The formula should have virtually guaranteed a championship. It did not. When Christie looks back at her time on the team, she recalls that the players were unaccustomed to such treatment. They couldn't deal with it. But a lavish lifestyle can't have been the sole reason. Indeed, the issue stemmed from something we've been stressing...

Our problems came from a lack of communication.

On paper we were the best team created, but we weren't committed to one another. We didn't commit to the journey we could have had as a team. We didn't talk to one another.

Abby and I were team captains that season and also close friends, but, as the season progressed, we rarely discussed soccer. We never planned or created team strategy the entire time we were captains. It wasn't that we didn't care. We just thought we had a team that would take care of itself. Abby took control of the attacking side of the game and I was responsible for how we defended. We just worked separately, which meant that the team lacked a cohesive plan for our journey together. We didn't have team goals or milestones, or a shared list of skills we wanted to develop over the course of the season.

Incredibly, we never had a purposeful, face-to-face meeting with the intent to discuss, share, or plan anything about the team for the entire time we were captains. We worked separately. We allowed the owner to take control of the on- and off-the-field decision-making, something we should have been talking about.

We lost many games we hadn't expected to lose that season, and it taught Abby and me a vital lesson. Even though the women on our team were exceptional, those individual skills don't matter without solid communication. A team with no communication will always be vulnerable to a team with great communication. In the end, Abby and I realized that there is much more to the game than the players themselves, no matter how extraordinary. This made for one of the biggest lessons of my entire career.

We were all at the top of our game, all leveled up, but still, without communication, the team could not succeed.

The Neuroscience of Communication with Young Athletes

Can a seven-year-old in their first year of sports understand the same feedback a fifteen-year-old athlete can? Of course not.

Much of the literature in developmental psychology recommends that teachers, coaches, and parents not treat children as if they are miniature adults. When communications do not match a young athlete's developmental level, information can be lost, frustration may set in, and a disconnect can form between a parent and child or athlete and coach. As we communicate to our children, it is important to recognize that the skills and abilities associated with decision-making, impulsivity, and problem solving are still developing throughout childhood and well into adulthood. In fact, Jay Giedd and colleagues at the National Institute of Mental Health performed research using imaging on the developing brain and found that the human brain develops throughout adolescence and well into the twenties.[3] Have you ever noticed that even the brightest teenager can make random, impulsive, even deleterious decisions? This is because their frontal lobes are not fully developed. This is the area of the brain responsible for attention span, organization, and, most important, problem solving.

An athlete's emotional control and decision-making at the time of play may reflect their level of frontal lobe development more so than their ability level. This is not to say that young athletes will always make irrational decisions. It suggests that young athletes need guidance as their brains develop, well into their teens, specifically in the areas of controlling emotions and making better decisions. What better place to learn this than on the field, in pressure situations, and in front of family and peers? Parents and coaches can help teens progress as they develop by keeping communication open and setting clear boundaries about their behavior.

Spatial awareness is a common problem with younger children, likewise to do with brain development. Spatial awareness, which originates in the parietal lobe, is also responsible for the function and processing of sensory information and is similarly not fully developed until age twenty-five. This is why young athletes need reminders about where they are relative to their positions, as well as about on-field spacing and movement on the ball. Kids don't respond well to hearing "You lacked movement" or "You are out of position." They aren't equipped to understand. Instead, you need to show kids visual fixes. Even that takes tweaking: some young athletes can't translate markings on a clipboard to positions on the field. Some kids need to see an action done to then mimic and learn it.

When communicating to young athletes, Christie shows more than she tells. For example, instead of shouting, "Just work harder," you should explain what that means: when the ball moves, you move. Teach the kids not to stand and yell, "I'm open!" Instead, show them how to move to an open space by showing them how the pros do it on TV or even hands-on in their own backyards.

Here are some tips for teaching younger children:

- When they ask, "Why?" show them in a concrete way.
- Distinguish between what you are seeing and what they are seeing.
- Give kids alternatives to teach them problem solving.
- Ask for their opinion instead of telling them how you would do it.
- Expect conversations rather than doing all the talking.

When communicating with your child, it is essential to consider their developmental level, their sports IQ, and the impact on the game of their age and intellectual skills. A more effective critique of your child's play can stem from addressing the issue of problem solving instead of the technical elements of the play. And you should also look for clues.

Communicating Priorities

Last year, Dr. Keane's son Christian asked if he could miss a team pasta party before a game.

I told him that he should go. I reasoned that even though he didn't want to drive an hour to the party, he was part of a team and he should show his commitment. My son said, "I haven't missed a practice all summer, even when they were voluntary. I'm tired. I just want to stay in tonight. Why can't I make that decision for myself?"

I found this reasonable, and I let him stay home. I told him he would be the one to communicate his decision to his coach and he had to prepare for repercussions, including being benched. But that was his choice. Of course I didn't want to see my son benched. But he and I agreed on the bigger lesson: he had the right to decide when he needed a break. It was more important to teach him to trust and respect himself than to sacrifice when his body was saying no. But, again, he needed to understand that not every coach, parent, or teammate would necessarily agree with this approach.

To my surprise, his coach understood. Christian wasn't benched. The coach said that he, too, was a two-sport athlete in high school and knew what it was to be responsible to two teams and two coaches while keeping up with rigorous academics. He told Christian he really respected his honesty. He could have just feigned an illness and the conversation would've never come up.

Consider the message you send your child when they tell you they need a break from sports and you are not willing to honor it. Though my son's scenario could have played out very differently, he would have come away with the same lesson. Sometimes, the demands of sports force you into tough life decisions. Taking care of yourself and taking the time to relax or be with family and friends are essential for balance and self-care; that said, not everyone will appreciate your needs. I told my son that his feelings were more important than the game, but also that his decision could have unanticipated consequences.

These things happen at all levels of play, and it's never too early to start talking to kids—or modeling behavior—about handling things that take precedence over athletics. For instance, when Christie's teammate on the national team missed a game for her sister's wedding, she was forced to sit out for several games.

My teammate had to earn her way back into the starting lineup. I had to sit her down several times to calm her down. She almost quit! For her, it was more important to attend her sister's wedding than to make that game. We understood that. But the coach wasn't as understanding. With the help of teammates, she persevered. But, in the coach's eyes, she had missed something vital—and the coach made her pay for it.

The funny thing is this: she wouldn't have changed a thing about attending her sister's wedding. And, ironically, the coach seemed to regret her decision to limit the woman's playing time. These things happen in sports: coaches and team staff are likewise imperfect. They too learn from their experiences.

Communicate your intentions with purpose. If family comes first, then encourage your child to miss a game if needed and acknowledge that the consequences for missing a game pale to those for missing vital family events. If your child's feelings come first, let them make decisions for themselves, while teaching them to honor their commitments to their coach and team. Childhood is not a practice or a dress rehearsal. We need to communicate our positive messages intentionally, and then act accordingly, even when it hurts.

Actions Speak Louder than Words

How many parents do you know who rehash stories from their high school athletic careers? How many of these stories still conjure strong emotions, even twenty to thirty years later? These are powerful times for a young, developing mind. These parents' high school stories typically lionize Mom's or Dad's accomplishments while simultaneously causing a teenage eye roll. "Dad, I can't believe you're still talking about that. And around my friends!" As a parent,

you are instrumental in the creation of your child's influential memories. You are there to augment your child's life experience, not live
yours again through it. Your part as a sports parent is so valuable.
It is sacred. Know your intentions and be clear, as your communications will have a powerful and lasting impact on a young life. What
message of yours do you want your kids to remember twenty to
thirty years from now?

Most parents intend to communicate positive messages about
sports to their children. We suggest that you take the time to consider what it is you're communicating to your children. What do
you want them to learn from your sporting experiences—to cling to
past accolades or to understand how the past shapes the present and
future? For reference, we've compiled this list of messaging points.
Please feel free to add your own preferences.

- Winning isn't everything.
- Learn from your mistakes.
- Sports are an outlet.
- Have fun and enjoy yourself.
- Show good effort and attitude.
- Be a good sport.
- Be kind to your teammates and opponents.
- Be kind to yourself.
- Don't be afraid to take risks.
- It's okay to lose.
- It's not how you fall down; it's how you get up.
- Relationships are important—it takes a village.
- A leader is not just a title.
- Sports are medicine for the soul for life.

Sometimes, we directly teach these things to our children with
our words. Sometimes, we send our kids affirmations via text, be

it an inspirational quote or something humorous we found on the web. But, as communication is 93 percent body language, the way we behave packs a powerful punch in terms of communicating to our children. How many parents verbalize the importance of sportsmanship, only to villainize a referee for a bad call? It happens every day. To this end, take the time to write down and reflect on some of your routine sports parent behaviors and the inadvertent messages that accompany them. Here are some examples:

Remaining calm at the game. When a parent is emotionally and verbally reactive during a game, they have a huge impact on their child. A parent's yelling on the sidelines is often embarrassing for kids. Yelling angers the referees and coaches and reinforces messages about poor sportsmanship and winning being everything. Meanwhile, remaining calm reinforces messages about attitude, fun, and positivity.

Reacting positively after a loss. Kids come off a loss with multiple emotions, ranging from anger and disappointment to sadness and even self-deprecation. It is natural to kick into parenting mode and to support and console them. It is also natural to feel empathetically disappointed and find yourself picking apart the game, or even talking negatively about coaches or players. Sometimes emotions get the best of parents, too. However, take the time to evaluate your emotional reactivity and the inadvertent messages you convey to your children. Realize that you are a powerful role model in dealing with disappointments. The stronger your emotions, the stronger your message to your family about the importance of a game.

Letting your child take a break when they need to. Sometimes, kids ask to skip a practice to hang out with friends or participate in a different activity. Many parents fear for their commitment to the team or the affiliated repercussions. When your child asks for a break, listen. Pay attention to their reasoning. Do they deserve a break? Clearly, you do not want to foster routine irresponsibility; however, there can be legitimate reasons. Fatigued. Overworked. Not feeling well. Prioritizing another event. Overall, parents are responsible for making this tough decision with their child. Ultimately, you want children to understand the meaning of commitment while balancing the rest of their childhood interests.

Key Points to Remember

1. Understand your child's communication style and body languages. Teach your child to effectively communicate with and without words.
2. Become clear on your goals and intentions. Whether you are planning for your child to win a World Cup or just to make a few friends, your intentions should be clear and consistent. Avoid hidden agendas.
3. Deliver messages at an appropriate developmental level. Make sure that what you convey matches your child's level of understanding.
4. Determine what kind of dialogue to have with your child and look for feedback that your message was received as intended.
5. Use active listening to teach your child to value their own perceptions, beliefs, and opinions about themselves. Remember that some things in life we can only learn through our own experiences.

CHAPTER 3

Get Your Head in the Game

Soccer practice begins at 6:00 p.m. sharp. By 5:30 all three kids are fed. Their homework was finished by 4:00. Their soccer bags are packed and neatly aligned in the mudroom, awaiting pickup. By 5:45, each child has their shin guards on and their cleats dangling from their shoulder as they clamber into the car. Cell phones are left on the kitchen counter in charging stations. No one is fighting. Everyone is happy, well fed, and eagerly awaiting stepping onto the field with their beloved teammates.

LOL.

Here's the reality. Soccer practice begins at 6:00ish. By 5:30, one of the three children has come downstairs for dinner. Two of the kids have their faces in their cell phones and are still in school clothes. At least one set of shin guards is missing. One of the practice T-shirts never made it to the laundry basket. One of the kids doesn't want to go to practice tonight. At 5:50, everyone is racing toward the car with remnants of dinner in their hands. Kids are fighting. One won't put down her cell phone and listen.

If paragraph one sounds familiar, then skip to the next chapter. Nothing to see here. If paragraph two sounds more like your life as a sports parent, then read on. If you are like most parents of athletes, you feel like there is not enough time in the day to get everything done. You might also have found yourself outnumbered by children, by practices, and by events. Not enough cars in the driveway or even adult drivers to get everyone where they need to go. This chapter is about the mental game that goes into being a great performer, and it's about how we prepare to perform.

Some experts say that up to 90 percent of sports is mental and only 10 percent is physical. Whatever the exact proportion, most experts put the mental number at least at 50 percent. Clearly, a large part of your child's performance is influenced by the situations, mind-set, emotional tone, and behaviors leading up to a given event. Athletes require different things in order to be focused and confident walking into a competition; that's true of anyone heading into a test, preparing for public speaking, or getting ready for a job interview.

In Christie's experience, the US Women's National Soccer Team purposefully and strategically planned their pregame experiences, as do many professional and college teams. Younger athletes are often unable to choose what they do prior to sporting events because they aren't in control of the family dynamics, responsibilities, and other obligations of parents or siblings. If you're in a position to help create a pregame environment, think about what you can do to make it as controlled as possible.

Have you thought about your child's mental state prior to leaving your home for a sporting event? What frame of mind is your child in when they head to a practice or game? What family dynamics influence the emotional state of your athletes? We've found that families don't think much about the impact of the time before games; rather, most parents are on autopilot. Families are engaged in normal routines: talking, breaking up fights between siblings, or rushing out the door.

The transition times prior to an event can be a crucial element in your child's success. If you consider transition times as part of your child's development and growth, instead of a means to an end, you will likely see improvements in their performance; better still, you may also witness more satisfaction with their experiences in general. Get the emotional pulse of your child. In addition to being aware of your family's climate or environment prior to games or events, consider adhering to certain rituals. Christie and her national teammates, for example, all stuck to different runups on game day.

Every time I had a big game or event, I would make sure I chilled out all day. Sometimes I would go shopping with some teammates. I walked around to loosen up my legs. But mainly I would not think about the game. I didn't need to be mentally prepping all day before a game. I just needed to take care of myself. My mental preparation started during the bus ride to the game. That's when those inner voices would start talking in my head. During the bus ride, I sat quietly and did nothing except focus on the mental game. I wanted to feel my emotions, and I concentrated on them. I wanted to understand my tension, my body, and my thoughts.

Ordinarily, the national team bus was very quiet. I can still visualize exactly where everyone sat, who was in my periphery, and what they were doing. We were always very routine, and we respected one another's pregame routines. A lot of girls liked to listen to music or read on the way to the game, and some would binge-watch Netflix series with their seatmates. Abby, for example, had to win at least one game of solitaire before she got off the bus. That was her ritual. If the ride to the game was short and Abby did not win at least once, she would panic. In her mind, she had to get that solitaire game done in order to succeed. We were great seatmates because I needed quiet and she needed her game.

Most if not all of my teammates routinely texted a family member or loved one or had a last phone call right before stepping into the locker room. They wanted that last moment of positivity from someone they loved and trusted before they stepped into battle.

Take it from the pros. The things you do and say to your child will have a lasting impact on their performance. If the message is positive, it doesn't matter exactly what you say; communicate that no matter what happens out there, you are there for your children. Remember, athletic success depends on having the courage to take risks, and the game itself can put athletes in vulnerable spaces: penalty kicks, quick decision-making about passing or shooting, going for a tackle or playing it cautiously. The decision-making process alone, in front of dozens or thousands of people, requires bravery. As a parent, you are their first resource. In order to develop bravery, a person must first develop feelings of safety.

Abraham Maslow, an American psychologist, is best known for his personality theory, the hierarchy of needs.[1] He said that a person must first achieve basic feelings of safety and security in order to progress to a focus on higher-level needs such as self-esteem and self-worth. He said that people are anxious when their lower-level needs are not met. He believed that until these needs are met, people cannot achieve the highest levels of human functioning, which he deemed self-actualization. When a person is self-actualized, they are considered to have reached their full potential. He believed that when physiological safety, self-esteem, and belongingness needs are met, only then can a person become everything they are capable of becoming.

Of course, the time before a game or practice isn't the time when a child becomes fully self-actualized. That takes a lifetime. But we use the paradigm here to illustrate that when basic needs are unmet, such as when a person feels unsafe or unloved, it hinders their ability to perform at their highest level. While we have countless examples of athletes performing phenomenally despite their lower-level needs being unmet, these athletes were playing with some level of anxiety, according to Maslow's theory. In the context of youth sports, imagine what a child's game looks like when their feelings of safety, love, and belongingness needs are continually met and reinforced. Dr. Keane recalls seeing Maslow's concepts come to life on a high school soccer field.

When my daughter Cameryn told me that she typically played better in the second half because she was nervous during the first half, I was shocked. I knew that she had nerves at the very beginning of a game, but I was surprised to hear that she was nervous the entire half.

Cameryn told me that she believed having nerves was normal, and, while that was true, she also believed she would never be able to do anything to change them—that is, until one of her friends did something completely unexpected and changed her game. It occurred on Fan Day, the first night game of her high school soccer season. The Fan Day game is usually the season's most attended game: many students, families, and faculty come out for the annual event.

My daughter told me that when the game started, her anxiety was even higher than usual. Just as she was lining up midfield, she heard her friends calling her name on the sideline. She looked up to see three of her best friends smiling and waving at her. When things got quiet and the first whistle was about to blow, her friend Kate, decked out in blue and orange war paint not unlike the character William Wallace in Braveheart, *waved her hands wildly and yelled, "Cameryn! I love you! I love you!"*

Kate's cheers sliced through the quiet night air, and my daughter, initially embarrassed by the attention, started laughing. Kate's sweet and funny comments broke the cycle of nerves in Cameryn's mind, jolting her out of her habitual first-half performance anxiety. The cheers snapped her out of her own head.

The scene made me look inward. What had I said to her before that game? "Score one for me"? *That's likely.* "Have a good game"? *Probably. It made me think even more about the power of pregame experiences as a prelude to performance, since our kids glean from us their deep-seated feelings of safety, love, and belongingness. Parents put a unique, inimitable, and lasting stamp on a child's confidence, mental game, and performance.*

As working parents used to shuttling our kids to different practices and games during the week, we often use the time prior to games and practices to take work phone calls or problem solve the workday. Instead of being a necessary respite for mental preparation—the kids for the game, us for the rest of the day—the car rides can become extensions of everybody's own personal chaos. When Christie felt emotional or stressed, her tone would change while driving to her daughters' practices and games. When she was in the middle of a divorce, she often felt irritable or even disconnected from her daughters. She was so busy that she would rush to practices and games, often showing up late, creating stress, and causing emotions to run high.

All parents and families have responsibilities and stressors that impact our interactions with our kids. Simple awareness of our own behavior can impact our levels of stress. Just thinking about being present—taking a deep breath before getting out of the car; asking ourselves, *What am I thinking about?* periodically throughout the day; not allowing distractions or irritants to derail our goals—can result in incredible change. As adults, when we establish healthy pregame habits like mental and physical preparation, we set an example for our kids about getting into their own strongest mental states.

This chapter is about getting into a clear mental headspace before a big event, whether it's the big game, the big test, the big presentation, or the big dance. It's about understanding the preparation needed to perform at our best and at our most authentic. Above all else, it's about making the last word, the last thing you said before your child exits the car, positive: Tell them you love them. Tell them you are there for them. Make them feel safe and worthy. With these aims in mind, it's important to establish healthy, head-clearing habits for this preparation time.

Sleep

Being rested is not just about sleeping the night before a game; how we sleep up to three days prior to the game can influence performance. Adequate sleep hygiene is vital to game-day performance because sleep allows the body to replenish, heal, and recover.

Many kids fall asleep during long car rides. Fittingly, the National Sleep Foundation recommends a power nap—sleeping for twenty to thirty minutes—before a game if needed.[2] While some kids like to sleep longer, especially during long rides, research shows that excessive sleep prior to a game can actually degrade athletic performance. After a half-hour nap, athletic performance may decline.

Much like a Navy SEAL in advance of a mission, Abby Wambach would nap all day before a major competition. She napped before every game. No one would believe that a powerhouse player like Abby would be snoozing before the World Cup. But napping benefitted her.

Parents should make decisions about napping and sleeping on an individual basis. Though a power nap might improve performance in one athlete, it can hamper performance in another. Pay attention to how your child reacts. Overall, too much napping can interrupt the body's natural sleep cycles. Napping during the day can prevent you from falling asleep at night. For most people, an adequate amount of uninterrupted sleep during the night coupled with routine exercise and good nutrition renders a power nap unnecessary.

Eating

The number one need for youth athletes is water. Kids tend to think they are not thirsty, and many avoid water. Athletes should be well hydrated prior to the game, sipping even on the way to the game. We recommend packing another water bottle or jug in their bag for during the sporting event. Four to eight ounces of water an hour prior to a game is recommended. Christie remembers:

My daughters grew up around the US Women's National Team. They learned to drink water through observation. All the women on the team were constantly sipping water. Everyone seemed to have a bottle of water with them everywhere they went. There were cases of water lined up in our hotel rooms. I never have to tell my kids to drink. They grew up understanding how important it is for their body because of how much water everyone around them was drinking.

I remember so many times when we had to stop the bus to go to the bathroom. Many times the girls would run off of the bus, dying to get to a bathroom after a long ride. We were always hydrated. We knew how vital water was to our game-day performance.

Many athletes eat carbohydrates the night before a game because carbs provide the body with glycogen, which delivers lasting energy. Without a glycogen store, the body begins to burn fat. While that is great news for people who want to lose weight, for athletes it means more susceptibility to fatigue or muscle injuries.

Basically, the best pregame foods are pasta, bread, fruits, and vegetables, in reasonable amounts. Encourage kids to stay away from fried or fatty foods. The pregame meal should occur one to two hours before a game; a good rule of thumb is to eat half of a normal portion size. Quick options prior to the game include protein bars, yogurt, bananas, protein shakes, and whole-grain toast. Teach athletes to view food as fuel and to monitor how food choices affect the way they feel. Many young kids, quite understandably, don't spend a lot of time thinking about the ramifications of improper eating. Also, don't overlook this vital idiosyncrasy: have your child eat what agrees with their stomach prior to game time.

Emotional Preparation

As noted, parental behaviors influence children's emotions. Your stress becomes their stress. Your irritability can result in their feeling distracted, disconnected, or overwhelmed while playing. The car ride to the event is a time to give your child peace of mind so they can be present during their practices or games.

Christie's daughter Rylie often stresses about homework. On the way to practice, she agonizes over it. She fears that she won't be able to get it done.

I always tell Rylie that I will help her with her homework no matter how long it takes. I want her to go and enjoy practice. I want practice to be a stress reliever for her, not a stress producer. I encourage her to take her mind off of everything else when she is at practice because I know that's how she will get the most out of it.

When I was a kid, I was always anxious before a game to the point that I would nearly throw up. I wanted to do so well. I felt overwhelming anxiety about letting my teammates down. In fact, I never learned how to get past my pregame anxiety as a kid. It wasn't until I learned that the game wasn't about me—it was about we—that I was able to alleviate my stress before I played.

Anxiety and stress are the two most common emotions experienced by athletes before a game. Kids worry about whether they will play well, the caliber of their opponents, how their coach will behave toward them, and how they will perform in front of their coach, peers, teammates, and families. So often, it is who attends the game that unduly influences a young athlete's performance.

A lot of kids talk to us about being afraid of messing up, looking silly, or being ridiculed by peers. Playing time is another source of anxiety. Incredibly, some young athletes admit that it is not the amount of playing time but rather their parents' reaction to allotted playing time that they most fear.

Mental Imagery

We recommend that kids take at least five to ten minutes before an event's start time to visualize success. When you visualize yourself doing something, your brain responds to the visualization as if you are actually doing it; visualizations allows you a trial run of an activity from the safety of your own mind![3] Countless studies show how performance improves after bouts of visualizing success.[4] For example, when a football player visualizes themselves completing a fifty-yard pass to a receiver, the chemicals and electrical impulses in the brain respond to the thoughts as they would if the athlete were physically performing the task. By the time athletes arrive to the field at game time, their bodies are already mentally conditioned for success and are more likely to perform well.

This is why professional athletes use visualization regularly to enhance performance. Alongside countless hours of physical repetition, athletes also train their minds by visualizing their goals. While visualizing, they activate the sights, sounds, smells, and senses involved in athletic performance—the more detailed, the better. Christie learned about mental imagery as part of the Olympic team.

I was extremely anxious before games until I was introduced to imagery in 2000. Once I understood the power of imagery, my nerves changed and my game improved. I would take a personal highlight video and set it to one of my favorite songs, which changed every year I played. I used songs like Alicia Keys's "Girl on Fire" and Rachel Platten's "Fight Song" for my videos.

You get the picture. Christie watched the video so many times that it was captured in her mind's eye. She could watch it in her mind during warm-ups or while on the sidelines. Today, kids can use their phones to make their own videos. Apps let them set their highlight reels to music. Even without a video, you can make a ritual of visualizing your child's great moments by talking about them. Jot down a few of those moments beforehand, and read them aloud on the way to the game.

Music also has a powerful influence on emotional states. These days, most kids are plugged into their technology prior to a game. Given music's impact on mood and confidence, encourage your kids to listen to mood-enhancing music before important events.

In a study conducted by sports psychologist Costas Karageorghis, music was shown to improve athletic performance in terms of endurance, power, productivity, and strength.[5] Music that is stimulating and enjoyable can help distract from anxiety-provoking thought processes, get athletes into the zone, increase confidence, and enhance the joy of playing. Given the unilaterality of the results, Karageorghis concluded that music is a "legal performance-enhancing drug."

Talk to your child about what kind of music makes them feel good, and encourage them to listen before they get out of the car. Your child might prefer to keep some of that private. That's okay. Or maybe everyone in the car can listen to it together. That's okay too. Get silly. Stay flexible. Respect the difference.

Rituals

Rituals and superstitions can also combat athletic anxiety.

For ten years of bus rides to and from practices and games, I sat in the fourth seat on the left side with Abby. We saw the game similarly and were comfortable with each other. We liked to talk about the game on the way home—soccer talk about how we were connecting or how the practice had gone. I remember exactly where Megan [Rapinoe] and Alex [Morgan] sat, too. When I had Rylie, she would plop in between us. This went on every season from 2006 to 2015.

When Abby retired, her absence was strange for me. So strange, in fact, that I started questioning whether it was time for me to retire too. Maybe it was time. All the rituals that I never realized I had were gone. The players I was used to seeing were gone. I wondered if I could still do it without the people, the sameness, the familiarity.

Consistent routines lead to enhanced performance. They lead to feeling safer and more prepared. Clearly it is not the actual behaviors that lead to better performance; it is the belief system behind the behaviors that packs the punch. For example, Michael Jordan always wore his blue North Carolina shorts under his Bulls uniform. Alex Morgan always wears a pink headband. Shannon Boxx always wore a French braid. Baseball players often spit into their hands before picking up a bat. Basketball players believe the last person to take a shot during warm-ups will have the best game. Football players think taking a new number when they are traded to another team is bad luck. Hockey players won't cross their sticks.

While playing on the national team, Shannon Boxx and I realized that we both loved banana pancakes. We developed a ritual of ordering banana pancakes on game day. It got so important to us that, no matter the conditions, we had to have them; this got pretty challenging at some of the international games. Even our team nutritionist got involved in our quest for banana pancakes. With banana pancakes in our bellies, we believed, we would always have a good game. We believed it like we knew the sky was blue. It was such a simple, comforting ritual, but it was also enormously effective. It is a memory that I will always cherish.

We could write a whole chapter on rituals, but their power really lies in our belief systems. The rituals themselves distract from the true pressures of the game. They help athletes get into a positive mindset. Investigate what your child is doing before events and then figure out why. Even if these behaviors haven't taken on formal ritualism, identify and encourage positive behaviors. Pregame consistency and routines are known to enhance performance. Feel good. Look good. Play good.

I *Am* and I *Can*

Two of the most powerful phrases in human language are "I am" and "I can." These statements are known to strengthen a person's ability to heal, to forgive, and to cope with difficult times. You can help your child achieve a positive headspace by taking turns finishing a sentence that begins with "I am":

- I am a good teammate.
- I am a selfless player.
- I am good at keeping my head up.
- I am a kind player.
- I am worth it.
- I am strong.

This powerful exercise uses real, possible, and believable examples and gives parents a clue into their child's self-image. You can use this ritual to positively shape children's thought patterns. The older the child, the more you can get out of this exercise and, ultimately, learn about pregame positivity.

We are all susceptible to the stressors of daily family and work life as well as the busyness, even chaos, associated with practices, teams, coaches, and sporting events. As parents, our emotional state on the way to events may be tied to influences outside the game. We may also find ourselves caught up in the excitement and competition of the game and thus eager to coach our children on the way there. Sometimes, a good talk prior to the game is fun and adds to the enjoyment of the moment. We invite you to try one of the suggestions detailed in this chapter prior to your child's next game. Even a shift in your awareness can make an immediate impact on your child's performance. A season of mindfulness and awareness can make lasting changes. You are what you think. You become what you do. And so do our kids.

When Christie talks about *being all in*, she means that her athletes need to bring all of themselves to what they're doing. Whether you're heading into a big game or getting ready for a big test, being all in is about being present in the moment, feeling prepared for the unknown, and daring to take risks. When an athlete is all in, they know they have everything they need to succeed. They know they are enough.

When my athletes arrive at a game, I tell them that the moment you step on the field to play, you can't get fitter, you can't get stronger, and you can't work on your technical ability. Your time is right now. You can't change who you are right now. You are enough. I tell them to step on the field and embrace it. I am trying to instill confidence in each athlete, assure them that who they are right at that moment is perfect. The time is now. There is no need to question themselves prior to performing.

Knowing how to physically and emotionally prepare for this kind of commitment is a skill that takes time to develop, but it is so worth it. The sense of calm, control, and preparedness enjoyed by a kid who knows how to get their head in the game will serve them throughout their lives—and will probably help you, too.

CHAPTER 4

Accountability

Accountability is the obligation or the willingness to accept responsibility for, or to account for, one's actions. When athletes are accountable, they take ownership of their mistakes as well as their progress. Teaching kids accountability ultimately fosters a sense of courage and humility. Regardless of your age, it can be hard to take an honest look at yourself and your good, bad, and ugly. When we teach kids accountability, we help them develop into conscientious and responsible adults. Without accountability, kids tend to blame others and find ways to justify their behavior, regardless of how their actions might be affecting others.

Responsibility is the first step in teaching accountability. It is defined as the carrying out of agreed-upon actions, being dependable, and honoring commitments. Accountability, meanwhile, is a personal choice that takes responsibility one step further. Accountability is something you hold yourself to in the wake of a task, be it done or undone. It is about transforming your responsibility and effort into reliable and actionable results.

Take a standard, albeit ideal, team practice: when practice is over, all the kids join in to put away the practice equipment, including picking up cones, putting balls in the ball bag, and making sure all the pinnies are removed and sorted. All the kids know that once practice is over, everything must be cleaned up. Only after the coaches conduct their final team meeting and everything is put away are the players released to go home.

Consider an alternate: after the equipment is put away, some of the kids grab their bags and cell phones and walk with their friends, as wrappers from protein bars, empty water bottles, and sweatshirts litter the ground. Responsible athletes put away the equipment as instructed; accountable athletes throw away garbage even when it isn't theirs. They bring the abandoned sweatshirts to the coaches or their parents. Some athletes will take it one step further and color-code the cones or send out a mass text about the sweatshirts. It is a personal choice, a nod toward accountability, to look out for your teammates and make sure your playing environment is clean, rather than doing only what you were told.

This same scenario plays out on the field. It is the difference between the athlete who does exactly what they are told but never more and the athlete who plays outside the box, giving that little bit extra, every time. These are the athletes who move out of position to chase down an opponent for a teammate who couldn't get there in time, the athletes who fill in for an injured or fatigued teammate. Accountable athletes can be trusted to solve problems on the field, even when they did not create them.

Accountability is a concept that contains a lot of different elements, all of which are important on and off the field:

- Personal responsibility: being aware of what's expected of you and fulfilling those expectations
- Team responsibility: being aware of what's expected from the group at large, getting involved to ensure that everybody is doing their part, and likely picking up some slack in the meantime
- Personal pride: feeling like your value is tied up in the larger outcome

- Ownership: believing that your contributions make a difference in the overall success or failure of the group
- Self-analysis: being able to assess where there is room for you to influence the outcome and results as a whole, and being able to identify areas for improvement
- Commitment: being a reliable presence with a consistently dedicated attitude

In this chapter, we're going to discuss all the facets of accountability and explain how to teach it and how it contributes to important growth and development in our kids—both as athletes and as people.

What Is Your Ripple Effect?

A ripple effect occurs when an event or idea produces a reaction, spreads, and produces a further effect. In sports, showing up to the field feeling positive and strong creates a positive ripple effect. Talking negatively to a teammate, on the other hand, can negatively affect the whole team. You can teach your child about the ripple effect by showing them how powerfully their actions affect others.

The same thing goes for parents. One bad play, one bad referee call, and parents on the sidelines get louder and angrier. I once heard a mother at a heated soccer game (particularly for nine-year-olds) yell, "Ref! That was clearly a bad call. Everyone can see he was offsides!"

Another mom on the opposing team yelled back at her, "You are not a referee!"

To which the first mom replied (and lied), "In fact, I am a referee!"

"Well, you are not the referee of **this** game!"

We all have our moments. It is easy to get caught up in the emotion of a sporting event, especially when everyone's emotions are running high. It's even more difficult to maintain your composure when it is your child being yelled at, getting hurt, or being unfairly fouled. Sometimes you feel justified in yelling back. You might even lose your temper.

Eventually, the mom who'd triggered the argument paused, took a deep breath, and moved her seat away from the offending parents and away from the negativity. She could have stayed and continued arguing. Heck, everyone else was yelling too. Instead, she chose not to say another word. She chose her ripple effect.

If you are responsible, your behaviors and choices can create a small, positive ripple. But if you are accountable, your behavior and choices can have a significant positive ripple effect. Don't make excuses—be accountable and create that big positive ripple.

Ways to Foster Accountability in Your Kids

Parents Create the First Mission Statement

A family mission statement is a combined, unified expression from all family members of what your family is all about—what it is you really want to do and be—and the principles you choose to govern your family life.

—*Stephen Covey*, The 7 Habits of Highly Effective Families

Companies have been putting together mission statements for decades, and when families do the same, both the process and the result can be incredibly powerful. A family mission statement is just what it appears to be. It is a description of a family's values, standards, goals, and raison d'être, or reason to be. When married couples first get together, they rarely talk about why they got together and what their life goals and purpose will be. Much of this is implicit, subtle, and often assumed between partners and later their kids.

When we reviewed our own family missions, we both realized we had similar values and standards but had never formally presented them to our children. For example, both of our families value attitude and effort. Our children know that because we repeat it to them so frequently, on and off the field. We often tell them that it doesn't matter if you won or you lost, got a bad grade or an A; what matters was that your attitude and effort were in place. It is our golden rule.

Our kids know that they are accountable for their attitude and effort, over which they have direct control regardless of coaches, teachers, or other outside circumstances. This awareness gives them an internal guidance system in any environment. As part of a family mission statement, family members get a sense of who they are and what standard they hold themselves to.

After writing the first draft of this chapter, we sat down with our families and formally wrote our mission statements. What initially felt forced and awkward turned out to be a laughter-filled hour of mindful soul-searching. Everyone in the family meeting had a voice and contributed to the final draft of the family mission statement. The kids came up with words like "loyalty," "respect," "fun," "determination," and "love." They talked about how the words translate to actions, like what to do when one of them ate the last brownie. Or who should bring the laundry upstairs, even when they didn't use the pool towels or it is not their clothes. These discussions were quite different from those we have when things are unraveling and everyone is arguing, blaming, and justifying what they did or didn't do. There is power in putting your purpose and your goals into words; having this statement lets family members evaluate one another's behaviors, articulate the standards, and encourage one another to live by the mutually agreed-upon mission.

Without this vision, Stephen Covey argues in *The 7 Habits of Highly Effective Families*, kids can "be swept along with the flow of society's values and trends...It's simply living out the scripts that have been given to you. In fact, it's really not living at all; it's being lived."[1]

What we make our kids accountable for in the home inevitably shows up on the field. For families with athletes, their family mission statement should include a specific mention about what it means to be an accountable athlete. Remember, parents are the first exemplars when it comes to playing sports, being a good teammate, and behaving at sporting events. Kids throw their first baseball, shoot their first basket, or score their first goal in their backyards, long before stepping onto a field. They attend their first sporting events with their families, whether it is an older sibling's game or a professional event. Parents wield the most powerful impact in teaching accountability in sports.

Athlete Accountability Questions to Ask Your Child

- Is your bag ready?
- Is your uniform clean?
- Did you go to bed early enough?
- Did you eat properly and prepare yourself?
- Are you hydrated?
- Are you preparing three days prior?
- Is your homework done?
- Are you honest with the coach if you are playing on two teams?
- Are you fully committed to the team?
- Do you train away from sessions with your coach?

- Do you ask questions at practice to get better?
- Do you express yourself so your coach knows how you are feeling?
- Do you plan ahead and alert your coach if you're not going to be there?
- Are you on time? If not, why?
- Did you show good attitude and effort?

Athlete Accountability Exercise

1. Draw up a family mission statement about sports. Choose at least seven values that you and your children believe define their mission in sports. Include topics such as fun, attitude and effort, competition, hard work, good choices, sportsmanship, preparedness, and readiness to learn.
2. Each season, list two values that most resonate with your child and two things they would like to focus on moving forward.
3. Post these words somewhere visible in your home, or on their hockey stick, or in their soccer bag. Tape them inside their helmet or on their bat.
4. Throughout the season—on the car ride to or from an event, at dinner, or before practice—talk about how they showed their values at the last game or practice. Reflect on how they were accountable to those values.

Revisit this exercise with each season and with different teams. Discuss how your child engages in these concepts. The exercise teaches a child to look internally while learning new skill sets and developing physically. The exercise highlights the unique personal contribution your child makes to each team and teaches accountability that comes from within. It leaves the coaching to the coaches and the parenting to the parents.

Communicate the Standard

You can't hold someone accountable if you don't first communicate your expectations. At back-to-school night, teachers discuss their curricula and teaching methods, as well as parent, student, and classroom expectations so kids and families can meet them. We suggest that sports parents inform their children about their expectations at the start of each season. For example, discuss responsibilities such as who prepares game gear and who is responsible for getting rides to and from practice. Discuss whose job it is to pack the bags, fill the water bottles, and clean the uniforms. As kids get older, scheduling can become quite chaotic, so teens should be held accountable for time management and scheduling changes.

Christy Holly, a twenty-year veteran of youth coaching, is the US Women's National Team recruiter and developer and also the assistant coach of the US Women's U17 and U23 teams. When Coach Holly took on his first professional team, he communicated his standard on the first day of practice. He created the mission statement much like a family statement, and he asked all the athletes and coaching staff to contribute to it. He told the team that once the mission statement was created and received, every team member was accountable for everything on the statement, on and off the field. His team agreed. Their mission statement honored seven core values: trust, teamwork, honesty, integrity, work ethic, perseverance, and accountability.

Coach Holly believes that the core values instilled in youth athletes later become a natural touchstone when things go wrong. He repeatedly preaches the core values of the mission statement to his athletes, to remind, to instill, and to create a sense of solidarity. He believes that players need to develop a mind-set of accountability when things are going well in order for it to kick in when things start going poorly.

During his second season of professional coaching, Coach Holly's team endured some tough losses. He noticed that several athletes were beginning to lose sight of the team values. During one game, what would be an eventual team loss, two of the athletes refused to high-five their special teams coaches. One athlete was upset about playing time and the other was angry about their position. The spirit of the team seemed to be unraveling, and their negativity caused a ripple effect.

Coach Holly relied on the mission statement. At the next team meeting, he reminded the players of their agreed-upon core values. He told them to reflect on their recent behaviors on and off the field and to hold themselves accountable for any behaviors that did not reflect the team's core values. He told them that they had twenty-four hours to come to him if they had concerns about living up to the team's mission statement. After those twenty-four hours, he said, he was going to make roster changes according to core values.

Coach Holly expected two of his eighteen players to own up to the unsportsmanlike behavior he saw on the field; they had outwardly disrespected the coaches in front of their teammates. Those two players did come forward, admitting to feeling beaten down by the losses and for unfairly taking out their frustrations on the coaches. Even more incredibly, fourteen other players came to him and owned up to potential lapses in core values. Many admitted to insufficient effort. Others lamented their attitude toward their teammates and about the game. Still others confessed to behaving selfishly, to prioritizing their own playing time over the process and the team.

Coach Holly was proud of the turnout because it reflected a culture of accountability. The players all thought themselves to be the root of the problem. He had instilled a set of core values, and the players had called upon it in times of adversity. This was part of Coach Holly's larger methodology of teaching players to "Live Above the Line," a concept that outlined player expectations before the season and stood as a reference throughout the season.

Live Above the Line

Being a Role Model

Parents who do not model accountability cannot expect their children to behave accountably. Again, accountability is a choice and a mindset. There are times when teaching accountability can seem daunting or even impossible, but the behavior you exhibit now will ultimately manifest in your child's sense of accountability. For example, when you apologize instead of making excuses, you demonstrate personal responsibility. The values that we hope to instill in our children and teach them to feel accountable for, such as their politeness, respect, eating habits, fitness level, work ethic, cleanliness, organization, and even grooming habits, start with our own.

To be a role model for accountability, you must be brutally honest with yourself about your own day-to-day behaviors. Note how often you grumble, "I don't have time for that," "I can't," or "If we didn't have so many games this week, I would be able to..." Pay attention to how many times you say "sorry" or make excuses. We can't just mandate accountability in our children; we need to live it. When Christie's daughters were growing up and accompanying her on the road with the national team, they learned a lot about accountability.

My position on the national team inherently made me a good role model when it came to how I took care of my body. My kids got to see me working out consistently for years. They saw me making excellent food choices and not consuming too much alcohol because that would affect my ability to play well. They have seen me drink and have a good time, but always in moderation. They also spent time with twenty other great female leaders and role models. And talk about accountability: they saw me continue to work out, eat well, and hydrate even during the off-season. They saw me have a chance to play in my forties because of the lifestyle I led.

Providing Just and Reliable Consequences

Many times, usually in the heat of the moment, we reprimand our children with unduly harsh and unjust consequences for things they do, saying things like:

- "That is it! No using your cell phone for the rest of the year!"
- "I am taking away *all* of your electronics."

■ "I am tired of you leaving your sweatshirts at practice. I am going to give away your gear to someone who actually appreciates their stuff!"

Obviously, when we stack the deck with empty threats, we rarely follow through. Worse yet, we haven't scratched the surface of accountability. When consequences are too harsh, kids spend their time being mad at us instead of learning the lessons we are trying to teach. When we provide just and reliable consequences, we not only help them internalize our rules and values, we also maintain a healthy relationship with our children.

The best methods of discipline for teaching accountability are those that employ natural consequences, are least restrictive, and create an opportunity for the child to learn by themselves. When Christie was raising her daughters while playing on the US Women's National Team, she had to be creative. With the chaos of traveling and the stress of playing in the world arena, Christie often found herself brandishing heat-of-the-moment consequences, though she never lost sight of the consistency needed to teach her daughters a sense of responsibility.

Christie and her daughters usually ate their meals with the team at hotel restaurants. To instill discipline, a friend told her about using "bad-girl medicine" as a quick and reliable consequence. Bad-girl medicine is actually Tabasco sauce, which is conveniently available in most hotels and restaurants. The idea is to place a tiny dot of Tabasco sauce on a child's tongue so they would feel the burning sensation. If Christie's daughters misbehaved in public, Christie would place a bottle of Tabasco sauce in front of their plates: bad-girl medicine. She never even had to use it.

Mealtime for my team was a time for players to relax and unwind. My daughters had to behave well in an adult environment at a very young age.

They learned early about proper manners in a restaurant and at team meals.
Sometimes they were able to run around, depending on the mood or the
particular restaurant. But after a tough loss or hard practice, they needed
to behave and understand that when Mom told them to sit down and eat, it
wasn't playtime.

The women on the national team had a running joke about Abby and
Tabasco sauce. Since she loved it and used it regularly when we were dining
out, she used it on her food in secret from my kids. My daughter Rylie loves
and admires Abby. If she ever saw how much Tabasco sauce Abby used on
her food, she would never believe it was "bad-girl medicine." Abby wasn't
a bad girl, and Tabasco sauce clearly had no effect on her. We all used to kid
that parenting was the art of deception, so, with the help of the team, I would
always distract Rylie when Abby asked for Tabasco sauce.

Parents hold their children accountable via multiple disciplinary
methods, but the success of any given method depends on the parents' *own* ability to be accountable. Effective parenting comes from
controlling our own emotions and behaviors so we can remain reliable and consistent. In employing these methods, and to benefit from
the efficacy that comes with consistency, parents must be prepared to
discipline their child every time, without failure. Otherwise, children
learn quickly that the threat may not be real. This plays out on the
sidelines, on the car ride home, and wherever else you are modeling
accountability in sports.

I always loved how Abby taught Rylie to be personally responsible and
patient. She taught her not to interrupt adults. Abby would tell her, "My
hand on your arm means I hear you and I will get to you. I am not able to
talk right then, but you should know if my hand is on your arm, I know
what you have to say is important and you must wait your turn." Rylie
loved it, and she never interrupted. In fact, she never interrupted any adults

when she was growing up. I think Rylie felt important when Abby squeezed her arm. And Abby always kept her word. When Abby finished her conversation, she gave Rylie 100 percent of her attention. She made Rylie feel special just by that touch; it gave her something to rely upon so Rylie never had to worry about going unnoticed.

I really admired Abby's consistency and dedication to teaching Rylie. To this day, my daughter is very respectful and does not interrupt. My younger daughter, Reece, however, is still learning...

Accountability isn't about making your kid feel like they're on their own. It's really important to explain that you're teaching them the personal responsibility skills that will help them thrive as they grow. As you put more responsibility on their shoulders, offer them more support and assurances that you're still there for them, even if you've let them fail on occasion.

Giving Honest Feedback

It is *so* hard to give negative feedback, especially to our children. Research on management consistently shows that leaders tend to avoid giving feedback, especially negative or corrective feedback.[2] This holds true for parenting as well. Parents are afraid of hurting their children's feelings or doing damage to their self-esteem. On the flip side, they are afraid of inflating a false sense of pride and fostering cockiness or self-absorption.

Positive reinforcement assists in the development of children's self-esteem and self-worth. Feelings of safety and security aid the development of internal models needed for tackling problems and handling adversity. Children need both rewards and ramifications to perform well. Indeed, bad behavior brings consequences, and parents need to be the first line of defense for teaching that lesson as well. Christie recalls that teaching accountability was one of her toughest tasks as head coach of Sky Blue FC in 2009, during their run to winning the Women's Professional Soccer national title.

A year after the US National Women's Team won gold at the Beijing 2008 Olympics, we were on a high. Natasha Kai was a key member of that team. She had so much talent and could be relied upon to score all types of goals for us. When she was on her game, she was incredible.

Natasha played for me on Sky Blue FC in 2009 and, naturally, was one of our big names. Even though she had been starting every game, she was not performing to her capability. When I was appointed coach midseason, I realized that I had to have a very tough conversation with Natasha. Understand this: at the time, Natasha was one of my closest friends. She was actually living with me! But, despite our friendship, I knew that she needed to be held to the same standard as everyone else. It didn't matter if she was considered a big name. If she wasn't playing to her potential, she wouldn't be starting. This conversation with Tasha was difficult; so was subsequently pulling her from her starting position. But I knew—as her coach and teammate—that I would be doing her and her teammates a disservice by failing to address her play or hold her accountable.

We went into the playoffs with Tasha, one of our main attacking threats, serving as a substitute player. I was hoping that subbing her out would be her wake-up call.

Tasha was struggling with her eating habits off the field. She was not giving herself enough nutrition to last a ninety-minute game. We talked about it often. Since she couldn't last for ninety minutes, I would sub her in only at the end. I needed to reduce her playing time so she could be more effective on the field. I could've coddled her and let her play, and I wanted to because she was one of my best friends. Tasha is a phenomenal soccer player and an even more amazing person. She had all the right intentions, but I knew I had to pull the plug on her playing. If I didn't, I would have hurt her more.

Eventually, Tasha realized that she was coasting through games without performing, and that it was no longer acceptable. As the team progressed to the championship game, Tasha won back her starting position. She scored one of the team's most vital goals that season. I held her accountable for the team's expectations, and Tasha eventually held herself accountable for the same. She made a huge contribution to our success. In the end, not only did Tasha forgive me, but she thanked me for my part in her success.

Remaining Grounded in Reality

Accountability isn't about an athlete's taking the blame for a mistake or for a loss. It's not about a declaration of guilt or a confession of sin. Accountability is simply about taking responsibility for an outcome. It is being aware of how your own actions affect the outcome of the team.

At home, parents should focus on how their child's behaviors impact their family, siblings, or friends. Take a look at how you handle disputes between siblings or conflicts with your child and their peers. Do you let them fight it out? Do you have a tendency to blame your child's friends?

Regardless of whose "fault" it is, the reality of every situation is that everyone involved has a role. Use these experiences to keep your child grounded in their own reality. What part did they play? Step back to evaluate the situation and ask, what do they think of their own behavior? How did it contribute to the escalation of the circumstances? You can teach your child to regularly look for their role in every situation. In doing so, your child will develop the ability to look for solutions, not problems. Key to the development of accountability is the ability to look for results. If your child is accustomed to getting caught up in problems, this will ultimately hinder them on the field.

For the 2012 London Olympics, Pia Sundhage was the coach of the US Women's National Team. She was a terrific coach and someone I really admired and loved to play for. Coach Pia loved to have positive vibes around the team at all times and always worked on ensuring that the energy was right—whether that was on the field, in the locker room, or in the hotel. That bled into the video room too. During our video analysis sessions, Pia would never share many negative clips. She didn't want to hurt her players' confidence.

I wasn't used to this. I always felt that video helped me remain accountable for my performance. Nobody likes to see themselves fail or make mistakes in front of their teammates; however, I learned to take my ego and emotion out of the equation and use the video review to help me grow. I didn't want to repeat those same mistakes. I remember one particular game when I wasn't happy with my performance. I knew that I needed to own my mistakes to improve and help contribute to the team. Video review, always a key tool in my development as a player, felt even more important now that I'd been named team captain.

When the next day's video session began, I was prepared to see my face and feet all over the footage. I was ready to accept these mistakes and move on. However, not one of my clips made it into the team video review. Had I really played that poorly after all? Was it all in my head?

I made sure to get access to a laptop with my video clips, even though it wasn't something Coach Pia required me to do. I felt the need to be accountable. I needed to ground myself in my own reality.

We can't, and shouldn't, realistically hold our children accountable for everything that happens on the field. Many parents feel the need to hold their kids accountable for scoring or for not surrendering goals or points. However, playing sports is not all about scoring. In some cases, a coach may not put your child in a position to score. Sometimes your child may be up against superior competition. Sometimes whole teams have bad days or are out of rhythm, so there aren't many scoring chances. In cases like these, consider holding your child accountable for values and personal attributes instead.

Ultimately, your focus should be on big-picture concepts like productivity, supporting teammates, attitude and effort, and turning effective training into good performance. The goal or the win should be considered a child's reward for the work, the fun, and the connections made with teammates. It's the icing on the cake.

CHAPTER 5

Mental Toughness

When Christie was in high school, she made the varsity soccer team as a freshman.

I was quickly recognized on the team. Within a few games, I was racking up goals and handing out a lot of assists. I made the headlines in our local newspapers. At the same time, at fifteen years old, I was painfully shy and timid. I was easily intimated by upperclassmen and was generally quiet and reserved off the field. Off the field, I never talked about or celebrated my success.

During that year, one of my teachers pulled me out of class and asked me to take a walk with her. I followed her onto the soccer fields. I had a feeling something was wrong; at the time, I would never dare defy a coach or teacher. She led me to the end of the fields, where we were out of anyone's sight.

The teacher told me that I was "too good" and that I needed to tone it down. Since I was a freshman, I needed to let other people shine. She told me to back off and play at 50 percent so I could give the other girls chances for success. It was a very short talk, but it made a lengthy impression on me and how I came to play the game.

She said, "It's not like you're going to the Olympics or anything."

I was angry that she didn't care how her words affected me. I knew not to tell my parents because that undoubtedly would have caused more drama. I knew it wasn't life threatening; if it had been, I would have told them. I knew this was my problem to solve, my problem to deal with. That teacher came to our games; every time she was there, I could feel her eyes on me. I felt uncomfortable and embarrassed when she was around me at school. She rattled me. I had never had someone challenge my ability. Everyone was usually trying to make me a better player, and she was actually telling me to stop being productive and just exist on the field.

Apparently, the teacher was looking out for the seniors who weren't feeling good about their own play. Several were headed to play Division I soccer the following year. The teacher told me that this was their year and I should let them shine, let them be the superstars for their last year at the school. Since I was a freshman, I would someday have the same opportunity. This teacher very easily could have shattered my confidence, but I didn't let her. She mistook me for someone with a big ego who just took over games without thinking about my teammates. The funny thing was, I was painfully shy, and I was always avoiding the limelight. But when I played, I was in the zone. I loved fighting and competing and being part of a team with my friends. I never once thought about stealing someone else's spotlight.

After the "talk," I did change my playing style somewhat. I would be aware of opportunities to score but decide not to take all of them. But I would never surrender my effort or identity. When I played, even if that teacher was standing there watching, I refused to let her affect me. I respected myself and the game too much to change for her.

You have to truly believe in yourself and your talents. That mentality will get you through the tough times, the backlash, the thoughtless comments, and the jealousy that unfortunately but inevitably come with success. I took that negative experience, and I let it open my eyes. Instead of being mad, I used it as a reminder to help others. I never changed my productivity like the teacher asked me to. Instead, I increased my awareness of how to assist my teammates and become a better all-around teammate.

That is mental toughness: the ability to persevere in the face of adversity. Some people believe it is a gift or an innate quality. Some say it is a choice. We say both. Some kids are naturally mentally tough, while others learn to become mentally tougher over time. Some kids need a good kick in the butt as motivation, while others require reassurance. Ultimately, mental toughness is a skill that can be learned by routinely choosing to push forward instead of backing down when faced with adversity. Mental toughness is about being creative and deft and agile in the face of the unknowable. It's about choosing to never, never, *never* give up, even when everything is going wrong. It's not about being angry or aggressive; it's about taking a hit and bouncing back up. About staying and persevering when you are tired, sad or think that you don't give a shit anymore. That's mental toughness.

The world of sports is a wonderful microcosm for studying mental toughness; be it in a team setting or competing in an individual sport, you will inevitably face opportunities to win and to lose. It is said that success is good for building confidence but that failure is the greater treasure. Parents, take note here. We tend to celebrate the wins and mourn our children's losses. But here's the thing: how they win and how they lose is all a part of making your child mentally tough. The losing is teaching your child to *choose* perseverance in the face of adversity. This is something you can only learn through experience. No one is getting through life without some negatives. We want to raise kids who are prepared for hardship.

When the Going Gets Tough, the Tough Get Going

Why were the highly accomplished so dogged in their pursuits? For most, there was no realistic expectation of ever catching up to their ambitions. In their own eyes, they were never good enough. They were the opposite of complacent.

And yet, in a very real sense, they were satisfied being unsatisfied. Each was chasing something of unparalleled interest and importance, and it was the chase—as much as the capture—that was gratifying. Even if some of the things they had to do were boring, or frustrating, or even painful, they wouldn't dream of giving up. Their passion was enduring.
　　　　—*Angela Duckworth*, Grit: The Power of Passion and Perseverance[1]

Mentally tough people see challenges as opportunities. Yes, a supposed obstacle actually appears that way to them. It's a matter of perception. When a door closes, mentally tough people don't pout in front of it or try to beat it down. They start looking for other doors, windows, or any kind of opening to get to where they want to go. When Christie was invited to her first training camp with the national team, the team was overloaded with forwards—to the point that she was asked to play defense. Christie had not played defense her entire career. Instead of feeling bitter that she was being forced out of the position she loved, she saw it as an opportunity to get playing time on a new team. Better still, she saw it as an opportunity to earn a spot on the best team in the world. Christie eventually became a starting outside back for the Olympic team. She turned an ostensible negative into one of the biggest opportunities of her life—something that's opened countless doors for her since. Changing positions was no small feat and came with a steep learning curve, but Christie set her mind to harnessing the opportunity. She didn't let her doubt, fear, or disappointment get in her head; she believed that she would succeed and then did what it took to get herself there. This goes back to our power of visualization discussion.

In a different arena, Dr. Keane recalls that chasing her dream of opening a private practice was riddled with challenges and the possibility of failure. She, like Christie, saw opportunity instead of implausibility.

When I was completing my doctoral degree, we students were provided with a colloquium on the first Friday of every month. The colloquium involved a presentation on various subjects from an outside professor or professional. On some occasions, doctors who chose to work in private practices—rather than in research, clinic, or hospital settings—were asked to talk to us about their experiences. Participation in the colloquiums was optional, but I never missed a presentation that involved private practice.

As soon as I realized that I wanted to become a neuropsychologist, I dreamed of having a group practice offering multiple disciplines of psychology where we could treat patients and meet regularly to meld our minds; be fun, fresh, and creative; and provide a warm, caring environment to everyone who came to us for treatment. That was my mission.

I would get so excited every time a private practice doctor spoke at the colloquium. I carried a notebook littered with questions (and my dreams). Each doctor would begin the same way: how rewarding it was to set their own schedules, work within the community, and do what they loved and still make a living. But, inevitably, they would end up complaining about strict compliance regulations, paperwork, and certifying services with insurance companies—a more recent and challenging development. Some of the private practice doctors confessed to needing a second job in a hospital or clinic due to reduced insurance rates. Many warned us that it was a real liability to get into private practice: too time-consuming; less lucrative every year; not worth the effort.

Their stern warnings didn't dissuade me. I listened intently to every word. I absorbed every complaint. Perhaps curiously, nothing they said ever made me doubt that I could or would open a private practice one day. I knew they were right, that their experiences were truthful. I knew that circumstances for rising doctors would be far different from those for veteran doctors. But here was the biggest difference: I had completely expected to have problems, and I was okay with that.

When I first started my group private practice, I had very little training in business or leadership. So I took courses in small business management and read every book about effective leadership that I could get my hands on.

One statement by Barack Obama particularly stood out to me: no one can become a great success without having many significant failures.

He said, "The real test is not whether you avoid this failure, because you won't. It's whether you let it harden or shame you into inaction, or whether you learn from it; whether you choose to persevere."

I came to realize that failure was inevitable. The doctors at the colloquium might have thought that they were sharing problems, even caveats, but I saw them as imparting wisdom learned the hard way. No one starts a business without first falling on their face. I know I did. I also went on to create multiple group private practices and stuck to my mission of fun, innovation, teamwork, and community.

Mental toughness is a choice. It's not that the scoreboard doesn't exist; it's about trusting your skills and, more important, your ability to learn and adapt to thrive in any circumstances. Adopt a mind-set in which you see wins and losses as inherently the same in the end— opportunities to learn, grow, and improve. When you are passionate about something, you have the desire to become mentally tough. When you trust yourself and your skills, you can be tough. We can teach kids that winning and losing are equally important parts of the process of reaching their goals and dreams.

The Power of Positive Thinking

Think about all the things you routinely say to your children. Do you focus on their strengths and positive qualities? Do you point out their weaknesses? Do you talk about their sports performance in a way that influences their overall perception of their ability to handle adversity? Ultimately, what impression are you leaving as to their ability to affect situations in a positive or negative way?

Just thinking about something can change your brain on a structural and a chemical level. Negative talk impacts how a child might think about and talk to themselves. Count how many times you say something negative to yourself. When you bombard your brain with toxic signals from negative thoughts, you train your brain to reproduce negativity.

Mental toughness is built on the power of positive thinking but is not necessarily just about repeating positive messages that have no grounding in reality. Sometimes, when we direct positive messaging at our children, we may inadvertently attempt to protect them from disappointment. This can be a disservice. Hard as it may be, parents must sometimes let their kids fail and later help them to see the positive side of that failure. It's painful to see your child miss every shot or get scored on. It's easier to tell our kids that it was no big deal; don't worry about it; it wasn't their fault. But getting though the game, persevering, and playing despite fear can only be learned through experiencing adversity. When we mask obstacles with positivity, we subtly send a message that losing is something to fear. Make it clear to your children that we see everything as a learning opportunity and that the outcome that matters is personal growth, not a scoreboard.

Sports-Specific Messaging for Kids

- You are so dedicated to your training.
- You have great stamina.
- You are a skilled player.
- You are a strong competitor.
- You push yourself hard in practice.
- You are not afraid of making mistakes.
- You are becoming a great athlete.
- Each day your technique gets better and better.
- You have great attitude even when you are disappointed.
- You give 100 percent effort.

The essence of positive thinking in sports psychology is a constructive focus on an athlete's goals. Athletes who measure their success by their stats are always going to be worried about the numbers. Instead, athletes should set goals based on honing a skill, increasing endurance, or improving focus and attention. Research indicates that teaching kids to direct their thoughts, as opposed to letting them wander in a negative or anxious direction, has a positive effect on their overall performance.[2] With this training, athletes learn self-control within a sea of uncontrollables such as opponents or scoreboards. Christie tapped into the power of positive thinking while facing her greatest opponent.

Marta was my biggest competition, as she was known to be the best soccer player in the world. She was unstoppable. But I couldn't wait to oppose her. I knew that if I wanted to get close to her, I needed to play to the best of my ability. My aim was to recognize her tendencies and then use my strengths to limit her overall impact. Essentially I was playing a game within a game. With this mind-set, I told myself that no matter how good she was, I could rise to that challenge by sticking to what I was good at. When the battles with Marta got tough, I would remind myself of the small victories I had already tallied within the game, and that my years of training had prepared me for these big moments. This gave me the confidence to make it difficult for her tactically, physically, and emotionally. It didn't feel like a World Cup or Olympics unless I faced Marta, since her greatness made the games that more special. If I focused on how good Marta was, and believed she was better than me, I would have been defeated before the game even started.

If you think you can't do it, you won't. You will have a hard time finding a successful athlete who doesn't use positive affirmations, a mission statement, or other ways to talk positively to themselves. Professional athletes in all sports have conquered enormous physical challenges because of their mind-set. Many top athletes will tell you that when they thought they had exhausted their strength or physical talent, their thinking carried them across the finish line to success. Believing in yourself gets you to the final whistle—in sports and in life.

> ### The Power of "I Can"
>
> In both of our households the word "can't" is a red flag. If our kids use the word "can't," they are asked to reword the sentence and take the negativity out of their verbal communications. When they are forced to avoid "can't," they realize they can turn the negative into a positive. I can...

Believing You Can Make It Happen

The psychologist Albert Bandura defined the concept of self-efficacy.[3] Put simply, self-efficacy is your belief in your ability to affect situations, achieve goals, and overcome challenges. Children who have high levels of self-efficacy bounce back from problems more quickly, are less emotionally reactive to negative situations, and are more motivated and interested in learning. In sports, self-efficacy is considered one of the most important factors that affect performance. It is a can-do belief system that can be taught and modeled.

When athletes with high levels of self-efficacy are faced with a challenge, they don't waste their time blaming coaches, teammates, or situations. They take responsibility because they believe they have the power to make a difference. Kids learn this through what Bandura termed "verbal persuasion." It is a commonly held belief, especially during childhood, that the voices that are the loudest and most repetitive are those that are internalized. They not only affect children's self-efficacy but also become part of their subconscious. Young athletes are often besieged with opinions about their ability to perform—by parents, coaches, and teammates. If you want to know how your child is thinking, listen to how your child's teachers, coaches, other parents, and authority figures in their life speak to them. Those messages form their belief in themselves.

Kids learn self-efficacy through vicarious experiences, such as watching their own performance or observing someone else's. When kids see their peers succeed in sports, they develop the belief that they themselves are capable. Recently, a friend posted on Facebook about her son Aiden's participating in a football training clinic. They first showed video of a quarterback making a play on the training field. They then showed video of the previous night's football game, in which Aiden made the same play with the same success. The video provided three additional examples of things Aiden learned at the clinic, coupled with footage of him performing the plays successfully during the game. It was both a great advertisement for the clinic and a direct boon to Aiden's sense of self-efficacy: video proof that if Aiden puts in the practice, he can succeed.

Self-efficacy is a child's ability to say, "I know I can do it." It's not arrogance or conceit but self-confidence. It is the faith you have in your own abilities, unrelated to anyone else on the team. Some kids are afraid to express big dreams because it seems arrogant. Parents can talk to their kids about how self-efficacy and dreaming big are not the same as self-importance or doubting the other members of the team. Christie often speaks about self-efficacy to parents and coaches.

It's not about one comment. It's about reassuring the child and building habits around that child's believing in themselves. You foster it by your own belief in the child. Everyone wants immediate gratification and satisfaction through this journey of sports; however, the roller coaster of emotions that sports provide is something we have to embrace and teach from. You're only as good as your last game, unless you inherently believe in yourself and it becomes your habit to show up and compete every day. With strong self-efficacy, you are less susceptible to the highs and lows of the game.

How Do We Foster Self-Efficacy in Children?[4]

- Talk to your child about the importance of failure and how to use it to learn.
- Help your child set realistic short-term goals.
- Praise attitude and effort over outcomes and wins.
- Be authentic and honest in discussing your child's abilities.
- Identify your child's strengths and repeat, repeat, repeat.

Thought Stopping

Sydney Leroux, a professional soccer player, Olympic gold medalist, and World Cup champion, was born and raised by her mother in Canada, while her father lived in the United States. Sydney learned to play soccer on Canadian soil but dreamed of playing professionally in the United States.

As a result, Sydney decided to leave her mother and Canada for the United States. Since her father was a US citizen, she was eligible to try out for the US Women's National Soccer Team. She believed that the US soccer program had better opportunities for her than the Canadian program, and she was right. She moved at the end of high school and attended college at the University of California, Los Angeles. While at UCLA, Sydney was asked to play for the US Women's National Team.

In 2013, Sydney found herself back in Canada, playing for the US

National team in an international friendly against her native Canada. Her homecoming was bittersweet: the Canadian fans were angry with Sydney for having switched alliances early in her career. No country wants to lose one of their greatest players. When she stepped on the field, and every time she got the ball, the Canadian fans erupted in boos. Christie remembers that game vividly.

I think about how intense that game was for her and where her mind-set must have been. I knew how much stress she was under, even without the booing. I was hoping for her that the booing wouldn't get into her head.

I knew how hard she worked. I knew she took a huge risk when she left Canada to play for the United States. What if she was wrong? It would have been safer for her to stay. I was thinking about how this game could change her soccer career forever.

But Sydney made it through, thanks to her mental strength and her mental preparation. Despite the crowd's negativity, Sydney was able to maintain her focus and remain productive throughout the game. When she scored during that game I remember her face. It was a mixture of happiness, sadness, anger, and excitement. It was everything she was. She looked up at the crowd, pulled on the US badge on her shirt, and put up a finger to her mouth to silence the crowd. Sydney took that risk and it was part of the process that led her to her success. I could not have been happier for her.

Sydney ended up winning the World Cup in Canada—while playing for the US team—only two years later.

The Mental Game

The mental side of sports is bigger than the play itself. Christie believes it is everything. When she first began training with the national team, she mistakenly believed she was being trained to increase her fitness level. She recalls intense fitness testing sessions with drills that were emotionally and physically exhausting. She remembers that the most intense fitness trainings took place on the 1999 national team, which won the World Cup. Christie understood later that the testing had very little to do with concern about her actual fitness and everything to do with developing mental toughness.

We always had to beat the clock, and everything was recorded: How many wins you had, how many losses, and one v. one battles, four v. four challenges, and seven v. seven small-sided games. After completing all those tasks, the shin guards came off, and we had to run again. They were relentless. We had to get to one side of the field in eighteen seconds and had thirty seconds to get back. You did ten of them. If you couldn't do this, you weren't considered fit. You failed. Boy, did I fail!

When Christie compared her statistics from the 1999 team to her fitness levels on the 2004 team, the difference is staggering. Her fitness improved much later. She realized that she was being taught mental toughness on the 1999 team. She was being trained to handle pressure, push herself to her potential, perform when she wanted to quit, and control her emotions and her mind. She believes that the training in mental toughness on the 1999 team was the reason why they won the championship. They learned how to outhustle and outfight their opponents. They believed they could do anything. The team was a powerhouse of technical and athletic abilities, but the mental toughness ultimately gave them the edge they needed.

Parents should talk openly about skills like grit, perseverance, reframing, goal setting, and adaptability. If a kid wants to quit, parents need to be prepared to push them to honor their commitments but also to listen to their reasoning: are they quitting because they've gotten everything they can out of it or because it's harder than they think they can handle? A parent's role is to be trustworthy, a guiding force and an active participant in deciding the child's goals.

Life isn't fair. One of the biggest lessons in sports is learning to be uncomfortable. Sometimes you have to hold your head up, even when you don't see results. In life we face adversity all the time. There will always be the job you didn't get, the promotion you were passed over for, the disappointing SAT score, or the team you didn't make. What you do with these adversities defines your life. Mental toughness sets kids apart from their peers and gives them the life skills to succeed.

If a player, no matter how talented, is easily distracted by the circumstances surrounding play or influenced by outside factors, that player likely needs help developing their cognitive inhibition. This is the skill of tuning out any stimuli that are irrelevant to the task at hand. Some things that need to be tuned out are emotions, noise, people, outside situations, and even physical discomfort. The more an athlete is able to tune out inhibiting factors, the more successful they can be. Mental toughness is about selective attention, the ability to remain focused, and the ability to remain free of distractions.

One of the high school teams Christie volunteered to assist with was losing a game 4–0 in the second half. Worse yet, five of their starting athletes sat on the bench. The coach said to her, "How could we possibly make a comeback? Five of my best players are hurt."

Christie told her, "Those five players have their feelings hurt; they aren't physically hurt." She knew the athletes were having a difficult time losing in front of their peers. Five injuries were just too convenient.

When an athlete is injured in a game, their perception of pain and cognitive inhibition can dictate whether they will return to the field. Sometimes, players sustain major physical injuries and return to the game anyway because they are so focused on their desire to win and play; other times, an injury is physically minor but drastically impacts an athlete's confidence and faith in their ability to keep going.

When a person is injured, their pain is processed in the brain. For example, if you pinch your skin with a clothespin, it will be momentarily irritating. But, over time, you will become distracted by other things, and you may not even feel the clothespin anymore. It is well known that anxiety and depression make pain worse. They don't make the *injury* worse; the emotional state makes the *experience* of the pain worse. When athletes are in a state of distress, not only are they more prone to injury, but they are more prone to experience the pain of the injury. ***This excludes major physical injuries where players are advised not to go back out onto the field of play.*** If an athlete has been evaluated and told to sit out, there should be no negotiation. But if after an evaluation the decision is up to the coach and the player, it's important to find out where the athlete's head is in order to figure out how best to coach them.

When Christie was training for the US Women's National Team, she recalls that the fitness training was so physically painful, she had to learn to distract herself from the pain to complete the task.

I told myself, instead of having to be the first one in line to run this drill, I could be the first soldier in a military battle. Drills were nothing compared to what other people have to face. I would think about being left in the middle of the ocean during a perfect storm; no matter what I had to do in training, it was never as bad as drowning at sea. My worst fear is of drowning, and thinking about how hard I would have to work to prevent myself from drowning was a helpful way to motivate myself when I wasn't sure how much I had left to give to the drills. I always told myself that no matter what I was facing, it could be worse. This isn't really that bad. *I went to my deepest, worst fears of my life to get me through.*

One of the most mentally challenging drills was called the beep test. It is a multiple-stage fitness test, a shuttle-run test whereby coaches can estimate an athlete's maximum oxygen uptake—in other words, running 'til you can't run anymore. The test involves running back and forth between two cones twenty meters apart. It is synchronized with a prerecorded audiotape, which beeps at set intervals. Every time a player hears a beep, they run to the opposite cone. As the test progresses, the intervals between the beeps become shorter, which means you must move faster to get further in the test. You have to be at the cone when the beep sounds. If you don't meet that task, you are eliminated from the test and the coach will call you out.

My mentality about the beep test changed over time. Early on, all I could think about was getting better at it, even mastering it. It mentally took over my preparation leading into a national team camp. As I got older, my inner voice matured, and I saw it as helping me be the fittest player I could be for the team. Initially, my adrenaline would pump and I would feel overwhelmed. I second-guessed whether I did enough. Later, when standing on the line, I would tell myself, At this moment, right now, it could be worse. I could be floating in the water trying to survive. I could be on a front line in active duty. *I put myself into mental scenarios that I thought were more mentally and physically taxing than what I was doing. It put me in a more relaxed state. My heart rate was lower than during previous years when I started the test.*

When I was able to distract myself from the anxiety, the beep test became more satisfying and enjoyable. No one wants to push themselves to failure, especially when surrounded by peers. In the end, the test became a gauge for my fitness; this would help me be the best I could be rather than compare myself to other players or freak out. The question became, "Can I beat my own time versus beating a teammate?" In the beginning I just didn't want to be the worst, and later I was competing with myself, to be at my personal best.

Christie's story is reflective of cognitive inhibition, a term that describes the mind's ability to tune out irrelevant information. Sometimes we purposely select what we pay attention to and sometimes we just tune things out without realizing it. Cognitive inhibition in sports is limiting the distraction of feelings, friends, parents, and boo-ing Canadians from the time the game begins until the final whistle. You can teach kids mental toughness not by eliminating distractions, but by training kids to cope with them.

Mental Toughness Strategies

Track your thoughts. Many athletes keep a diary of all thoughts related to game-day performance and training. Keeping a record of your thoughts helps increase your awareness about your thought patterns and helps you to make changes as needed. Encouraging your child to keep track of their thoughts both surrounding and during their activities can help them identify where their strengths are and where they need more support. You can also ask your child to communicate three positives about the game, themselves, or their teammates.

"Stop" techniques. If an athlete tends to self-deprecate or feels that negative thoughts are uncontrollable, they can try thought-stopping techniques. When a negative thought comes to mind they can say, "Stop," out loud and shift to a positive or affirming framework instead. Dr. Keane likes to recommend visualizing a stop sign or a garage door closing between the negative thought and the positive thought.

Change the story. Teach children how to reframe a negative thought into a positive one. If your child is upset that the weather is bad for a game, teach them to reframe it by thinking about how the rain sets up the opportunity for more tackles. When the best player on the team is injured and the team feels they can't possibly win, here's the reframe: the other team doesn't know how to beat you without your best player. This can be the opportunity to shine or step up with-out them. This is about teaching kids that it is not about what they can control but rather how they frame it. It is a matter of teaching constructive ways to reinterpret things on the field—from negative to positive.

Word washing. Telling someone to calm down when they are nervous rarely works. If it did, psychotherapy sessions would require only a few minutes of your time. Instead, try to use different words to describe the same feelings. All athletes feel a rush of adrenaline before a big event. Many successful athletes call their nervousness excitement instead. Instead of calling it anxiety, they call it passion, and they describe it as feelings that show how much they care. Teach kids that uncontrollable feelings can actually be used as fuel for a great performance.

- When you are exhausted, you are really working.
- When you fear failure, you are invested.
- When you feel angry, you turned up your intensity.
- When you feel frustrated, it is because you care.
- When you are playing aggressively, you are competing.
- When you are emotional, you are enthusiastic.

Meditation

Sara Lazar of Massachusetts General Hospital and Harvard Medical School hurt herself while running. She was a longtime marathon runner and also a longtime physical therapy patient due to repeated running injuries. Her physical therapist told her that she needed to stretch. She advised her to take up yoga, suggesting this would reduce the potential for injury. She also told her that yoga would increase her level of compassion and open her heart. Dr. Lazar, a neuroscientist, initially scoffed at the idea that yoga would influence her level of compassion, but she opted to try it as a method of stretching.

After several weeks of yoga, not only did Dr. Lazar's body feel better, but she was surprised to find that her mind-set was beginning to change. She noticed that she was calmer at work and better able to handle stressful situations. She was able to see things from others' points of view more easily than before.

Dr. Lazar researched the literature on mindfulness and mediation. She found a huge body of research demonstrating that meditation decreases stress, depression, anxiety, pain, and insomnia while also increasing quality of life, for both children and adults. Studies showed that people who meditated long-term had increased gray matter in several areas of their brain, including their auditory and sensory cortexes as well as their insular and sensory regions.[5]

Meditation helps slow down the mind and assists in the conscious awareness of the present moment, including physical sensations such as breathing and ambient noise. Mental toughness is all about conditioning the mind for emotional control, attentional control, and creativity. Neuroscientists have found that long-term meditators had more gray matter in their frontal cortex, the part of the brain responsible for attention, decision-making, creativity, and memory.

Dr. Lazar was able to replicate these findings in her own lab, but she also went a step further. It was clear that people who meditated for years had substantial changes in their gray matter, but many people don't have time to meditate for long periods. In her study, Dr. Lazar put people with no experience in meditation into an eight-week meditation and mindfulness program. Her study found that practicing meditation and mindfulness even for two months could substantially impact the brain. Dr. Lazar asserts that even fifteen to twenty minutes a day may be enough to reap the benefits of meditation.

While the research on kids and meditation is not as robust, it is growing. Studies show that kids who meditate have better grades, better school attendance, decreased ADHD symptoms, better self-control, an increased sense of well-being, and a greater perspective-taking ability. Studies on meditation and athletes yield similar results and suggest that meditation improves concentration, self-regulation, relationships, and attention span and reduces stress.[6]

There are many ways to help your child learn to meditate; the first starts with you, the parent. Kids are much more likely to become interested in meditation when they see their parents doing it. Parents can teach kids simple breathing exercises, or even practice silence for a few minutes a day to help get them started. Parents can also turn meditation time into a game. It is a good idea to set aside a consistent time and specific place in your home for meditation. It can be any quiet area of the house: you and your child can design the space with a mat, pillows, or other comfortable accessories to remind your child of the comfort derived from meditation. Taking pediatric or family yoga classes is another great way to start your child meditating at a young age. The benefits will last a lifetime.

"Mindfulness" is a term often used synonymously with "meditation." It is defined as the process of living in the moment rather than thinking about the past or the next thing in line. It helps athletes experience all the stimuli associated with a moment or event rather than focus on winning or goal achievement. Mindfulness in sports involves remaining focused on the process and spending more time thinking about self-improvement. Christie knows that even the best drills aren't enough. Mental acuity and clarity achieved through mindfulness are essential.

I learned about mindfulness during my last years at Sky Blue FC. Our goal was to be the best possible version of ourselves. Each day we focused on being better than the day before. The coaches encouraged a mind-set focused on self-improvement, which allowed us to enjoy daily training and better understand each week what was working for us. When we lost a game, it wasn't viewed particularly as a defeat; we would review it and decide whether we were still getting better. Every part of our performance had to be measurable; otherwise, we were an adrift boat, floating without sails.

A hybrid of goal orientation and process orientation can provide kids with balance. Stay true to the process of developing your child, and allow them to grow toward their goals. Help them to understand that throughout the process there will be successes as well as setbacks. Knowing this ahead of time helps kids avoid the bitter disappointment that typically accompanies defeat. When kids are solely goal- or results-oriented, a defeat can feel like the end of the world.

Mental Toughness on the Floor

Liz, a fourteen-year-old gymnast, was falling just short of a national-level ranking. She had athleticism, advanced skill, and amazing technique; however, her parents believed she just wasn't "tough enough" to make it to the top. They hired additional trainers to help her improve her overall scores, but with no success. To them, mental toughness meant training harder, and she did.

When Liz was on, she was incredible, and her parents and coaches marveled at her talent and ingenuity on the floor. When she was off, she looked like a novice. When Liz reached her teens, she became increasingly distracted by outside influences as well as things well out of her control. Liz's parents finally sought out sports psychology counseling with the hope of helping their daughter.

Liz had been very close with her teammates since her child-hood; however, they had become increasingly jealous of her success and more vocal about it. It wasn't fair, they said, that she won all the awards when they were all working just as hard as she was. They told her that she shouldn't always be the one handpicked to compete, and that she should let someone else have a chance for a change.

Liz felt terrible that her friends were not enjoying the same level of success, and she felt responsible for helping them perform better. She became consumed with helping them so they would not be mad at her. Liz's parents couldn't understand why Liz would care so deeply about what her teammates thought of her. They explained that they wanted to see her get tough. Who cared what the girls thought of her? But for Liz, it wasn't that easy. She cared.

Liz's feelings toward her teammates are normal and developmentally appropriate. Most teens care a lot about fitting in and having friends. Liz needed to establish appropriate boundaries with her friends—what responsibilities she had within their relationships. Her mental toughness focused on teaching her how to get into the zone, stay focused, and to use cognitive strategies to improve her performance.

Working with a sports psychologist, Liz was first instructed to review and re-create her pregame routine. She learned to use the time to mentally prepare herself to compete: having a good conversation with her coach, visualizing herself succeeding, engaging in positive self-talk, and having a good warm-up. She agreed to sit apart from her teammates prior to events so she wouldn't be so distracted. She switched her focus from taking care of her teammates to thinking about her own needs on the day of the event, such as her pre-event nutrition and sleep habits.

Liz's big shift was to focus on herself. Over the course of only a few weeks, Liz fine-tuned her routines, and her overall scores improved. Mental toughness came from within Liz, not from a focus on training harder or from the scoreboard.

Mental Toughness Training

You can teach your child how to harness their powers, whether they are leaders in the making or soldiers more prepared for battle than

they realize. They can make a conscious decision to choose perseverance. Teach them that making the decision to never give up assures
them of true success.

- Losing doesn't hurt physically.
- What counts is progress every day, not immediate results.
- Get your mind off the scoreboard; focus on what you can
  control.
- When things change inside you, they will change around you.
- Shift your focus to how you can assist your teammates.
- Say positive things to yourself during the game.
- Stick around teammates who pull magic from you.

You can't change a kid's DNA, and you wouldn't want to, but all
kids can learn to be mentally tough and agile. We can teach kids how
to understand and change the world around them and how they can
change their perception of their environment. We can plant seeds.
This goes for those at the top of their sport, too. Early in Christie's
career, she sought the help of a sports psychologist because she was
having problems adjusting to a new coach.

*In one of our sessions, the psychologist told me that I had leadership quali-
ties. I was shocked. I had never thought of myself as a leader and I told him
that. He said that I needed to adjust my perception of what a leader looked
like.*

*During that session, the psychologist told me that because of my intro-
version, I would sit on the outside of the huddle, looking in from afar, all the
while witnessing how the prior captains led the team and what made the
team tick. I observed personalities, strengths, and weaknesses. I talked a lot
less than most of my teammates. But I was always observing and listening
and very self-aware. He said a good leader thinks of others. They are willing
to adapt to make themselves and the team better.*

I said, "But I don't speak up. How could you say I am a leader?"

He told me that there are many ways to lead people, but I didn't believe him. Then there came a fateful day: Coach Pia asked me to be a captain on the US Women's National Team. Despite some initial reluctance, I thought back to all those messages that told me that I could do it. Even Coach Pia had seen leadership qualities in me. I stepped up.

The seeds were planted. Eventually, Christie became known as Captain America. How's that for mental toughness?

CHAPTER 6

Authenticity

Authentic parenting means letting go of who we think our children are supposed to be and teaching them to become who they truly are.[1] It is the ability to behave in line with your truth rather than external influences. It is the awareness of your whole self, your good, your bad, and your ugly, as well as your ability to express yourself honestly. Authentic parenting engenders character, courage, and compassion.

Authenticity in youth sports is about guiding children to play the sports they want to play, rather than the sports their parents choose or the ones they happen to be good at. When you allow kids to choose the sport they are passionate about, kids show more commitment and better overall performance. Kids who play sports out of pure joy get into the zone naturally. When kids choose their sports, they tend to have healthier physical habits, such as better fitness and attitude, making sports injuries and burnout less common.

The way you behave toward your neighbors, coworkers, kids, and family members; the way you speak to teachers, other parents, and coaches; and the way you handle life's multiple stressors reveals your authenticity as a parent or coach. It is not what town you live in, how much money you make, or your title at work that makes you authentic to your children. It's the match between what you say and what you teach your kids, and what your own behavior ultimately looks like on a day-to-day basis. For kids, it's not whether they started, what team they play for, or how many goals they scored. It's about how they conduct themselves on the team, the way they play the game, and the way they repeatedly show up during times of adversity and conflict.

This chapter asks you to look inside yourself and evaluate whether what you are saying and doing with the kids in your life is a match with your values, your intentions, and what is really going on inside yourself. Our lives with our children are so short. In Dr. Harley Rotbart's *No Regrets Parenting*, he reminds parents that we have only 940 Saturdays with our kids from birth until they leave for college. To us, this time together is too precious and sacred to go around pretending.

> Character first, ability second.
> —*Shinichi Suzuki, creator of the Suzuki Method*

How do we teach authenticity in a youth sports culture that is grounded in values such as chasing medals and championships and winning at all costs? Many of us grew up in that culture. We might find ourselves wanting to give our kids the things we didn't have when we were playing sports as children.

When John was growing up in the eighties, he played football, soccer, and baseball. Back then, if a child was a decent athlete, they could get away with playing three sports with no additional training or without a commitment to a restrictive elite club or travel team. He laments that his parents rarely attended his games, and he often rode his bike alone to the fields after school. However, he knew that both of them needed to work to support him and his two other siblings. Attending all his games just wasn't possible.

John played three sports into high school, excelling at soccer.

He was always put into the goalkeeper position despite wanting to play midfield. Repeated pleas to his coaches fell on deaf ears; he was always asked to play goalie because he was "so good at it." By high school, he was well-known as a great goalkeeper, and he made the varsity team as a freshman. Still, he wasn't satisfied. He believed that he was coerced into playing keeper because his parents were never present to lobby his case to coaches or to put him on a team that would let him play his preferred position. By his junior year, John quit playing soccer for good. His coaches hadn't budged, and he grew to hate the game.

John had retired from competitive sports by the time he got to college. He dabbled in basketball "just for fun," playing intramurals in college and participating in over-thirty leagues while raising his kids. When John's children Harper and Kenneth began playing sports, he was all in. He never missed a practice or a game and even coached a few seasons. He signed them up for additional training camps, and both children had personal trainers in their respective sports. Additionally, he attended all of Harper's violin lessons.

When Harper was a high school freshman, she told her father that she didn't want to play soccer anymore. John was flabbergasted. She had been the best midfielder on her middle school and travel teams. Every time John watched her play, he saw a bit of himself out there. When she said she didn't want to play anymore, he couldn't for the life of him figure out why. He'd given her everything he didn't have when he was a kid.

What John didn't realize was that he never gave Harper permission to be herself. He never let Harper really explore with him or share with him what she liked to do. Like many parents, he saw her athletic ability and concluded that if he parented her better than his own mother and father had parented him, he would have a happy powerhouse of a soccer player. In fact, John learned that he was not letting his daughter choose for herself.

Luckily, John came to this realization quickly and allowed Harper to quit playing that season. John wanted his daughter to be happy and fulfilled; forcing her to stay in a sport meant replicating the disillusionment from his own youth. Without the pressures of training and elite teams, Harper rediscovered her love of soccer. She then asked for additional training and opportunities to try out for other teams. John realized that his daughter could not play from an authentic place if she was just trying to please him or live out the childhood John had been denied.

Modeling Authenticity Ourselves

When Christie was in eighth grade, she played in her middle school basketball championship game. Her father was the coach of the opposing team. She remembers this game distinctly because she made the layup that should have won the game for her team. But her father yelled to the referee that she had traveled; her points should not count.

"The layup was perfect. I didn't travel," she recalls. "But the referee agreed with my dad, the layup didn't count, and my team lost."

Of course, Christie was mad that her father had interfered with her winning the championship. (*Author's note: She may have learned a little bit about competitiveness from her father as well.*) Kidding aside, the lesson she internalized from that game and from her experiences with her father was that being authentic to your truth—during a game, in practice, out in the world—is important, despite the difficulty of a given situation.

My dad didn't let the fact that his daughter scored the winning layup stop him from coaching from his truth. He believed then that I traveled, and, to this day, he believes that I traveled. End of story. If he hadn't spoken up, he would have been letting his bias as my dad outweigh his responsibility to his truth. That's what he instilled in me: to respect the game. I consider my father to be one of the most authentic and honest people I know. He taught me this powerful, lasting lesson through sports, even when it hurt.

Christie's father taught her that victory comes from a place other than winning. It comes from integrity, from an internal resource of acting from your truth that can only be taught and cultivated through experience. Figure out what makes you the happiest and the proudest and follow through with it. Christie attributes much of her success to being true to herself regardless of circumstances, and she carried what her father taught her right to the World Cup.

The Impact of Our Choices

When we stop to look around, it's easy to wonder where all the time is going. Between the obligations in our own lives and everything our kids add, we too often end up racing from one activity to the next without stopping to think about why. Life offers so many different options and choices that it can become all consuming. Regardless of what kind of player your child is, there are endless opportunities available—if only you have the time and money to devote to them. This can foster a nasty sense of FOMO, in both kids and parents.

FOMO (the fear of missing out) is a pervasive feeling of anxiety that occurs when people start wondering what exactly other people are doing without them. Am I missing out on fun? Is my child missing out on something important? While feeling dread about missing out is nothing new, we now have perpetual, vicarious access to what other kids are doing, what teams they play on, what championships they have won, and who is training them.

FOMO is one of the biggest obstacles to authentic parenting.

It disrupts youth sports by engendering a ceaseless yearning for dreams of elite teams, scholarships, and stardom. FOMO parents often feel like they are letting their kids down by not providing every opportunity, despite time constraints, costs, stress on the family, and missed vacations. Social media images of other, apparently successful athletes can cause parents to wonder if they are doing enough for their kids. *Are my kids well rounded? Too competitive or just right? Am I fostering my child's talents and drive?* When we get caught up in youth sports FOMO, we can easily lose sight of the things that really matter, such as family, friends, and even educational pursuits.

Tough Love to Combat FOMO

- Stay in your own lane! Don't look over the fence into your neighbor's yard. Stay focused on your own children's happiness, well-being, and growth.
- Focus on the here and now, not on the future. Courageously accept that the decisions you make are guiding your child on the right path. Unconditionally love where your child is right now.
- Allow your child to have a social life when they want to. There is always something to miss out on. Empower choices and balance.
- Find your JOMO, the joy of missing out! Teach your kids the value of downtime, family time, and playing sports and games in their free time, just for fun.

Guided Discovery

The rationale for putting kids in sports varies from parent to parent and depends on life experience ranging from having never played to having played at a professional level. When asked, most parents tell you that they put their kids into sports because of what sports teach: leadership, teamwork, perseverance, commitment, and accountability. However, when we look at some of the realities of youth sports, many of these values get lost in the hectic shuffle of competitiveness and fear.

Children are born parent pleasers; it is in their nature. They are praise junkies. This is great because it molds and shapes their self-esteem. But how do you know if you are pushing your child to achieve in sports past the point of their interest or ability? How do you know if their interest is authentic or rooted in their innate need to please you?

We believe you should allow your child some leeway to figure out what they want to do. There is a difference between showing your interests to your child and pushing your interests on them. Make an effort to look out for their unique strengths and abilities in everything they do, not just on the field. Make time to let them explore new things, then sit back and watch.

Again, every child is different. Some may need a push to participate and discover they love the sport. Others crave external praise and find themselves playing for it. Some say they wished their parents pushed them harder. We encourage taking every opportunity you can to let your children figure it out for themselves. And they will figure it out. Ironically, both external praise and punishment can inhibit their internal guide. Try to show interest rather than push with praise or punishment. Try to understand their perspectives about why they play and what they like about it, while withholding judgment.

Christy Holly, the US Women's National Team talent scout, talks about the use of guided discovery with his athletes. He uses bowling with children as an example. Basically, when children are learning to bowl, we put bumpers along the alley so the ball does not repeatedly roll into the gutters. Without the bumpers, learning to bowl could be extremely frustrating, not to mention time-consuming.

Holly sees the bumpers as analogous to guided discovery. The bumpers do not tell the bowlers exactly how to bowl. They don't ensure a strike every time. Instead, the bumpers guide the ball in the right direction. They steer the kids to the ultimate outcome: using form and technique to throw the bowling ball straight while avoiding pitfalls.

When Holly coaches, he never gives kids all the answers. He never directly tells players how to solve problems. Rather, he uses his guided discovery technique. Holly assigns exercises and problems with multiple possible solutions. He gives players a set of paradigms to work within and observes their solutions. He believes firmly that you need to let the young players use their own imagination and creative skills to problem solve. Holly strongly prefers to observe and understand each kid's approach to the problem. Ultimately, this helps him as a coach gain a better understanding of the child's thought process and perspective. He stresses, as we have, that it is okay for them to fail while solving problems; it is key to achieving a feeling of ownership and enjoying the experience of getting it right. He believes if he tells his players exactly how to do things, he is setting them up for future failure: if they can't solve the problem as instructed, he fears they'll think they're doing something wrong. Through guided discovery, Holly wants his players to use the skills they already have to experiment and further develop their problem-solving skills. Much like the bumpers kids use when bowling, Holly will redirect the players when he feels they are headed in the wrong direction.

Each year, Holly gives his teams the month of December off in order to move them away from too many structured practices. Most kids are at practices because their parents tell them to be. During the season, kids learn commitment and respect for their team by consistently showing up for structured practices. In December, he lets kids decide whether they want to use their free time to play soccer. Not every athlete chooses to be there if left to their own devices—and that's okay. "It's important to have free play in sports training so the players have a chance to play in an environment where they can play their sport without having to worry about being evaluated," Christy says. "I want kids to figure out the game for themselves and play with that freedom. When they are being coached and they can't do what their coach is telling them to, they feel inhibited, afraid to take risks. In free play, you get to play any way you see fit."

Many parents today look back at their childhoods and remember a time when free play took up the majority of their free time. The act of going outside after school and meeting up with friends to play sports is oddly a thing of the past. Much of this free-play time has been replaced by video games, excessive homework, and rigorous trainings, practices, and games. Abby Wambach is the youngest of seven siblings and grew up in Rochester, New York. Abby attributes much of her success to playing with her siblings in the backyard. She credits her brothers for her toughness and her reaction time: she fondly remembers one of her brothers shooting hockey pucks at her.

Conditions of Worth

Carl Rogers, the father of person-centered therapy, coined the term "conditions of worth" to describe how we believe that our self-worth, or value as a person, is dependent on external factors or meeting certain conditions others place on us.[2] Conditions of worth are common in children and can be problematic when carried into adulthood. Parents sometimes create complex conditions for their children to live up to without realizing they are doing so. Children easily learn that if they do certain things, they will please their parents and receive love. As a result, they strive to do these things. Because conditions of worth are derived from parents' hopes and dreams for their children, they may not match a child's true abilities, interests, or talents.

Conditions of worth often show up in sports, as children aim to please parents, coaches, teachers, and teammates. This is a very subtle concept, easy to miss, but it's extremely powerful. Ask yourself, what do you feel you need to do, have, or be to be of value in the world? Typically, to teach their children how to be successful, people say things like:

- Never let them see you sweat.
- Get mad.
- Be tough.
- Work hard.
- Do as your coach tells you.
- Don't show them your pain.
- Outsmart them.
- Show them you are stronger.
- Be a champion.

Sometimes these expressions are helpful; they can motivate and guide kids to achieve great success. Sometimes, however, they are a mismatch for a child's actual ability level, feelings, and talents and can lead to unhappiness, nervousness, or a lack of satisfaction. Sometimes they make a kid feel that their parents' love is conditional. Examine how and why you are saying some of these things to your child. Do you show more love when they win a championship? Do you pay more attention when they outsmart their opponents? Do you encourage them to hide their feelings? Learn to recognize what you praise and punish, as well as what you judge. When you do, you will free your child from conditions of worth and enable them to find out who they really are.

Taking Care of Yourself

Parents all over the United States tend to arrive at games thirty to forty-five minutes before game time—often carrying tents, water bottles, cell phones, video cameras, coolers, and lawn chairs, almost always absorbed in multiple responsibilities. Parents drive hours on the weekends to tournaments. They drive from one end of town to pick up one child to the other end of town for another practice. They get dinner on the road. They drive kids for hours after work only to get to their emails at ten or eleven at night. Life in youth sports often interrupts family time, academics, and even peace of mind.

Though many sports parents wouldn't trade any of it for the world, there are moments in every parent's life when they feel overwhelmed, stressed, and frustrated at their children for seeming ungrateful. These emotions are definitely par for the course. However, if you find yourself blowing up frequently, having regular conflicts with your children, or constantly feeling like you are at the mercy of someone else's clock, consider making yourself a priority too.

Take care of yourself. When your actions toward yourself don't match what you are trying to teach your kids, you lose credibility. Why should your kids take care of themselves when you don't? How will your kids learn to pay attention and be focused when you are complaining and distracted? Take the time to make sure that you are comfortable with the sports lifestyle and schedule you have created. If you frequently complain or lose control of your feelings, consider how it impacts your children. Kids thrive when they believe that their parents are interested in them and available to them. Your kids will be more open to telling you how they really feel if you model self-respect and self-care. With you as their model, kids can learn to give these gifts to themselves.

Being Consistent

When the research professor Brené Brown speaks about authenticity, she talks about the choices you make every day. She talks about how honest you are about when you show up every day. Authenticity is not a big-picture concept; rather, it is a culmination of the consistency of daily rituals. While you keep your big-picture goals present, you remain mindful of the process every day. You can teach this to your children. Sports naturally teach this to children.

Get Real

How many times have you heard the expressions "Just be you," "Be yourself," "Get real"? But some kids don't yet know who they really are, an idea that can give them anxiety. Model acceptance of yourself so your child can learn to do so for themselves. Accept your own weaknesses; talk confidently about yourself; acknowledge your good, bad, and ugly to your child; and let them know all of it is okay. Can you imagine how awesome it would feel if you thought you were enough? Amazing!

Who Are You?

When an athlete steps on the field on game day, they need to know who they are. They are a Laker, for instance, or a Red Bull or a Rocket. They need to know what is expected of them—not just "to win," but, on a deeper level, how they are expected to comport themselves. They are offense, defense, a pitcher, a quarterback, a goalkeeper. They know the strategy. They know how to play the game. But when a parent steps on the field, can they say the same? Do they know what is expected of them on game day? Are they thinking about how their parenting might affect their child's athletic performance, self-concept, or future perceptions of the game and themselves?

On game day, do you unfold your lawn chair and sit quietly as you view your child on the field? Do you pace the sidelines? Who are you? Consider the following common sideline parent descriptors:

Achievement Orientation: Parents in this category place a high value on winning and achievement; they are focused on their child's individual development and growth as well as the team's competitiveness and ability to win games.

The yelling parent: You provide a running commentary of the game. You critique what you see during the game. Your voice can be heard on the other side of the field.

The stressing parent: You pace during the game. You are emotionally reactive. You need to unwind after the game.

The side switcher: You move yourself, your chair, and your family to the side of the field your child is playing on. You find yourself having a hard time paying attention to the game when your child is not playing. You spend much of the time focused solely on your child's performance.

The referee abuser: You contest any call the referee makes that you do not agree with. If a referee has spoken to you directly at any time during the game, you fit nicely into this category.

The blamer: When you are dissatisfied with the outcome of your child's or the team's performance, you place blame on the coach, other team members, the field conditions, and so on.

The loner: You watch the game from the other side of the field, away from other parents, or even with the opposing team. You avoid socializing with other parents.

Social Orientation: Parents in this category tend to place a higher value on the socialization and individual growth of their child, regardless of the sport, as well as on the development of relationships with players and families involved with the team.

The overencourager: You encourage participation trophies. You aim to see your child happy regardless of their performance, effort, or motivation. You place a high value on praise and encouragement.

The soccer mom: (This applies to any sport.) You are well prepared at every game with first aid, refreshments, and a response to any natural disaster. You are well liked and well respected by the other parents on the team. You place a high value on relationships and serving others.

The socializer: You spend a large percentage of the game time speaking with other parents. You value the connectedness of the team over the outcome of the game.

The partier: You tend to invite other families or the entire team to your home, or you organize outside activities or celebrations for the team. You are involved in the setup or organization at weekend or sleepaway tournaments.

The Facebooker: You are connected to the team families on social media. You photograph and post most or all of your team events. You are excited about and proud of your child and their teammates.

You may have occupied one or more of these roles at different times in your life. You might be thinking of other parents who fit easily into one or more category. There is no role described here that is considered good or bad, positive or negative. Note the behaviors you have engaged in or identify with and understand whether your behaviors match your intentions for your child. If you intend your team experience to be fun, consider the effect of yelling on the sidelines. If you intend for your child's experience to be one of achieving success, consider the effect of continuous praise on your child's motivation to perform.

It is helpful to understand our own sense of character and what values we want to instill in our children. Every bookstore has at least two aisles full of parenting books, overflowing with opinions on how to parent and teach our children. Authentic parenting is about understanding and becoming aware of your values and examining whether your behaviors match your intentions.

When Authentic Parenting Works

Allyssa was an only child to two doting, affluent parents, both highly competitive college athletes. She had attended private school since the age of five and enjoyed multiple sports and recreational activities. When Allyssa was interested in a sport, her parents provided her with at-home equipment and private trainers and access to elite teams. Her parents were ecstatic when Allyssa narrowed her interests to soccer and basketball when she was in seventh grade. They were all in.

Allyssa was a true athlete. She was one of those kids who stood out no matter the sport or how often she practiced. She had the it factor. Allyssa was highly sought after by coaches at her school and in her local area. She trained daily and played passionately. Her parents marveled at Allyssa's zest for everything she did.

Allyssa was a middle school soccer standout; by the seventh grade, she had already scored the most goals of anyone at her school. Her parents were enthusiastic members of her club soccer team, volunteered regularly at the fields, and even assisted with the management of the overall club program. They became a locally known and loved soccer family, with Allyssa at the center of it all.

Allyssa's parents shared her triumphs on social media, talked soccer with parents on and off the sidelines, and created friendships with many soccer families. They were pleased that Allyssa also continued to participate in other sports and activities. They knew it was important for her development to be exposed to a variety of activities and environments, and they wanted her to make her own choices about what she wanted to do. And Allyssa seemed to do all of this effortlessly; she excelled at all of it. Since Allyssa spent most of her time playing soccer and showed so much promise, her parents planned for her to begin specializing in soccer when she began high school.

In New Jersey, high school soccer usually starts in July, in the form of "voluntary" captains' practices for the current team and incoming freshmen. High school coaches are not permitted to begin coaching practices until August, so many high schools hire an outside coach to run the July programs. In reality, many high school coaches surreptitiously attend the sessions in July, which, unsurprisingly, is when evaluation for new players begins. You'd best be there if you plan to make the team, especially varsity. The head coach called Allyssa's father to make sure she would be at the practice. Her parents beamed, dreaming of her future.

One week before the captains' practice, Allyssa announced to her parents that she no longer wanted to play soccer or basketball, and therefore would not be attending. She told them she wanted to specialize in one sport, and that sport would be surfing. Record scratch. Surfing?

Allyssa had surfed a few times, but she hardly showed any real interest in it. Her family had never considered surfing a sport, or even worthwhile, unless vacationing. Allyssa's parents immediately protested. They talked to her about attending captains' practices to give high school soccer a try while still being able to surf all summer. Perhaps she was just nervous about playing high school sports.

Allyssa reminded her parents about a conversation they'd had not long prior, when she had asked to quit the church youth group because none of her friends were in it. Her parents had asked her to think about what was in her heart and said that she could quit if she really wanted to. She had thought hard about it and decided to stay in the group; it mattered to her personally even if it meant not spending as much time with her friends. She told her parents that she knew in her heart that surfing was something she loved.

Reluctantly, Allyssa's parents agreed to let her pursue surfing, having no idea how to help her succeed, other than buying her the best wetsuits and surfboards. Surfing was different from the sports her parents were accustomed to. There were no surfing moms on the sidelines. No referees, fouls, or buzzer beaters. Where was the excitement? Whom would they socialize with? Over time, they realized that soccer might have been more about their dream than Allyssa's, and they knew she would not find happiness living out someone else's dream.

Allyssa's parents eventually figured out how to be "surf parents." The experience was remarkably different, and surprisingly wonderful. They were able to find Alyssa specialized training, too, just to make sure she had an edge on her competition. By her junior year of high school, Allyssa had tallied more accolades from surfing championships than peers who had been surfing their entire lives. By her senior year, Allyssa had earned her first national sponsorship.

Guided by her parents, Allyssa stayed true to her authentic self and found joy and success in surfing. To this day, Allyssa remains an active member of her church group.

CHAPTER 7

The Car Ride Home

The car ride home is a critical time in the relationship between parents and athletes. This marks a window when the events of the game or practice are the freshest, when disappointments are raw and emotions run high. While the ride home from a sporting event might at first glance seem harmless, routine, or even insignificant, many articles and even a book written on the matter underscore its magnitude in terms of a child's interest and attitude toward participating in sports.

Ask any athlete about the car ride home with their parents, and they will have an anecdote. Over the years, we have asked youth, college, and professional athletes about their experiences. The range was staggering:

- My parents were great
- A barrage of questions
- An argument every time
- A dissection of my performance
- Fighting about where to eat
- A discussion of my sport that my parent knows nothing about
- Judgment day
- A list of the things I could do better

- A bashing of my teammates
- A heated discussion about my coaches
- Compliments I didn't deserve
- Comparing me to my brother
- My playing time
- Compliments and love
- How much money my parents paid for the sport
- How much traveling they do for me

After a sporting event, an athlete needs to rehydrate, reenergize, and rebuild. They have lost water, electrolytes, carbohydrates, and muscle protein; moreover, they're still riding high on adrenaline, which can influence a barrage of thoughts and emotions.

Racing from one intense physical activity to another can increase the likelihood of injury and burnout, so it's important to take care of an athlete's physical needs after a game. To do so, hand your child a bottle of water, take them for lunch, or let them play video games or watch TV when they get home. But even when you schedule in time for physical recuperation, a child's emotional needs often go unaddressed. Cue the car ride home as a critical piece of your relationship.

What's Happening Biologically Post Game

An athlete's emotions can range from euphoria to despair to excitement to anger, even after a win. These emotions are a sign that your child's sympathetic nervous system, or fight-or-flight system, is still activated. These emotions can be set off during the game, afterward as a result of the outcome, or during the coach's postgame talk. When your child gets into the car for the ride home, they may be knee-deep in their emotional fight-or-flight response, or beginning to recover from it.

The fight-or-flight response is a reflex that occurs whenever we are faced with something we perceive as stressful. It is a primitive reflex that once served as a survival instinct. When our ancestors were met with potentially life-threatening danger, such as an approaching enemy or bear, their body was able to respond before they could even think about it: stand and fight or turn and run.[1]

In modern times, the fight-or-flight response is rarely generated by real danger and is commonly activated by perceived threats such as the loss of a job, a relationship, or money. Sports are a breeding ground for activating the stress system due to the pressures created by coaches, parents, and fans—not to mention the perceived loss of prestige, scholarships, playing time, and future opportunities. Athletes also experience the fight-or-flight response during games or practice, in direct response to an opponent, an error on the field, or a loss.

Athletes experience the fight-or-flight response before, during, and after a game in the very same way all of us do. Top athletes, like Tom Brady and Carli Lloyd, make this look effortless. They execute winning plays during times of extremely high pressure, looking unruffled and flawless. Top athletes understand the fight-or-flight response, and they learn to use the increased adrenaline, cortisol, and oxygen to their advantage.

However, like the rest of us, sometimes even the top athletes experience fear beyond their control. They, too, can be overrun by emotion. When fear kicks in, athletes may experience heart pounding, increased sweating, changes in breathing, nervousness, fear, and reduced ability to concentrate, as well as worry and rumination about their play. Athletes experiencing severe anxiety play reactively, have tunnel vision, and have difficulty returning to their usual style of play. Some get locked in and take themselves out of the game without even realizing it.

The neocortex is the area of your brain responsible for abstract thinking, higher-order thinking, sustained attention, creativity, and imagination. The neocortex is also home to our autobiographical memories, which enable us to think, write, drive a car, or play soccer.

The limbic brain is like a first responder. Whenever the brain receives information about a real or imagined threat, the neocortex takes a back seat, and the limbic system is the first on the scene to make sure you are safe. You react to threats without thinking.

Have you ever seen your child shut down after discussing the game by putting on their headphones or tuning you out? Did your child ever burst into tears or seem completely irrational after a game? It's not that they can't handle the pressure: these are examples of how the limbic system hijacks the brain while in a state of excitement. When your child gets into the car, they may be in the process of psychologically switching off the (imagined) threat response. By forcing a conversation on someone who is in an emotional state, you are much less likely to have a rational conversation.

After a game, you may also be recovering from a fight-or-flight response. Taking time to think before you speak to your child gives you time to make your own switch. When you are relaxed and clear about what you would like to say to your child, you will speak more purposefully.

Take the example of Murray, a top-level executive who lived his life in a fiercely competitive environment. He was habitually stressed out about his son's playing time on his high school basketball team. After all, Murray had played Division I basketball for four years. His son was taller and faster than him but was not receiving the recognition that Murray believed he deserved. He assumed that his son was not trying hard enough.

To help his son, who was also frustrated with his playing time, Murray constantly reminded him of setting goals for himself during the game. Driving home from games, he tried to talk about what he'd seen:

- "Why do you pass to John all the time? He doesn't ever set you up."
- "It looks like you are coasting rather than competing. Do you want to be out there?"
- "I think you could be a little more selfish. Why not try taking more shots or driving to the basket?"

On one of the car rides home, Murray noticed a pained expression creep onto his son's face while enduring his father's line of questioning. He never answered and completely checked out, looking at his phone instead. Murray's wife sat beside him in silence. He realized that both his wife and his son were frustrated with his constant questioning, and that he felt the same. He realized his behavior wasn't accomplishing his actual goal, which was to help his son become a better basketball player—and to love the game like he did.

When it comes to helping an athlete with postgame talk, you must first establish your intentions before you deliver your message. Murray genuinely wanted to help his son have the success that he felt he deserved. How he went about it, however, got in the way. Murray was too emotionally lit up after a game. Everybody needed to cool down before talking about basketball. On future car rides home, Murray planned the day with his wife while his son played on his phone. Eventually, they were able to talk again. Murray found that he had to understand his son without first judging him. He also learned to trust that his son was doing the best that he could. He decided to approach his son later in the day or at dinner, in a safer environment where his son could leave if he wasn't happy with the conversation. Murray learned to listen.

If you have been enduring difficult rides home, rethink your goals for the ride. If you're trying to run errands after a practice and your child is being unusually surly, it might mean that they just need to get home and decompress. Instead of using the time right after the game to analyze every play, change your goal: simply enjoy a calm ride home or, as in Murray's case, begin to restore your relationship with your child. It's not necessarily that you have to set aside your intentions for helping your child succeed; you just need to rethink your timing based on what your child is ready to discuss on their own timeline.

Parents don't yell at referees, get thrown out of games, or start arguments with opposing parents on the sidelines because they hope to harm, shame, or embarrass their own child. It's just that parents often miss the forest for the trees. They get so caught up in the details of the game—referee calls, playing time, or positioning—that they can be oblivious to their own behavior and its negative effect on their child or the team. It's important for us to consider how our actions impact our kids before, during, and after the play.

It's time to change the way you think about the car ride home. Rather than use it as a coaching session or a chance to strategize, consider it your time to assist your child in cooling down. While the sympathetic nervous system controls unconscious thought and automaticity, the parasympathetic nervous system engenders a relaxed, clear, and focused mind that is better able to listen and problem solve.

While preparing for the 2008 Olympics, Christie recalls elevated anxiety. Her teammates, meanwhile, were running on adrenaline due to the excitement of competing against high-level international teams while the world watched. They were feeling the power of attending the Olympics. It is one thing to tour an Olympic arena, quite another to be enveloped by the Olympic spirit, including the teams, the medals, the Olympic village, and the celebrity. Athletes know they aren't there for themselves. They are representing their country! The US Women's National Team had the added pressure of previous gold and silver medals and wanted to remain the best in the world. Emotions ran high, but Christie and her teammates instinctively knew that the best problem solving was done via the right mind-set.

After a training session before the Olympic Games, our goalkeeper Hope Solo didn't like the way I was running someone down and the angles I was giving the attacker. I felt comfortable with my tactics, but she didn't. We got into an argument one day on the field. Hope and I weren't seeing eye to eye on anything. Our arguing escalated; it even continued after practice. Finally, the coaches said, "Enough is enough! Get on the bus!"

Hope and I instinctively sat on different sides of the bus and let our disagreement wane for the time being. We knew that was best; we needed to cool down before revisiting the issue back at the hotel. Hope didn't like how I was defending. I thought my defending was not only fine, but something that had brought me success. When we arrived at the hotel, we resumed our discussion and broke down film with our defensive coach, Erica Walsh. We eventually came to a mutual agreement on how we would play collectively. In the end, we both compromised and left feeling confident about the changes we made. After the incident, our relationship was even stronger because each of us could see how the other was reading the game.

Hope and I were able to solve our problem because we took the time and space to calm down on the way home from the practice. We both cared so deeply about the game. We respected each other enough to know we could reach that level of discord and still overcome it. For me, communication is huge in sports, and it was vital to talk about what we were feeling as we headed into the Olympics. We had to express ourselves, to get into a relaxed state of mind, and to listen with respect to each other's very different opinions on the game.

One of Dr. Keane's children had a high school soccer coach who began each soccer season with the same speech to parents. He explained that there were only three roles available at his soccer games: the coach, the player, and the parent.

He said, "I am the coach and there are no other coaching positions available. I have already chosen eighteen boys to play on my team. That leaves the parent. I expect the rest of you to fill that role. The coaching and player roles are taken."

For him, this meant that the car ride home needed to be a time to emotionally and physically cool down, to transition away from whatever happened rather than relive it. He believed that the role of the parent was just as critical as the roles of coach and players. He said that parents are primarily responsible for support. He asked that they help their sons follow through with their commitments, encourage them to have fun, and, most important, make their sons feel loved no matter how they performed.

If your car ride home is usually heated or highly emotional, or ends up in family arguments, consider an alternative approach: no game discussion on the car ride home. Leave the coaching to the coach. This step away from parent coaching may be exactly what some children need, especially those in higher-level competitions. There could also be ancillary benefit: the less you direct the conversation on the car ride home, the more your child may want to talk to you. Without pressure, your child may spontaneously return to discussing the game with you.

How do you do this? Ask them if they need water. Stop for lunch. Dry their tears. Give them a new Band-Aid. Listen if they want to talk, and get comfortable with quiet if that's what they need. Allow them to shift gears from the competitive and pressured playing mode, and let the game end on the field. You can be supportive and leave discussions, reviews, and critiques to your child's coaches.

The majority of professional and elite athletes we spoke to on this topic say that their parents never criticized them or gave negative feedback during the ride home. In fact, most of the college-level and professional athletes we surveyed say that their parents were supportive and that sports was a source of joy for their family. Many elite athletes told us that their parents made playing sports fun for them and that their parents' love and support never felt contingent upon winning.

The first question my mom or dad would ask is, "Did you play your best?" If the answer was yes, they would usually respond, "Good. That's all you can do." After that initial question, we would get into more specifics of the game. But they never stressed about winning or losing, rather giving 100 percent, because that is what matters.

—*Phil Costa, former center for the Dallas Cowboys,*
National Football League

When They're Ready to Talk

When Christie was a child, she never wanted to hear the words "good game" or "bad game." The words were meaningless to her.

Kids want constructive feedback. Although a simple message gives them a sense of relief, they still want more purposeful information regarding their play. When I am coaching, I always like to say something detail oriented and specific to the individual player.

If I feel a player didn't play well, I speak to them about specific parts of their game that need improvement. For example, instead of criticizing their effort, I talk to them about addressing fundamental skills that can aid their overall development. I relate the feedback to one of five different components within the game: where the ball is, space, teammates, situation, and goals.

The same can be said when someone has a "good game." Rather than say "good game" or "well played," which seem generic and somewhat unhelpful, I talk to them about something specific that went well, such as their movement off the ball or ability to problem solve under pressure. These conversations are vital to a child's learning curve, and we as coaches need to embrace this in detail so the players can grow.

"Good game" doesn't give the child any information about how to

self-evaluate or have a repeat performance of the wanted behaviors. They could have had a bad moment, but it doesn't mean they had a bad game. Just because you scored a goal doesn't mean you had a good game. One moment doesn't define an athletic performance. That's why details matter.

It is important to create and maintain a clear feedback loop with an athlete. Ask how they think they performed. This is typically a good initial segue into a productive conversation. Allow them to communicate first instead of setting the direction of the conversation by throwing a negative or a positive. The first thing I say to my athletes at halftime is, "How do you think you are playing?"

During my professional career, I had a coach who would walk into the locker room at halftime and ask straightaway, "How does it feel out there?" Questions like this allow the coach or parents to glean an understanding from the athlete's perspective.

After all, the kids are the ones who are out there competing and absorbing all the stresses, which we, as parents, may not appreciate. From this point, we can then build a more meaningful and beneficial two-way conversation. This not only forges trust among all involved but ultimately helps the athlete gain the confidence to evaluate their performance without the fear of criticism.

It is a parent's job to be a source of support even when a child makes a lot of mistakes, plays poorly, or does not get much playing time at all. Ask supportive questions and actively think about being a good listener. You can help your child reflect on their experience as well as help them see the big picture. Teach your child that life is not about just one game or one play. Use questions to help them get to the answers they seek on their own. Create a safe space for your child to talk as they sort out exactly what they're processing.

Some kids may look forward to the debriefing on the way home, going over what happened and who did what, and reviewing the highs and lows. Many parents note that their families prefer to have the conversation on the car ride home so as to avoid having it in front of other parents or teammates. They believe this is a safe place to talk privately about the game. While this is true, it's important to strike a balance here. When beginning conversations, avoid judging a child's playing as good or bad. Many times, children will mimic your voice and they will also regard the game or their playing as good or bad. They may also become hypercritical of themselves and point out only mistakes—theirs and others'—after a game.

It can be tempting to talk about other players or to recap your kid's own playing time, but Christie likes to focus on two topics on the car ride home.

When I talk to my kids after their games, most important to me are their body language and their effort. They are the only things I comment on. Many parents are more concerned about kids' playing time and whether they started the game. For me, it is all about attitude. If one of my daughters didn't feel like showing up for a game, she would lose playing time. If a child shows a lack of commitment or interest in playing that day, they should face consequences. I believe it's a teaching moment that reminds kids not to let their teammates down, regardless of their level of interest that day.

I remind myself that this time together is an opportunity for my daughters to tell me their emotions. On the car ride home, my girls know that I will always ask about their attitude. But I don't jump to conclusions based on what I saw, either. If they didn't seem focused or engaged, I will ask them why they didn't want to play or whether they were tired. I am aware that, as children of divorce, my daughters could be grappling with something that has nothing to do with athletics. Sometimes it is difficult for my daughters to play when both sets of grandparents are on the sidelines. They can't always handle that. It's important that my girls understand how those factors impact them and that they learn to recognize their feelings while they are playing.

During the car ride home, I talk to my girls about their teammates, too, but not to judge their performances. I want them to realize that the other girls on the team are dealing with things unrelated to the team as well. This is a life skill that I teach through sports. Difficult situations arise, but when you are on a team, try to be present and not let circumstances affect the people who rely on you.

Regardless of how much you know about your child's sport, there are always ways to open dialogue when your child is relaxed and able to communicate with you. By opening up a conversation, regardless of your understanding of the game, you may find critical teaching moments like the ones described in this chapter. The following is a list of simple conversation starters that can reinforce lessons you are trying to teach your child through their participation in their sport.

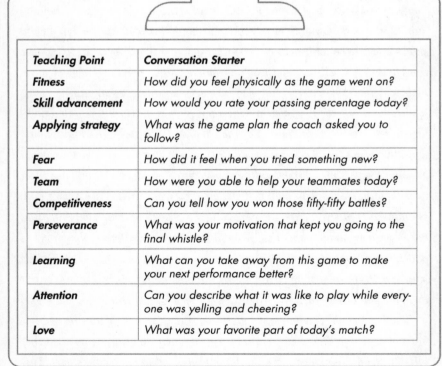

Teaching Point	Conversation Starter
Fitness	How did you feel physically as the game went on?
Skill advancement	How would you rate your passing percentage today?
Applying strategy	What was the game plan the coach asked you to follow?
Fear	How did it feel when you tried something new?
Team	How were you able to help your teammates today?
Competitiveness	Can you tell how you won those fifty-fifty battles?
Perseverance	What was your motivation that kept you going to the final whistle?
Learning	What can you take away from this game to make your next performance better?
Attention	Can you describe what it was like to play while everyone was yelling and cheering?
Love	What was your favorite part of today's match?

How to Talk About Mistakes

All sports, whether individual or team, youth or professional, indoor or outdoor, are made up of mistakes. Let us repeat that because it is one of the most important concepts for a parent to grasp when considering what to say to their child on the car ride home. *Sports are made up of mistakes.*

On bus rides with the US Women's National Team, Christie recalls that her teammates used the time to self-reflect as individuals and as a team.

My bus rides home with my teammates were often about problem solving. And sometimes the conversations led all the way back to the meal room with the national team. The communication on the bus ride home would be about how to solve a situation we could not fix during training or a game. I always sat next to Abby on the bus. We often discussed how we could get better. We talked about what we believed would be productive and what work was needed. This comes from all the training, from youth to high school to college and on to pro. It takes a long time to be able to self-evaluate and be honest about how you're really playing, to the point where most professional athletes are hypercritical of themselves. But for us, bus rides home were never negative or critical. They felt honest and constructive.

Reflection is a key component of development, and these conversations were a vital part of our continued growth as players. Being able to look at ourselves and understand what needed to be done to improve our performance allowed us to propel our game to the highest level. During these conversations, we relied heavily on our culture of trust. We were all in this together. We knew that if we grew and improved individually, it would collectively benefit the team. It was to our benefit to improve those around us, and, because of the shared reliance and trust we had for one another, we knew that even negative feedback was worth absorbing and would prove advantageous. I always looked forward to these internal conversations among teammates. They helped all of us thrive.

> I have not failed, not once. I've discovered ten thousand ways that don't work.
>
> —*Thomas A. Edison*

Pay close attention to how you discuss mistakes on the car ride home. The teams that succeed are the ones that capitalize on mistakes. Teams win because an opponent surrendered a turnover, misplayed a ball, or gave a foul. Every athlete up to the pro level understands that they *will* make mistakes, regardless of the sport.

It is important to have a realistic and healthy relationship with athletic mistakes. If you use a critical voice when talking to your child, the conversation starters listed earlier might be beneficial. Some kids are naturally hard on themselves, and, for that reason, you must teach them to identify several positive moments in the game, even if the stats or the score aren't necessarily reflective. Kids need to understand that their efforts can be productive even when they haven't won the game, scored all the goals, or made the headlines. Teach them to see their mistakes as learning opportunities.

Avery had played on youth lacrosse teams since she was eight years old. At age sixteen, Avery was part of a high-level academy team. She was a starting attacker and loved by her coaches and teammates for her enthusiasm and perseverance. Her mother, Kelly, had been a high school athlete who understood the game of lacrosse; that said, Avery felt that her mother could not possibly understand the pressure she was under.

After games, Avery would vent.

"My teammates don't pass the ball to me when they should. Sometimes I am wide open, but they think I can't finish the job. They keep the ball to themselves or they pass it to someone else they think can do better. It's so frustrating!"

Kelly would react to Avery's emotional outbursts by encouraging her daughter to see her teammates' perspective. "Maybe sometimes you don't pass the ball back to them? Maybe you need to be more vocal? Try moving to a different spot on the field?"

Kelly's suggestions were always met with more frustration, and eventually a heated argument would ensue. Kelly felt helpless, and Avery felt invalidated. All Avery heard was that her mother didn't understand her feelings and was taking her teammates' side. At sixteen years old, Avery was full of hormones, mood swings, and irrational thoughts.

Kelly eventually decided not to respond when Avery was so heated. Kelly simply allowed Avery to vent without interruption. She only asked questions to make sure she was hearing the situation correctly. She reflected on Avery's words. She said things like "So it sounds like you are frustrated because no one passed you the ball today" and "You are angry because no one on the team followed the coach's game plan?"

Kelly's methodology worked. It calmed Avery down. When Kelly listened without judging, interpreting, or correcting, Avery's postgame rants lessened. It just felt like talking. As Kelly continued to listen with curiosity, Avery felt safe to speak her mind and express her feelings.

Over time, Kelly was able to talk with Avery about her own perspectives on the game and how she might problem solve if she were in the same situation. Once Avery felt validated, she was able to hear and benefit from her mother's advice. Kelly taught her daughter about partnerships, what being on a team was really about. She taught her to communicate with her teammates in ways that would foster passing plays rather than hinder them. She also modeled good listening so that Avery might do the same for her teammates.

This breakthrough opened the opportunity to talk to Avery about being a good teammate, which Kelly explained as someone who invests time in understanding those around them. Kelly talked to Avery about the importance of communicating, in terms of words, tone of voice, and timing. She also helped Avery see the game from her teammates' perspective and understand that her teammates vary in ability, drive, and technical prowess. Courteous of this mindfulness, Avery improved specific components of her own game, which ultimately enabled her to play more cohesively and cooperatively with teammates.

When you let your children vent after a game, you are allowing them the freedom to express their feelings. As soon as you jump in with what might be perceived as judgment, criticism, or correction, your child is bound to feel invalidated, as if their feelings don't matter.

When a child is emoting this way, it is important to be supportive and keep your opinions to yourself: it's listening time, not teaching-moment time. You have to let your child know that what they feel is important and that you want to hear from them. On the other hand, don't feel obligated to validate what is invalid: frustration or sadness after a loss are valid; pouting or aggressive behavior are not. Validating a child isn't the same as cajoling or comforting. When Avery complained that no one was passing to her, her mother spoke about what she believed to be true. "It can be hard when the game doesn't go as well as you would have liked."

However, there are certain conversations that you *need* to have on the car ride home. These include if your child was rude or disrespectful to coaches or teammates or if they refused to listen during the game. These conversations need to happen in real time, despite heightened emotions or your child's disinclination to discussion. During these conversations, be clear and direct and keep it simple. Offer your rationale and explain why their behavior was inappropriate.

Don't dwell on what they did wrong, but rather direct the conversation to what they should do differently in the future. But for the most part, you'll get further with your child if you follow their lead.

Rules of the Road Home

Remember: your goal for your car ride home with your child should be to give them the support they need to recover and learn from their experiences, whether it was a tough practice, a heartbreaking game, or a triumphant match. Katherine A. Tamminen, Zoe Poucher, and Victoria Povilaitis, in *Sports, Exercise and Performance Psychology*, suggest several rules of the road home to guide conversations and keep children engaged and on board.[2]

1. Abstain from uninvited conversations.

If your child becomes emotional during your questions or conversations, shift gears. Having an unwanted or forced conversation can shut a child down and build resentment. When your child is emotional, their ability to problem solve, reason, and recall information is reduced significantly.

You may notice that your child provides short answers, shifts focus to their phone, or answers with an emotional or angry tone of voice. These are your cues to have the conversation at another time.

We also suggest that you give your child permission to say, "Not now." Teach your child to self-evaluate and decide for themselves when they are ready to discuss the game and when they are not. One family we know actually gave out red cards on the car ride home, to be used when any member of the family did not want to discuss the game. When a player is given a red card during a soccer game, they are thrown out of the game for engaging in inappropriate behavior on the field. For this family, a red card on the car ride home was a pass to stop discussing the game. A family red card throws out unwanted game conversation in a humorous, lighthearted way, while still respecting boundaries.

When you give your child the ability to decide whether they would like to discuss the game, without making them feel pressured or guilty, you essentially help them to develop a sense of compassion for themselves. You teach them that their feelings matter. When kids feel forced to speak, they may harbor anger and resentment. The conversation won't be authentic either.

2. Understand and be clear about your intentions.

Prior to communicating with your child, think about your intentions and motivations. Is your goal to teach or improve skills? To highlight examples of how to get ahead of the competition? Are you engaging them about a specific aspect of their performance or attitude? Thinking ahead about what you want your child to get out of the conversation can help you frame the discussion more productively.

Avoid rhetorical, passive-aggressive questions like, "Were you even trying in the second half?" or "You practiced that play so many times. What were you thinking out there?" They leave a child little recourse and no answer. Many well-meaning parents intend for these questions to foster their children's sense of accountability, or perhaps to enhance their next performance; however, a barrage of questions about an athlete's performance often leads to defensiveness or a complete shutdown.

Since your purpose is not to embarrass or punish your child, be extremely careful about your word choices and delivery. Do a self-check before you speak: Is what you want to say completely true in the big picture? Is what you want to say necessary for your child to hear from you? What's the kindest way to say what's on your mind?

3. Ask questions in a supportive manner.

Sometimes a child internalizes your voice as their own. If they perceive your feedback as critical, they may become habitually critical toward themselves. For example, a study published in *Clinical Psychological Science* asked participants to listen to one of five sets of audio instructions about themselves.[3] Some of the audio instructions were positive and self-affirming and others were negative and critical. As expected, the group exposed to negative, hypercritical voices showed an increase in fight-or-flight response symptoms. Also as predicted, participants who were instructed to be positive and compassionate toward themselves showed increased parasympathetic activity.

Remaining calm, modeling acceptance, and using a positive voice with your child after a game, despite the outcome, has a meaningful effect on their ability to listen to you, as well as how they talk to themselves in the future. When we model self-acceptance and kindness, even when things go wrong, we help our children switch off the threat response and give them a chance to heal.

Because of the heightened emotions your child is experiencing, the conversations on the car ride home can easily come to define their entire relationship with you. If you are not mindful, your communications can result in their feeling unloved—even though that's certainly not your intention. Be as gentle and supportive of them as you can. Ask them questions to help them review and remind themselves what their coach is teaching them.

Neutral Questions for the Car Ride Home

- Ask them about their position.
- Ask them what they did in their position during the game.
- Ask what their coach said after the game.
- Ask them what they learned during the game.
- Ask your child to teach *you* about the game.
- Ask how they might invent a way to do things differently.

4. Give them a sandwich.

The sandwich-feedback method involves giving your child feedback while surrounding it with praise. It starts the conversation with a brief reinforcement or compliment about something positive or productive your child did in the game.

Next, you deliver what you are trying to teach your child in a nonaccusatory tone. You provide your child with the information you want them to receive from the perspective of an opportunity for growth. You keep it simple.

Last, you close the sandwich with praise about one of your child's strengths, such as their attitude on the field, perseverance, competitiveness, or fitness. You may also close it with praise, for instance by commending their ability to make changes and to grow as a player. When you "close the sandwich," remember to include feedback about what they did that went well, what they improved upon, and what they can learn from their win or their loss. This helps them to internalize the notion that regardless of the outcome of the game or event, their efforts are meaningful and efficacious.

We are not suggesting that you generate artificial positive feedback or the dreaded participation award. If you cannot see anything positive that feels real or authentic to you, skip this time to speak. When Christie is coaching, she purposely opens conversations with a compliment.

I take this approach in order to gain the player's attention and trust. I follow that up with feedback I feel is critical for their further development. I then close out the conversation with another positive. It is very important to me to be sensitive to players' emotions. Timing is vital, so even as I begin the conversation with the compliment, I keep my finger on the pulse of the conversation. This may not be the right time to give them the corrective information I had intended. I can always finish the conversation at another time. If I do proceed with the critique, I layer it with positive, complimentary information. This technique softens the feedback and hopefully prevents them from becoming defensive. Ultimately, this makes for a more constructive conversation.

Your kids require you most of all to love them for who they are, not to spend your whole time trying to correct them.

—*Bill Ayers, education activist*

CHAPTER 8

Confidence

A few years ago, the fates of authors Keane and Pearce Rampone interwove. Dr. Keane's daughter Cameryn was playing on her eighth-grade school team, as well as for Christie Pearce Rampone on a travel team. Meanwhile, Christie's daughter Rylie was playing for a nearby middle school. At the end of the season, their daughters' schools met in the championship game. Dr. Keane recalls:

In the final moments of the tie game, my daughter was asked to take a penalty kick, a kick that would clearly impact the outcome. Not only were both schools watching intently, but both of Cameryn's travel team coaches were there watching as well. She set down the ball, composed herself, reared back...and missed it. She watched as the ball sailed over the crossbar. No goal. Her school lost.

Cameryn walked off the field with her head down. Her teammates and coaches told her "Good try," and "Don't worry about it," but their faces read otherwise. They were disappointed. They had wanted to win. Cameryn felt that she let down not only her school team but also the spectating travel team coaches.

The next day at school, one of Cameryn's teachers, herself a former soccer player, made choking noises and gestures at Cameryn in front of her peers. Can you imagine? When she got home, she said that she dreaded going to travel soccer practice because of what her coaches would say to her. To her surprise, the first thing Christie told Cameryn was that she was proud of her for stepping up to take the kick in the first place. She told her she knew firsthand how much courage that took. Christie also said that she would have taken the exact same angle and approach to the kick that Cameryn had. Christie focused on reinforcing the skill and the vision, something she emphasizes in practice, instead of the end result.

This was the ultimate mixed bag for a parent. Of course I was devastated that Cameryn had missed. No one wants to see their child fail or feel bad about themselves. But I was grateful that Cameryn could balance failure with support from a positive role model. Cameryn was lucky to be coached by someone dedicated to building her up. Christie taught her to work through the negative in a constructive and realistic way. This kind of coaching can impact her for life.

Three years later, Cameryn and Rylie were teammates on a travel team. Their team was unbeaten in a tournament and headed to the finals. The four of us were driving to the field. We were predominantly silent, save for the Christmas music that hummed low on the radio, reminding us not to take this stuff too seriously. But we were. I know, I know. I'm a parent too. I know that if you are not winning, you are learning . . . but who doesn't want their kid to win a championship?

We hopped out of the car and walked over to the field. Steps before the grass, Christie turned to face the girls, suddenly breaking the silence.

"Hey, Cameryn. Be prepared today. If there is a penalty kick, I want you to take it. Place it low to the corner."

"Okay. I got it. I can do it. No problem."

Christie turned around satisfied and didn't address the girls again.

The conversation made my soccer-mom heart skip a beat. Naturally, I secretly hoped there would be no penalty kick. Now, I may not be a helicopter or lawn-mower parent, but I have never acquired a taste for watching my child make mistakes, even though I know she needs them to develop. So, as regards this book: do what I say, not as I did.

Within the first ten minutes of the game, just as the laws of chaos predict, one of our strikers was fouled in the box. Cameryn lined up to take the penalty kick. I reluctantly pulled out my cell phone to capture the moment for her father, win or lose.

"I feel sorry for you," said a voice behind me, one of the other team moms. "It has to be so hard to watch!"

Just like that, Cameryn kicked it low to the corner. Not sailing above the goalie's head. Not blasted past her hands. Low to the corner, just like she was told. Goooooooooaaaaaaalllllll.

In three years, Cameryn's physical ability to shoot a penalty kick hadn't changed, but her confidence had.

Christie and her team won the championship.

Without confidence, athleticism and technical skills are moot. Parents often ask how they can raise a brave child who takes on challenges and consistently believes in themselves. The answer is this: preach confidence. Confidence is the opposite of fear. In our opinion, it is impossible to win until you are fully unafraid to lose. Kids who measure success only by wins and losses eventually get tripped up by performance anxiety, fear, and other head games that keep them from doing their best. In order to help your child develop confidence, it's important to create an environment in which they feel safe taking risks, learning from their mistakes, and developing their skills regardless of their current level.

Throughout childhood, children are exposed to coaches, teachers, authority figures, teammates, and peers who both build them up and pull them down. The trick is to identify who is who and to train your child to pay more attention to the builders than to the breakers. We don't mean that kids should automatically avoid the people or experiences that might break them down. Instead, we should more actively help them work through—and learn from—those situations.

Does Everyone Get a Medal?

Within pediatric psychology, there are conflicting views on how best to foster an environment in which kids aren't hyperfocused on outcomes. Some pediatric psychologists believe that parents should provide repeated praise and encouragement and purposely create positive experiences for their kids. They believe that positive experiences associated with mastery and success engender a sense of "I can do it." According to this approach, kids can then handle other life challenges, having learned to believe in themselves. Some psychologists advocate participation medals and equal playing time for all teammates irrespective of skill level. They believe that growing a confident child comes from fostering positive emotional experiences and rewards.

Others believe that without the experience of loss or challenge, children aren't able to develop the resources they need to handle adversity. Some psychologists argue that parents provide their children with too much positive feedback, to the point that most of the praise is groundless. Praising a child for everything renders moot the boost of real pride that comes with truly achieving something. Will a kid who gets so much praise for riding his tricycle want to do the work to ride a two-wheeler? Will a kid who thinks his somersaults are amazing be motivated to learn to do a cartwheel?

Every child and every situation is unique. Some kids may not be able to appreciate their actual accomplishments if they experience too many artificial milestones and awards. Other kids need a lot of positive feedback to keep developing. Some kids need just a few participation medals because, without them, they may not achieve any in sports. There are so many reasons why kids get involved in sports—exercise, leadership, teamwork, and so on. Shouldn't there be multiple approaches to coaching and parenting based on an athlete's unique personality and abilities?

We say, sign up for an activity that reflects the approach you think your child needs. Think about your goals and your child's goals for the experience. Are they desperate for a competitive position and do they need to be pushed to develop the qualifying skills? Do they love being involved in activities regardless of the outcome? Are they looking to hang out with a specific friend? Assessing the goals you and your child have for the activity will help you decide which approach is best. Consider a recreational team with equal playing time instead of paying thousands of dollars to play for an academy team. Or consider trying out for higher-level teams that value skill and technique over giving everyone a chance to play.

Focus on the Most Important Goal

Even the world's premier athletes can have their confidence shaken. When Christie was first invited to practice with the US Women's National Team, she took a significant blow to her self-confidence.

When you are successful throughout your career and you reach the highest level, it's easy to lose some self-confidence when you actually get there. When I got called to the national team in January 1997, I had been accustomed to being one of the top players on almost every team I played on, in both basketball and soccer. Now that I had made it to the national team, I was back to being a nobody.

The camp was ten days long; in this period of time, I had so many knocks to my confidence. The first thing we did was watch a video of the team winning gold at the 1996 Olympic Games in Atlanta. I had always dreamed of winning Olympic gold; it was that very moment when I realized I was surrounded by so many special athletes. My self-doubt kicked into overdrive. I wondered what I was even doing there. Soccer wasn't even my number one sport: it was basketball!

Prior to playing on the national team, I had always been a forward and goal scorer (seventy-nine goals in eighty collegiate games), which led to my being quite confident on the field. Aaaaand then I got to the national team, where my competition for a position on the forward line consisted of Mia Hamm, Michelle Akers, Tiffeny Milbrett, Shannon MacMillan, and Cindy Parlow. The competitions was so intense that the coach decided my best bet would be to play on defense. All of a sudden, the one thing that I was good at, that one thing that made me feel valuable, had been stripped from me. I was moved to a position I had never played and encouraged to figure it out if I wanted to remain part of the team. Naturally, this left me questioning whether I was good enough to contribute.

The real kicker to my confidence happened during the fitness testing on the second day of camp. To remain part of this team and prove to my new teammates that I belonged, I thought that I needed to show out during fitness testing. This was a terrible idea. I came out of the gate fast, pulling in front of everyone—but could not keep that pace up and got lapped by many players. My confidence was at an all-time low at a time when I needed it most: surrounded by some of the best women to ever play the game.

Eventually, I realized that I had to change my attitude, my mind-set. I told myself that I was going to give it one last effort. It wasn't the training that needed to change; it was my inner dialogue. I had to stop making excuses and get focused on my own playing style. I had to evolve my game, step up to the challenge, and keep moving forward.

Confidence always comes from your mind. Often, kids are looking for immediate results—especially when they're used to being the best. That is what Christie realized when she first made the national team. She was looking to be recognized as she had been in the past. This marked the first time she wasn't immediately acknowledged as one of the best on the field. Christie had to draw on her previous successes to conjure up the self-confidence needed to play on the national team. No one was going to believe in her unless she first believed in herself.

Comparing Yourself to Others Is a Losing Game

Many athletes look to their coaches, parents, and teammates for a sense of how well they play and if they are "good enough." The psychological concept of social comparison theory says that many people unconsciously compare themselves to others to determine whether they are faring better or worse.[1] Some people derive their sense of self-worth from how they measure up to other people. Research suggests that people who repeatedly compare themselves to others are prone to deep personal dissatisfaction, and tend to be overcompetitive and self-punitive.

Many young athletes compare how they are playing to others. "She's better than me." "He is the best player on the team." "I can play goalie better than her." "My scores were lower than his." Athletes at all levels talk about comparing their play to that of others in the same position. Christie admits to doing the same early in her own career. To boost their confidence, athletes can make a shift from focusing on judging other players and teammates to focusing on how to connect and communicate with them. Instead of criticizing them or sizing them up, productive athletes shift to trying to understand them and learn from them.

To model this, parents and coaches can eliminate talking to kids about other players, unless it is a communication about making the other player better. After a disappointing loss, it is not uncommon to hear a parent or player blame the offense or the defense, or to point out that one of the players on the team was responsible for a goal, or the fact that the team did not score enough to win.

Knocks to a kid's confidence happen at every level of play; however, confidence is paramount during transitions from team to team or from one play level to the next. In soccer, for example, athletes must eventually transition from playing on a small field to a larger one. Basketball players must transition to a higher hoop. As children specialize, they often move from recreational to travel to higher-level club and academy teams. As players get older, the pace of the game and the speed and strength required to play change too. Many of these transitions can affect confidence. Kids accustomed to being the star player at one level might find themselves on the bench at another. No matter the sport or particular level, virtually all athletes appraise their peers and wonder if they fit in or if they're even good enough to play at a given level.

The next level in any sport is made up of better athletes and bigger stars. Give kids confidence by preparing them for these transitions ahead of time. Educate your child about the impending changes and let them know to expect an adjustment, just as they expect new teammates, new coaches, and a new playing philosophy. Despite how they play at the next level, kids must be made to understand that they belong. The transition happened because of the accomplishments that preceded it. A kid might have the pedigree to move up, but they also need the confidence. Kids should be reminded to go into these transitions with open minds and realistic expectations. Many assume that they will remain stars no matter the team or league they join.

When your child transitions to a higher level, frame the change as an opportunity to grow and learn. Remind them that they don't want to be the smartest person in the room or the best athlete on the team. If they are, how will they grow? Who could possibly train them? Explain that transitions bring challenges that will not necessarily feel comfortable but will keep kids growing.

Athletes who identify what they want to learn from other athletes will do better than athletes who repeatedly tell themselves that they

come up short. As we mentioned previously, every athlete has something unique to offer, and no two play the same. Everyone comes
to the field, ice, court, or mat with their unique experiences, talents,
and knowledge, and the games are always in the eye of the beholder.
Teach kids to look for excellence, to measure up to their own standards instead of others', and know that their success will always be
unique and personal and will come from within.

How to Tell If Your Child Is Struggling with Confidence

- Avoidance of trying new things
- Reoccurring injuries or events that keep them out of play
- Repeatedly voicing self-doubt about ability
- Focusing on errors or losses
- Needing motivation from parents to try hard
- Perfectionism or unrealistic expectations about performance
- Comparing themselves to other athletes
- Attributing their success to luck instead of ability
- Hiding when they play; standing behind other players
- Fear of asking questions or speaking up to coaches and
  teammates
- A lack of ownership; blaming others for poor performance

Encourage Emotional Expression

After a disappointment or loss, parents are often quick to dry their
child's tears, promise that it will be okay, or assure them they can
beat that team next time. It is hard to see your child upset. Some parents are afraid that if a child feels bad about a loss, it could hurt their
self-esteem or make them less likely to try next time. We encourage

you to let your child experience negative emotion. Let them learn from it. To boost self-confidence, shift the focus to how they come back from a disappointment, rather than trying to avoid or bypass it with an affirmation or excuse.

In a 2017 study in the *Journal of Behavioral Decision Making*, researchers found that people who allow themselves to fully feel failure actually lay the groundwork for future success. In the study, ninety-eight volunteers were asked to find the cheapest price for a particular blender, with the promise of a cash prize to the participant who found the best deal. Half of the respondents were asked to focus on their emotional response to losing, and the other half were told to simply think about the details of their failure. In the end, nobody won: all participants were told that the blender was available for $3.27 less than the one they had found.[2]

Everyone then participated in a second, similar task, which involved shopping for a book. The researchers found that the group that had been directed to focus on their emotional response to failing spent 25 percent more time on the second task than did the group instructed merely to think about the details of failure. The results indicate that the group that emotionally reflected on their failure tried harder than the group that did not. In sum, the study suggests that when we don't recognize and embrace our failures, we won't learn from them.

Build confidence by allowing your child to experience the emotions related to their disappointment and reflect on things they can change and improve. Give them time to talk about it and reflect on how they feel and what they did. Do this with a nonjudgmental ear and offer no initial advice, only validation. For example, "I can understand how you felt embarrassed when you missed that shot," or, "It has to be frustrating when they don't pass the ball to you." Regardless of how irrational your child's initial appraisal of their failure or disappointment, it is important to let them verbalize their feelings You can later shift their focus to how they might change or improve going forward.

Emotional expression can be a really tricky thing to learn, but it's so important. Christie has struggled with it periodically throughout her career.

People who really know me say I don't show my emotions. My dad had a rule when we were growing up: don't show your fear. If you get knocked down, get right back up. He said that you show your emotion through your play. He told us to help our team with our energy and movement during the game, not afterward. He made sure that we did not celebrate in front of our opponents. You should always respect the efforts of the opposing team, he said. He used to tell us that you show your appreciation by doing your best for your team. So once the whistle blew and the game was over, I never celebrated a win. I went back to being a quiet, shy, and less-than-confident person.

I was the middle child of three. My older sister was also a great soccer and basketball player, but I was always a little bit better than she was. I loved her and admired her and I never wanted to rub it in her face. My sister went on to play Division I soccer and then semiprofessionally too. I believe that the only thing that separated us was my commitment level.

My younger brother played well too. He was also gifted in basketball and baseball. But when he was growing up, he was always compared to me—by other parents, in the newspaper, everywhere. He ended up quitting because he tired of the comparisons to his big sister. He called me when I was in college and asked if I would be upset if he left basketball. I told him that I just wanted him to feel confident and happy in anything he chose to do. Even though basketball made him happy, the environment brought out the worst in him. So he joined the bowling team (and he was a damn good bowler!) and he kept playing baseball. My brother wound up having a blast because he just wanted to play sports to have fun. We all had different athletic abilities and very different personalities.

At a young age, when my sister and I played basketball, the people who ran the league wouldn't allow me and my sister on the same team because of our skill level. So we always wound up playing each other. Any time my team would win, I wasn't allowed to talk about the game. I was taught to focus on something else afterward. I focused more on my sister's emotions than my own. I never held back my talent to let my sister win, but suppressing the celebration of wins inhibited my ability to enjoy my success. I became so aware of other people's emotions that I saw my victories as someone else's losses. I took celebrating as a negative. To this day, I have a hard time embracing my successes, and I tend to quickly move on to the next goal.

This is what we mean when we say sports experiences influence your life. I still get angry that I don't take complete care of myself emotionally. That missing skill is so hard to integrate now that I have this happy and evolving family life. Instead, I am trying to learn a new skill set by doing things for myself. My confidence always came from playing and taking care of others, but I am still working to develop the confidence to allow myself to be full of emotion.

I really draw from my past when I am coaching: allowing the kids to express themselves, to enjoy the win and feel the loss when they need to. This was one of the biggest things I took away from sports—allowing myself to feel. I want the kids to feel it, all of it, and learn that those feelings of passion are what make them competitors.

There is value in teaching kids how to express emotions rather than just telling them to. But we must also show kids that their success and pride should be based on attitude and effort and not just end results. Letting kids feel the hurt, disappointment, and pain is equivalent in terms of emotional development to their feeling the celebratory joy and exhilaration. Remember, emotional pain coupled with reflection means progress.

Public Disappointment

When athletes succeed, it's often in front of a crowd, and it can be incredible to feel like the world is celebrating your achievements with you. But when athletes experience crushing defeats, those too are often public spectacles. This is where having self-confidence becomes even more critical; not only does it help you bolster yourself as you recover from the disappointment, but it can help you block outside negativity.

Winning a silver medal in the 2000 Olympics was one of the biggest eye-openers of Christie's career. Prior to the championship game, the athletes are told what to expect when they win—the celebrations, the interviews, the parade, and so on. What they aren't told is that if they don't win a gold medal, none of those things happens. Everything is just canceled. Thus, America viewed this tremendous team as a loser.

When I got home, one of my family members repeatedly called me "second place" after I'd had an amazing experience at the Olympics. I was a little surprised, to be honest, to be seen as a loser. It was only the second-ever Olympics for the US women's soccer team, and, in my opinion, our team was one of the best the United States had ever fielded. Despite this fact, and coupled with others' reactions, coming home with silver still made me feel like I'd come up empty.

I think kids can only find true success after they've experienced negative emotions in sports. They need to feel it. Some people called me an Olympian; others called me a loser. In the end, the silver medal was part of a larger learning process. I don't regret the sadness. As devastated as I was, it made me a stronger person. Winning three gold medals after that didn't hurt, either. I appreciate that silver because it motivated me to learn and get better and to find lasting success. The silver reminds me that when I wasn't winning, I was still learning and growing.

When Christie brings her medals to speaking engagements, she makes sure to bring her silver as well as her golds. She explains that her silver medal was the best thing that happened to her. She talks about how she took the emotion of loss and carried it into her future training.

"A Winner Is Just a Loser Who Tried One More Time"

This quote from George M. Moore Jr. reminds us that we learn more from our failures than from our successes. Ask any elite athlete how many times they practiced a certain skill and they will tell you thousands. Our kids are bombarded with images on YouTube and on social media that repeatedly show highlight reels of athletic success. Given this rise in technology, college coaches ironically rely less and less on highlight reels; they know a video tells but a small slice of a larger story. Think about it like this: a highlight reel could distill two years' worth of playing into six spectacular moves—or it could feature six spectacular plays culled from just two games. Social media does not show how many failed selfies preceded that glorious one (twenty-four, to be exact). Or how many misses it took before finally making that basket. The foundation of confidence is internal, and the basics come from doing—over and over and over again.

Christie's daughter Reece made an elite soccer team when she was nine years old. She had a real passion and love for the sport but did not develop as the other players on the team did. She saw less and less playing time. She loved her coach and the training but became increasingly disinterested in attending games because she didn't play.

Reece and I talked about her disappointment with playing time and why she wasn't playing. I encouraged her to keep working hard at practice and to make the most of whatever playing time she had. But, despite her effort, she still saw very little playing time and continued to feel discouraged. Then the coaches starting shifting her around the field; as a coach, I know that often means her position on the team is insecure. They were just giving her time.

I asked Reece if she was having fun and if she felt she was learning. The more we reflected on that angle, the more she entertained the idea of playing for a different team. We kept everything positive, and eventually she told us that she wanted to take a break from soccer and try a different sport.

Reece made her decision, took her break, and played basketball. The following season she returned to soccer with a local recreational team and had an absolute blast. She played with a smile and got a lot of time on a team that rotated playing time. She felt like she belonged, and her confidence shot through the roof! It showed how she expressed herself on the field. If she had remained on the elite team, she would have missed many on-the-field opportunities to develop her game. At her age, sitting on the bench not only limited her ability to learn but clearly impacted her confidence.

Don't avoid discussing negative experiences with your child. You can use challenges as opportunities for learning and see them for what they really are: necessary for development. Reece made the same elite team the following year but chose not to play on it again. Christie had an open and honest discussion with her about her options and offered Reece the ability to make the choice for herself. Reece's soccer ability, interest in the game, and confidence continue to grow as a result.

Attribute Success to Their Effort and Abilities

In a study by Moe Machida, Rose Marie Ward, and Robin Vealey, the most reliable predictor of self-confidence in college athletes was their past achievements—but only when their achievements were coupled with their perceived control over events.[3] The same didn't hold when athletes felt external events to be out of their control. In other words, when athletes internalized their success as something they had contributed to, they were more confident than athletes who attributed their success to external events such as luck. The study indicates that athletes should focus on what they know they can do, what they know for sure about themselves, and what they *can* control, like achieving personal bests and maintaining high standards. If you don't feel like you influenced your success, you don't take it with you to your next game.

Christie's first experience on a professional soccer team was with the New York Power. This is where she met her teammate and later close friend Shannon Boxx, affectionately called "Boxxy." Boxxy was a perfect example of an athlete whose success was directly tied to her ability to focus on her personal bests—because when she arrived at the US Women's National Team training camp, Boxxy wasn't expecting to play at all.

Boxxy was traded to the New York Power, having recently been playing for San Diego Spirit. Her coaches and teammates labeled her an "unfit" player, as she had a history of failing fitness tests. Surprisingly, within three months of playing for Power, Boxxy was summoned to the US Women's National Soccer Team camp in advance of the 2003 World Cup. Unfortunately, her "unfit" label followed her; when she arrived, the head coach told Boxxy that she had no chance of actually making the team. She was called up into camps only to practice, as a reward for playing well in the league. Boxxy had no chance to make the World Cup roster.

The training camp lasted only ten days, so Boxxy decided to make the most of the opportunity. Just being invited, she thought, indicated her potential and the ability to make the team one day. Because she was so sure that she wasn't being evaluated for a spot on the roster, Boxxy wasn't overwhelmed by the moment. She just focused on her play. And, because she showed her most authentic self on the field every day, she actually wound up making the team!

Boxxy played up to her potential because she played freely. She was grateful and enjoyed the experience. She wasn't distracted by pressure or stress, and good things happened because she played with confidence. Not only did she make the squad, but she started the opening game and throughout the tournament.

Boxxy derived her self-confidence from practicing within a different mental space. She focused on enjoying the moment: scrimmaging with a world-class team, wearing Team USA gear, and embracing teammates she'd never dreamed of playing with. Since her fate had apparently been sealed, Boxxy played to her strengths, out of her head, and without the mental baggage that goes along with unhealthy perfectionism and an attachment to gaining something. Almost inadvertently, Boxxy was able to play to her highest potential.

When Christie first practiced with the national team, in 1997, she was unable to keep up with her teammates during fitness tests—as measured by her times for various full-field sprints and short-distance drills. For each drill, she was held accountable to meet or beat a specific running time. During her first season, Christie was often lapped by teammates during those longer-distance running tests, and she, too, was labeled unfit. Though she excelled in short bursts, she lagged behind on full-field sprints. Christie was painfully embarrassed, and her confidence suffered. She was embarrassed because she felt she was disappointing her teammates. Her confidence soared during the short sprints, but she'd sprinted so hard that she didn't have the endurance for the long-distance runs. She questioned whether she belonged.

Christie wanted to "fix her numbers." She believed the long-distance fitness tests were her wakeup call. She needed to get fitter to be taken seriously on the national team. So she focused on how many training hours she'd need outside of practice to improve her fitness numbers. Initially, Christie focused solely on passing those tests rather than actually getting fitter or making her body healthier. She was working on *not failing*.

Her self-confidence hinged on the results of her tests. She was so focused on meeting those numbers that she was closed to other growth opportunities. She played well, but not to her true potential.

These days, fitness tests have evolved and the approach to fitness is significantly different. Each player should be evaluated in terms of their personal strengths and weaknesses. Their fitness goals should be tailored to the development of their unique abilities and talents. In order to play at their best, athletes must focus on what they bring to the team and to the game. Confidence comes from homing in on their own personal strengths and weaknesses as opposed to dwelling on things outside their control, like winning or losing. Ultimately, Christie and Boxxy dedicated themselves to developing their own attributes and abilities; they didn't agonize over whether they would make the roster or pass the fitness tests. They learned to understand and push themselves, mentally and physically. By her third World Cup, Christie was one of the fittest players on the team. She had prepared herself to play a ninety-minute game, not pass a test.

Develop a Positive Inner Voice

In the 2012 Olympic final, the US Women's National Team faced Japan at Wembley Stadium. The United States was ahead 2–1. With ten minutes to go in the game, Christie's regular defensive partner was forced to leave the field due to a concussive blow to her head. Though her replacement was very good, Christie was not accustomed to her playing style. Christie received an unexpected pass and, unfortunately, took a very bad first touch of the ball. The Japanese forward pounced, stealing the ball from her and breaking through on goal with a great chance to level the game at 2–2. The forward unleashed a great shot, but US goalie Hope Solo made one of her incredible, nail-biting saves.

I hugged Hope and didn't want to let go. I hugged her for a long time. I thought I'd almost ruined everything! Why didn't I play it up the field? What was I thinking? After the game I had flashbacks to that moment. I couldn't even focus on celebrating. I dwelled on that mistake for months! Rather than celebrating a hard-earned Olympic gold medal, I spent my time reliving a regrettable but ultimately inconsequential moment. There were plenty of positives from that game and the Olympics, but somehow I chose to focus on the negative. I eventually had to realize that the game wasn't just about me. I was one person on a team full of very talented players. I reminded myself that I had reliable teammates and an amazing goalkeeper behind me. You are only as good as the people you surround yourself with. When you fully understand there is no "I" in "team," you play more confidently.

Though Christie typically followed a positive internal narrative when playing, every so often that pesky negative voice would creep in, usually due to an error on the field that she felt accountable for. That voice would linger in her mind for days, even weeks. One of the most powerful things you can teach your child is to recognize their inner voice. Many kids don't realize that there's a voice inside their head, talking to them all the time. When athletes make mistakes and get stuck in their minds, their self-confidence is rattled. Top-tier athletes are better than most at shifting their inner voice away from damaging criticism and toward productive self-feedback.

Teaching Kids to Shift Their Inner Voice

1. Talk to your child about recognizing negative, repetitive thoughts that cause them to feel bad.
2. Let your child know that they don't have to repeat a negative thought. As soon as they think of one, they can choose to replace it with a positive thought.
3. Help your child understand that they can observe their thoughts by paying attention to them. The problem is not the thought. The problem lies in their belief that they cannot change that thought and or that the thought is true just because they had it.

As discussed, Christie's inner voice came from her parents. She told herself it wasn't right to celebrate her victories and to express her emotions out on the field. If parents are repeatedly negative, critical, or judgmental, the child incorporates those words into their own lexicon and speaks to themselves just as harshly. Think about the times your child makes a poor decision, makes an error on the field, or causes a turnover due to carelessness or inattention. How do you react to them? What words do you choose to help your child?

Kids need years and years of training to learn how to self-regulate and deal with their emotions, good and bad. When helping your child develop a positive inner voice, try to remember the big picture. You are not trying to exterminate all negative thoughts from your child's life experience. Your role is to listen, to acknowledge their negative emotional expression, and to help lead them to self-soothing and problem solving, as opposed to dwelling, ruminating, or developing an automatic negative self-talk reel in their minds. Help them to understand that they have a right to feel their unique emotions at any given time.

Parents can help children by teaching them to mentally rehearse positive scenarios before a game. Avoid giving kids expectations like how many goals they should score. They might interpret those expectations as the value they have on the field; if they don't meet them, their confidence decreases.

There are multiple strategies you can use to model and teach your child how to develop a positive inner voice.

Model positive self-talk. Say things about yourself in front of your child that model a positive inner voice. When you are proud of yourself, say so. "I feel great that I got the lawn mowing done." When you have a problem, talk it out. "That didn't quite work out as I planned, but I will give myself another chance tomorrow."

Shift away from perfect parenting. Many times when a child has a problem or is struggling with a negative emotional state, parents feel that is a direct reflection on their parenting. "I should have picked a better team for him." "I should have known he wouldn't get the playing time he deserved here." When we beat up ourselves for how we parent, we aren't doing ourselves or our children any good. Our unhealthy cognitive habits are contagious, too. Instead of wallowing in our own disappointment about what we could have done better, or taking responsibility for things outside of our control, we can model healthy self-esteem by making a shift from being a *perfect* parent to being a *valuable* one.

Share your experiences. When you hear your child using negative self-talk, listen, reflect to them what you have heard, and question them. Get a deep understanding of how your child uniquely understood their problem without putting your own spin on it. Let them tell you if you didn't hear it right the first time. Once you feel like your child has been heard, share your own experiences with the same feeling. You may not have played lacrosse or missed a foul shot on a high school basketball court, but you have certainly had your fair share of disappointments or subpar performances.

Teach them perspective. One of the most important things you can teach your child is to understand or empathize with others. Your child's peers, coaches, teachers, and other authority figures don't behave the way they do solely because of your child. People act the way they do because of their own feelings and life circumstances. You can teach your child from a very early age that other people's behavior is not your child's fault so they learn not to hyperfocus on themselves as the problem.

Teach them how to problem solve. When kids know how to problem solve effectively, they are less likely to get into patterns of rumination and worry. When kids focus deeply on a problem, it can easily spiral out of control and seem a lot worse than it actually is. Once you feel that your child has had time to express their feelings, toss out possible solutions to get them accustomed to a shift from awfulizing to problem solving.

Take steps to understand your child's unique sense of self-efficacy in terms of their familiarity with mastery, vicarious experiences, repetitive verbal dialogue, and emotional functioning. Athletes are generally critical of themselves, so it is crucial to have the right support team.

CHAPTER 9

Beating Performance Anxiety

Grace was a professional soccer player who competed at the national and international levels. She was invited to one of the youth national teams at a surprisingly young age and began competing professionally as soon as she was eligible. Her stats were consistently amazing and she was indispensable to every team she joined. However, Grace's coaches were consistently concerned about her attitude, regardless of her outstanding skill, technique, and raw athleticism. They believed that despite her innate ability, she lacked the passion and intensity needed to compete with the greatest players in the world. Grace appeared indifferent, apathetic.

As a professional, Grace knew her real problem was her fear of failure. She cared so much about her play that her performance anxiety sometimes crippled her concentration, decision-making, and composure. When she made mistakes, she would be sad, cry, and worry about her future. The more errors she made, the more her anxiety grew. And when Grace was deeply embarrassed and ashamed of her performance, she purposefully wore a mask of indifference to others.

To everyone else, Grace appeared to be a strong, extroverted, funny, witty, forceful, and sometimes even arrogant player. She built these defenses subconsciously to please her coaches and teammates or to keep people from getting too close to her, so she wouldn't have to endure their criticism. She attempted to hide her true fear of playing badly, losing, disappointing others, or doing the wrong thing.

Dr. Keane met Grace when she was at odds with one of her coaches. Grace had confessed to her athletic trainer that her anxiety was spinning out of control; her athletic trainer suggested she come for a consultation. The coach was new that season, exacerbating her performance anxiety. She felt she had her "nerves" under control, she said, but her new coach made her feel overly criticized and attacked. Grace blamed him for her spike in anxiety and mistakes on the field, because she believed the training he was offering her was below the high standards she'd set for herself.

- "I'm miserable. I feel like a total letdown."
- "I feel like I don't have enough support. With this kind of coaching I just know I am going to fall behind. I am going to lose my skills."
- "I don't want to be nervous anymore. I just need to be able to play, get better, and be happy. I don't want to cry about this anymore!"
- "What if I find out I am not good enough?"

Grace's initial sessions focused on her breathing and meditation, so she could learn to calm both her mind and her body and listen more deeply to her thoughts. She resisted this at first, as most type A athletes do, instead preferring concrete methods and very specific "magic wand" ways to get rid of her anxiety. Anxiety festers when we look to exterminate it without attempting to understand its source and what it is teaching us. With persistence and practice, Grace learned to become aware of her inner dialogue and uncover core belief patterns about her striving for perfection.

Grace also learned to reflect on her thoughts rather than just accept them as true simply because she was having them. This was important

because Grace tended to be quite self-deprecating, as most perfection-
ists are. She learned that while she couldn't always prevent a thought
from popping into her mind, she could control the thoughts that followed. She had never even considered how hard she was being on
herself. She realized that she had internalized a number of voices
throughout her childhood, the strongest of which was her father's.

Grace's father was a former professional baseball player. When he
retired, he taught and coached youth sports. Grace was the youngest
of three, and she turned out to be his only child with athletic ability
that surpassed his own. Naturally, he took quite an interest in Grace's
development and success in sports, which resulted in his microman-
aging her play.

Grace told stories of her father standing on the sidelines, calling
out plays to her, correcting her, and scolding her. She was an outside
back, and he always stood within earshot of her—and within earshot
of most of the parents as well. At halftime, her father switched to the
other side of the field to make sure she could hear his calls.

If an opponent got past her or juked her, she was subjected to
harsh criticism. Her father repeatedly shouted directives at her, such
as "Move your feet," "Focus on the ball," "You have to make contact,"
"Be more aggressive," and "Don't let her get past you."

Sometimes her father would be quite specific and coach her to
"Move up," "Close the space," "Get tighter to the forward," "Tackle,"
or "Make contact." She told Dr. Keane that the only way to appease
her father and quiet him down during a game was to successfully
defend against a forward or to win the game. He wasn't impressed
by total effort: if she got beaten by an opponent, that was all that
mattered to him. She dreaded conversations with her father more
than those with her coaches or teammates.

Grace's father inadvertently taught her that she was only good
if she was winning. Since every athlete is going to lose sometimes,
she internalized a hidden fear that she was not good enough. While

she verbalized a can-do attitude throughout her career, deep down she felt she was a fraud, as if one day her coaches would realize she didn't belong with the pros. With meditation, reflection, guidance, and journaling, Grace uncovered beliefs about herself that she never realized were there. Her discoveries led her to rewrite her own internal script and create new, growth-enhancing, confidence-building dialogue that came from within. She no longer accepted the opinions of others without first checking in with herself. She was good enough. She learned to strive for excellence, not perfection.

What Is Performance Anxiety?

Performance anxiety is a fear that develops from the illusion of failing. It is a fear of not being able to perform, a fear of losing, or perhaps even a fear of embarrassing the family. Performance anxieties come from deeply rooted fears of disapproval, rejection, and abandonment and are rarely fully known to the person who is experiencing the anxiety.

Performance anxiety manifests in multiple self-defeating behaviors, such as inadequate or excessive warm-ups, poor pacing, and distractibility on and off the field. The symptoms correlate with the fight-or-flight response discussed earlier and involve increased heart rate, heavy sweating, rapid breathing, fatigue, muscle twitches, trembling, and sour stomach. Feelings can range from butterflies and nervousness to panic and terror. An athlete with performance anxiety may appear stiff and overcontrolled due to muscle twitching or fatigue. They may refuse to take risks—avoiding taking shots or participating in plays—or they may play in an overcontrolled fashion in an attempt to avoid mistakes. Athletes with performance anxiety may appear distracted or unfocused on the game because of a lack of confidence and overemphasis on the game's outcome.

Performance anxiety is often rooted in a person's core belief system, and the fear is oftentimes not readily available to the conscious mind. Core beliefs are typically formed during childhood brain development, and they become an individual's internal guidance system. Parents, coaches, teachers, and other significant people in a child's life influence core belief systems.

When Grace played soccer, she was amazing. It didn't necessarily look like she was listening to a continuously critical inner voice. But Grace often ran onto the field with tears in her eyes. She was beating herself up constantly and it was holding her back—and making her miserable.

Grace eventually created pregame routines including using learned cognitive strategies for maintaining a positive mind-set and reframing defeating self-talk. Later, we will discuss these techniques and how you might teach them to your children. While these strategies were powerful game changers for Grace, most important to beating her performance anxiety was her awareness of and understanding of her inner voice. Until she fully addressed her inner dialogue, she was unaware that she was focused on trying to please her father. The result was a sense of helplessness and a core belief that nothing she did was good enough.

Some Signs of Performance Anxiety

- Appearing disinterested while playing
- Injuries lasting longer than medically expected
- Looking for the parent after making mistakes
- Looking down while playing
- Laughing at mistakes
- Difficulty taking criticism from a coach
- Making light of losses
- Playing very well in practice and not in the game

Parenting Styles that Exacerbate Anxiety

What type of sports parent are you? In the field of pediatric psychology, experts agree that different parenting styles affect a child's risk for developing anxiety. Let's look at how some of these styles might manifest on the field.

The Helicopter Parent

The dictionary definition of a helicopter parent is one who takes an overprotective or excessive concern in their child. Key words here are "over" and "excessive." We are not talking about being interested in your child's growth and development, keeping them safe, or being actively involved. We are talking about hovering around a child in an attempt to control events in their lives so they avoid feeling pain. Helicopter parents are also anxious themselves.

A recent study published in the journal *Cognitive Therapy and Research* showed how helicopter parenting affects children with anxiety.[1] In this study, parents and their children were invited to a laboratory and tasked with solving multiple puzzles. They were given ten minutes to complete as many puzzles as they could. Parents were permitted to help their child with the tasks, but they were encouraged not to.

The researchers found that parents of children previously diagnosed with anxiety touched the puzzles more often than did parents of children who were not anxious. Even though they were not overly critical or harsh, the parents of anxious children offered help with solving the puzzles, even when their child did not ask for it.

This research underscores the idea that helicopter parents perceive situations as problematic or challenging even when their child does not. Many of these parents experience anxiety themselves and are trying to shield their child from similarly negative experiences. Over time, providing unsolicited help sends a covert yet powerful message to a child: they don't have the ability to succeed or solve problems on their own. This feeling in turn increases a child's anxiety and reliance on other people to do things for them; they may also give up prematurely when assistance isn't available. When parents prevent their children from experiencing vulnerability or frustration, their children may develop a fear of taking risks.

The Lawn-Mower Parent

The lawn-mower parent is afraid to let their child experience adversity. While the helicopter parent intercedes and assists with problems prematurely and unnecessarily, the lawn-mower parent removes obstacles before the child can even get to them. This way, their child will never experience painful emotions such as fear, pain, or shame—but will also never learn that all those emotions can be experienced and processed, as they are integral catalysts for learning and personal growth.

Shea, a defender on one of Christie's youth teams, typically responded anxiously to in-game coaching or guidance. If a coach yelled out to her with feedback, she would ask to be removed from the field just moments later, like clockwork—even if she'd been playing well and had no apparent injury. After the feedback was imparted, she told her coaches that she needed to "see it" and thus wanted to come off the field. The reality was that Shea felt criticized and too overwhelmed to continue playing. She would often appear pale-faced at halftime and complain of stomach or leg cramps.

One day, Shea's mother asked Christie if she would refrain from raising her voice or critiquing her daughter during play. She asked that all feedback be given during practice and in a one-on-one setting.

"My daughter isn't going to play Division I soccer, so she doesn't need that kind of intense coaching. It just makes her nervous. She's not like the other kids. She can't handle it," Shea's mother said.

When Christie asked the mother how she planned to help her daughter with her anxiety, she responded, "I don't know. I have anxiety too."

Christie explained to Shea's mother that the more obstacles she removed from Shea's path, the fewer chances Shea would have to learn. In the absence of challenge or emotional pain, Shea would never learn how to face problems or manage her anxiety.

When a parent stands between a child and constructive criticism, it interferes with a child's ability to grow. Shea's mother was inadvertently communicating that her daughter did not have the ability to problem solve. By mowing down the problems before Shea could deal with them, Shea's mother was teaching Shea to fear them. Every time a parent mows down a problem, the problem is magnified in the child's eyes—in both intensity and importance. Coaching, constructive criticism, and feedback are lifelong gifts, not reserved only for Division I college athlete hopefuls. On a team of eighteen girls, it is statistically unlikely that any of them will play at a Division I level, let alone continue playing past high school. But feedback from a coach or teacher has purpose well beyond the team or sport. Kids need to have permission to grow and improve, to not fear change but to embrace it in their pursuit of greatness—athletically, academically, socially, and personally.

Every time Shea's mother clears a struggle for her daughter, she perpetuates *both* of their anxieties. Eventually, Shea learned to panic at the mere thought of failure or struggle; she'd never dealt with it, so she had no reason to believe that she could overcome it.

We can all empathize with Shea's mother; no one wants to see their child in pain. But, again, children must endure struggle to grow healthily. A surgeon learns their craft first by reading a textbook, and then by practicing on models and simulations. You would hate for a surgeon to go directly from reading about an appendectomy to performing that surgery on you, their very first patient. Everyone learns by doing, experiencing, and feeling. Lawn mowing removes both the pain and the joy of learning.

The Tunnel-Vision Parent

We have all yelled from the sidelines at one time or another—sometimes with praise, sometimes in response to a bad call, and sometimes just to instruct our kid to move to the right. Tunnel-vision parents often coach their children from the sidelines, yell while they are playing, and sometimes fight with referees. They are overly emotional during a game and focused solely on what their child is doing. We call them tunnel-vision parents because they are completely consumed with how well their child is playing, measured by their own standards and criteria. They are solely focused on what they expect of their child, regardless of whatever plans or goals anybody else may have. They embody not seeing the forest for the trees.

Many times, tunnel-vision parents were high school or college athletes themselves. They feel that they know what is best for their child, especially a child playing the same sport as they did. They are often future focused; overly concerned with winning, scoring, and playing at the highest levels; and oblivious to the big picture or their child's emotional development through sports. They often define success through their child's individual effort and achievements, rather than how they contributed to the team.

Tunnel-vision parenting affects a child in several ways. Certainly, constant coaching during game time can be distracting, confusing, and downright irritating. When her father yelled, Grace, the professional soccer player we met earlier in this chapter, had a difficult time understanding whom she should listen to—her parent, her coach, or her own senses. She also grew to internalize her father's voice and was distracted by it even in his absence.

Tunnel-vision parents increase a player's stress, and not in a way that makes them sharper. When this happens, adrenaline, cortisol, and other stress hormones are released in the body, and the limbic system (the brain's emotional system) is activated. In this state, higher-order thinking and problem-solving skills become less efficient.

Yelling is known to be effective when your purpose is to get your target to act without thinking—to stop a child before they walk onto a busy street, for instance. In sports development, however, a coach is tasked with teaching athletes how to think and effectively problem solve. Some coaches do all their talking at practice and take game time to sit back and watch their athletes perform independently, using what they have learned in practice. Yelling negative statements only interrupts this process.

Have you ever been on the phone with a friend and been interrupted by your child? You have probably said, "Hey, I am on the phone. I can't hear over you. I can't do two things at once. I need to concentrate. Just give me a minute."

A child can experience similar parent coaching from the sideline. When you coach from the sideline, you add to an athlete's to-do list. The athlete needs to pay attention to the game, their teammates, their opponents, their coach or coaches, and the referee. Now mix in an advising parent. The parent coach on the sideline is an extra variable in the player's equation, which interferes with their ability to pay attention to the rest of the game. In addition, receiving coaching from a parent is often an emotional experience.

There is a difference between yelling and coaching. Obviously, a coach may need to raise their voice over the sounds of the game and the fans. This communication is about information the coach and players have been preparing both individually and jointly. It is heard differently by the players because the players know they are being developed and instructed. When a coach yells, it's to remind a player of the goals that have been set in advance of the play. And sometimes it is needed to instill a sense of urgency in the play.

A parent coach often directs the child differently than the team coach does. The parent coach is often disapproving, pointing out what the child is doing wrong and triggering a child's anger, rejection, and shame. When a parent yells a directive at a child, the child is taught to listen and respect the parent's wishes. Children expect consequences when they do not obey their parent's commands. Further, parents often have very little idea about the coach's method or message or the intended strategy in the moment. Also, the game looks entirely different from the sideline than from on the pitch. Meanwhile, children are also taught to respect and listen to their coaches. This can be very confusing. When both coach and parent direct the child from their divergent perspectives, the child inevitably disobeys or displeases one or both of them.

Another example of parental tunnel vision is what we call parent coaching "on the ball." The number one rule of coaching is not to coach on the ball—in other words, when the athlete is in the middle of a consequent action such as dribbling the ball, controlling the puck, swinging a bat, or taking a shot. Effective coaching occurs off the ball, when the athlete can process, hear, and implement what is being taught. For example, a batter steps out of the box to talk to a coach. It makes little sense to yell directives when they're in the midst of a swing. In other team sports like soccer or basketball, when the athlete is not directly involved in the play, a coach can shift them into another space, direct them to make a run, or give them information.

When a player is coached on the ball, they learn to second-guess their instincts and they eventually lose confidence.

If you give your child feedback during a game, try to do so when they are off the ball. Remember, the entire audience usually has tunnel vision. Everyone tends to watch the area of the game where the action is, where the ball is. That's where all the yelling occurs. Imagine that you are recording how many times your on-the-ball yelling causes your child to make a mistake. Now imagine how many times you let a play happen without saying anything and your child succeeds.

Game Time Feedback Exercise

We invite you to try this exercise. First, write down the top five things you want your child to learn from the game. During the game, try writing down everything you would like to say, rather than actually saying it. Review what you wrote twenty-four hours after the game. Does what you were going to say reflect your goals for your child? Are you aware of the coach's goals for your child? Would you share what you would have said with the coach? Also, make note of every time your child looks back at you for reassurance during a game. This behavior provides you with clues about your child's level of confidence and concentration, and possibly their need to please you.

One of Christie's daughter's coaches sent multiple emails to parents, urging them to stop coaching from the sidelines. The girls were eight years old and had yet to fully learn how to listen to their coaches during play—especially with parents yelling at the same time. Things had gotten so out of control that the girls obeyed their parents' commands while ignoring the coach's. They were too young to understand, and they were developing some pretty bad habits. You can imagine how this looked on game day, eleven players following eleven different sets of instructions!

When a parent loses control of their emotions, some children get embarrassed or worry about what their parent's behavior means to their teammates or their coaches. Such episodes confuse a child. When a parent behaves unpredictably, a child develops anxiety because they begin to doubt the stability of their perceived safety. When these parental behaviors occur solely at sporting events, the child develop fears specific to sports performance. In a futile attempt to prevent further episodes, the children come to believe that if they play well, they can control their parent's behavior.

It's critical that you honestly assess your involvement in the problem. Occasional out-of-line behavior doesn't automatically make you a bad parent or the sole cause of your child's struggles. Performance anxiety comes from a variety of sources, including genetics, disposition, social learning, and life experiences. However, if you have a role in developing an athlete, as most parents do, consider how and where you might be able to help.

As a child athlete, Grace did not develop a true sense of what success meant to her. Instead, she came to take her father's expectations as synonymous with her own. She learned to blame him for her mistakes and to fear making them. As Grace progressed, she charted her mistakes; in doing so, she realized that she had not made nearly as many mistakes as the inner voice in her head had claimed. She also journaled her own set of wants and goals while on the field. Grace eventually came to trust herself and to develop healthy boundaries with her father, coaches, and teammates. Wouldn't it be great to mindfully and purposefully teach your child healthy boundaries early on?

Coping Skills to Reduce Performance Anxiety

A few of the possible anxiety-provoking situations in sports are an own goal for a defender, an interception, getting beat in a one v. one, a yellow card, striking out, a handball, falling off the beam, dropping a teammate, getting pinned, shanking a ball, missing a breakaway, fouling an opponent who ends up scoring, or giving the ball away to an opposing player. Sports offer abundant opportunities for kids to learn how to deal with life's challenges. But we as parents must let them. Rather than try to avoid obstacles or downplay their importance, the best thing we can do for our kids is show them how to overcome an obstacle and learn from the experience.

First, we must understand the source of the fears that contribute to performance anxiety. Many of these fears transcend sports but manifest only, to our eyes as parents, on the field. There is the ironic but pervasive fear of success, of standing out. Children may fear social disapproval or criticism by peers. They may be afraid they are not wearing the right attire. They might be on a team with kids from school that they'd otherwise prefer to avoid or ignore. The opposite can also be true: the team is full of unfamiliar kids, which heightens the child's insecurity. They may be asking themselves, *Will I fit in? Will they be better than I am? Do I know anybody on the team? Will there be big kids there? Are there social penalties for winning?*

Many people ask Christie how she remained so composed during the World Cup and the Olympic finals. She reveals the secret to her calmness: preparedness.

I was relaxed because we made it there. I felt completely prepared. I had been in a lot of finals, and I came to learn that you can't prepare for these experiences right before the game. Preparation is cumulative; it comes from all the practice, training, and routines. They call the matches leading up to a World

Cup or an Olympics "friendlies" because they mentally and physically pre-pare you for the games that carry so much meaning.

The first time I ever doubted my playing ability was when I got to the national team. It took getting to the highest level for my nerves to take hold because I had grown accustomed to being one of the best players on any team I'd played on. The national team taught me, and fast, that I had a lot of work to do. It was a process, and I allowed myself to learn from my failures. I gained the most confidence when I grew fitter and stronger, understood my position better, and felt comfortable with the other players.

I worked off the field on my strength and conditioning and also on the mental side of the game with a sports psychologist. I learned that you don't just show up and play. I prepared every facet of myself as an athlete: from my individual skills, my fitness, and my partnerships on the field to under-standing the mind-set of my coach and the players. All that work made me feel more relaxed at game time.

Every little piece mattered before a game: hydrating, eating right, taking care of my body and my sleep, my relationships with teammates and staff, familiarizing myself with the opposing team and also particular offensive players, preparing mentally, preparation, and reviewing video. Eventually, I didn't need the video because I could visualize it right before the game started, even with a huge crowd in front of me. I was so prepared I could visualize myself heading the ball, winning fifty-fifty battles, making rou-tine passes, running down players, engaging in good one v. one battles, and shutting down certain players. I developed such a solid routine that when I touched the ball for the first time, I was already in the zone. I never fully relied on superstitions because my routine kept me prepared and relaxed.

Following is a list of routine things you can do to counteract per-formance anxiety. If anxiety continues, we recommend following up with a sports or pediatric psychologist to assist in objectively assess-ing the problem and making additional treatment recommendations.

Diaphragmatic Breathing

Diaphragmatic breathing is another way to describe deep breathing or belly breathing. The purpose of this breathing is to slow your heart rate, thus reducing anxiety and nervousness. Four-seven-eight breathing is a simple technique you can teach your child; it involves breathing in for four seconds, holding the breath for seven seconds, and then exhaling for eight seconds. When employed at least twice a day, four-seven-eight breathing can help prepare kids for an on-the-field anxiety response.[2] The amount of time spent practicing breathing does not matter. What matters is the four-seven-eight ratio, and that they take at least four breaths each time they practice. Make sure that their exhalation is twice as long as their inhalation. Slow and steady.

To teach diaphragmatic breathing, have your child get comfortable and sit or lie down with their back straight. Have them place the tip of their tongue against the ridge of their palate behind the upper front teeth. Instruct your child to exhale through their mouth, then close their mouth lightly and inhale through their nose to a count of four. Then have your child hold their breath for a count of seven, and exhale for a count of eight. They should be able to hear their exhalation. Have your child repeat four full breath cycles and then return to normal breathing. Talk to your child about how their body feels after the exercise. It is normal for a child to feel light-headed when beginning to learn diaphragmatic breathing. This will pass with practice.

Over time, regular practice of diaphragmatic breathing helps people to be centered, mindful, and present. It is a natural anxiety reliever, or anxiolytic. Try this for at least one month, gradually increasing breath cycles to eight. There is no limit to how often children can engage in diaphragmatic breathing if they find it relaxing. There are no side effects, only benefits.

Controlling your breathing works wonders. Once diaphragmatic breathing is mastered, an athlete can use it on command to engage the parasympathetic nervous system and calm down. Deep breathing oxygenates muscles so your child can build strength and move faster. You can also seek out sports-specific breathing exercises—such as a three-to-two ratio for runners—that enable athletes to breathe rhythmically, in coordination with sports-specific movements. Regardless of the sport, once deep breathing is mastered, an athlete can decide which breathing rhythm best suits them on the field, on the court, in the water, or on the trail.[3]

Christie knows well the significance of understanding and listening to her breathing on and off the field.

Early on when I was working out, I deliberately trained without music so I could listen to my heavy breathing and my heart rate. It was the best way to get my anxiety under control. To this day, I don't work out to music because I always want to understand myself and listen to my body. I want to notice things that happen to me during the game, like when my legs get heavy. I want to feel that every time. I purposely listen to my heavy breathing during practice because it reminds me to expect it during the game, and that it's okay and I'll get through it. You want to have the same breathing, bodily experiences, and self-talk in practice that you will have in the game.

Mindfulness and Learning to Be Present

Help your child put into words the sensation of performance anxiety. Is their heart beating faster? Are they sweating? Do they have butterflies in their stomach? Is their stomach upset? When children are encouraged to become aware of what's happening to them physiologically, they can begin to break the cycle and become more attuned to their feelings, especially when they escalate.

First, assist your child in understanding what it means to be mindful. Mindfulness is a term that describes nonjudgmental present-moment awareness. The term itself is often used synonymously with relaxation, yoga, and meditation. While these exercises assist in the overall practice of mindfulness, the term itself refers to a set of cognitive strategies aimed at becoming present, rather than allowing your mind to wander off to the past or to the future. Many athletes dwell on past mistakes or losses or worry about future outcomes such as beating their competition. When a child practices mindfulness, they focus on the present, without judging situations as good or bad. This allows them to focus on internal goals or strategies.

Teach your child to recognize their inner voice or internal dialogue by first helping them become aware of it and then listen for it. Whenever they come to you with a decision or problem, don't impose your own rules and decision-making process; instead, ask them questions that encourage their own analysis. Your questions can guide them to their own solutions. Providing them with the answers, by contrast, merely tamps down their ability to hear their inner voice.

Once aware of their inner dialogue, children must next realize what it sounds like in the heat of the moment. Bear in mind, you cannot do this *while* they are playing; you must create a teachable moment, a facsimile of a heightened experience. Remember, your child cannot functionally distinguish between excited and anxious. They don't know the difference. But as we mentioned previously, research indicates that your brain responds to the term "excitement" with less of a stress response than it does to the term "anxiety." So reframe inner dialogue that fuels anxiety by using the term "excitement" instead. When you replace "anxiety" with "excitement," you perform better, no matter the sport or activity, including examinations and presentations.[4] It is great to be excited!

Here are some examples of this methodology at work.

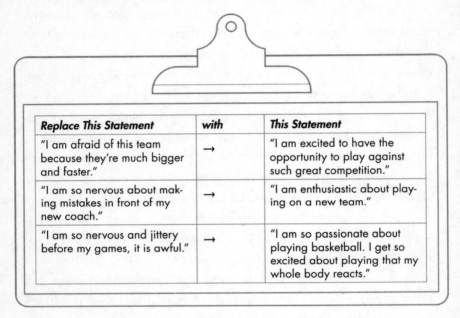

Replace This Statement	with	This Statement
"I am afraid of this team because they're much bigger and faster."	→	"I am excited to have the opportunity to play against such great competition."
"I am so nervous about making mistakes in front of my new coach."	→	"I am enthusiastic about playing on a new team."
"I am so nervous and jittery before my games, it is awful."	→	"I am so passionate about playing basketball. I get so excited about playing that my whole body reacts."

Teach your child that negative self-talk is a habit like any other: the more often you practice it, the more likely it is to recur. Indeed, unless you make an effort to reframe habitual, negative thoughts, the neuronal pathways to negative thought patterns in your brain will become stronger and stronger. You can be a great worrier with practice. You just don't want to be!

Override these pathways by actively creating healthy ones. Teach your child to recognize that thoughts are not things, and they can be replaced with reality-based messages such as the following:

- I got this.
- I have done this before so I can do it again.

- I am good at what I do.
- I have had multiple successes on this field.

Oftentimes, when we practice hearing our child's inner voice, we inadvertently get in touch with our own. You can also participate in meditation, yoga, and breathing alongside your child to cultivate your connectedness to your own voice. Journaling is another outlet. Much of what we say and how we behave toward others is actually a reflection of how we feel and think about ourselves. Listen to the things you say to your children privately, publicly, and in texts. You may notice themes or patterns in your own thinking that could benefit from positive changes.

Be Consistent and Prepared

Most kids respond well to structure, especially in situations where extra pressure is likely. When you drop your child off at a practice or game, have they taken the time to prepare their things? Do they have a game-day routine? To beat performance anxiety, help your child create a list of things they are afraid might happen as well as possible solutions to their worries. Take the time to help your child prepare before each game or practice in a way that addresses many of their worries or fears. This preparation may be physical and may include stretching, daily runs, or skills training during the week. Taking the time to practice could make the difference on game day. The preparation may also be mental and include affirmations, deep breathing, or listening to calming sounds or music prior to leaving the house.

Practice with Pressure

Getting comfortable with the uncomfortable is a critical tool for alleviating performance anxiety. This one is especially difficult for lawn-mower and helicopter parents, because it means being okay with exposing your child to discomfort—and not just any discomfort, but the kind that impacts game-day performance. To reduce anxiety, as Christie says, you need to practice at game speed.

Practice Like It's the Championship!

The penalty kick is one of the most pressure-laden tasks facing a soccer player. The penalty kick is taken by an individual player in front of both teams and coaches, with no assistance from any other players. It's just the kicker and the goalkeeper. Everybody's watching! It is high pressure for both stakeholders. And the outcome of the kick often impacts the outcome of the game. Sometimes penalty kicks happen in overtime, when every goal directly influences wins and losses.

The US Women's National Soccer Team practices penalty kicks before World Cup games in real time. Each player practices taking penalty kicks in an environment that simulates the enormous pressure of performing before the world's watchful eye. To simulate a game, coaches blast loud stadium sounds. Coaches also yell at the players over the music and distracting noise. This method has paid off. When Megan Rapinoe scored via penalty kick in the 2019 World Cup, she looked relaxed and the goal looked effortless.

The more experience you have in pressure situations, the better you can handle your emotions when called on to perform. This is why some professional athletes are deemed "practice players": they play very differently during practice versus during a game. Under the bright lights, practice players react poorly to the pressures of competition and perform below expectation, even poorly. Practicing foul shots and free throws in the safety of your backyard is great for mechanics, but it doesn't prepare your child for the real thing. Encourage your child to practice like they play—like it's game speed, like it's the state final.

Unbending Purpose

Teach your child that as an athlete—be it on a team sport or individual pursuit—they are part of something bigger. They are part of a community of coaches, trainers, parents, teammates, and other supporters. When you teach kids how to look outside themselves and how to connect with teammates or serve their coaches, they develop a sense of purpose. They become less focused on their individual performance or concerns.

Christie teaches her youth athletes to view obstacles as opportunities to cultivate their personal athletic superpowers. She encourages them to be unbending when it comes to their drive, attitude, and motivation. An unbending will to win, meanwhile, is a tired cliché—unrealistic and out of your control.

There is power in having unbending purpose, and it comes from training hard, working hard, working smart, working together, and being committed to the team. These things make you the best player you can be.

Teach your child to have an unbending sense of purpose to foster their gumption, drive, and intentions. Avoid preaching an unbending focus on winning. Teach them to home in on what drives them to play their sport. Ask them why they choose to play a given sport. What do they enjoy about it? If you play sports long enough, you will inevitably experience loss or failure. Instead, have them discuss their position on the field and the responsibilities that come with it. By focusing on purpose, you spend less time in your own head, and this calms the inner dialogue.

No one enjoys making mistakes, failing to meet goals, or feeling like they let other people down. But it's possible to learn new habits, create new routines, and retrain even the most ingrained performance anxiety to become a tool for preparedness. Grace learned to forgive her father and change her inner dialogue. She learned to create personal goals and gave herself permission to make mistakes and to define them. Shea developed the ability to take feedback from her coaches by experiencing it. Her mother learned how to face her own fear about seeing her daughter in pain.

These athletes needed to reconnect with their feelings and learn cognitive and behavioral strategies to manage and resolve their performance anxiety. Ultimately, the most integral component in resolving performance anxiety is self-compassion. These athletes learned to be more tolerant of themselves and others. They learned to focus on the amazing journey that is sports instead of on ephemeral and ultimately empty pursuits like personal achievement, glory, and wins.

CHAPTER 10

Concussion and Sports Injury

Christie's first concussion occurred during the 2007 World Cup in Shanghai, China.

We were playing Norway. It happened during the last ten minutes of the first half. I was playing on the eighteen-yard line in the center of the field. The ball came in from the left side while I was marking a player, and I jumped up to flick the ball out to my right, where there were no runners. As I jumped, our goalkeeper came out to clear the ball by punching it. So I got punched in the head.

I immediately fell to the ground. I slowly pulled myself to my feet, but I was dizzy and disoriented. I didn't have a good awareness of where I was. I rubbed my eyes to clear my vision as the game ensued. Instead of being smart and taking a knee, I continued to play with my vision blurred and with white spots floating in front of me. I couldn't make out faces, and I could only tell my teammates by their uniform colors.

Back in 2007, concussions weren't as huge a topic they are today, so I didn't realize what going on. Still, I managed to stay positive: I figured my vision would return if I just played on. But it didn't. When the whistle blew at halftime, I went into the locker room and told the trainer I had blurry vision and that I didn't feel good. The doctor gave me a concussion test, which I passed with flying colors. He gave me the "all good," and I returned for the second half. My vision was still blurry and my nausea remained, but since the doc had cleared me, I thought it was all in my head. I just couldn't figure out why I wasn't feeling any better, even after the halftime rest.

When I went back on the field, my confidence in my vision waned. It didn't seem to be returning. I felt nauseated because everything around me seemed to be moving. I turned to one of my teammates and asked her where the ball was.

"Christie, the half hasn't started yet."

I went down on a knee and pulled myself out of the game for good. Cleared or not, I had no idea what was going on. I had no business being out there. I couldn't even make out the field!

Sitting on the bench, my vision and nausea got worse. I felt overwhelmed and hypersensitive. The doc had told me I was okay. Why wasn't I? I became increasingly worried and emotional. In minutes, I left the sideline for the locker room because I couldn't take the noise and I still could not see the game.

This time I told the trainer that I was a mess. I felt like I was going to get sick. Worse yet, I felt terrible that I couldn't cheer my teammates on. I was overwrought at not being on the field with them. It was the semifinals of the World Cup, and I was stuck in a locker room!

I don't remember how I got to the hospital that day, but I remember closing my eyes the whole time I was there so I didn't get sick. Though the visit was quick, I felt claustrophobic and my head was spinning. I was given a CT scan and then released within hours with a diagnosis of concussion. They told me to rest.

The cab couldn't drive us all the way to the hotel because the traffic was so bad. Instead, I had to walk half a mile to get to my room. I felt like I was living in a dream. One minute, I'm playing in the World Cup; the next thing I know, I am in a Chinese hospital and then walking alongside an unfamiliar road, sick as a dog. Everything was a complete blur. No one was speaking English. I was scared because I had never been hospitalized outside of the United States before. At that moment, I felt so far from home.

When I finally got back to the hotel, I just chilled out. I wasn't able to watch TV because I couldn't focus on it. My nausea went away when I didn't concentrate on anything. My teammates checked on me as soon as they returned from the game. They had gotten third place in the World Cup. They took photos and celebrated on the field while I was in the hospital. At the hotel, however, the mood was subdued. Third place hadn't been our expectation.

Two days later, I flew home. I was out of it for two weeks. I could function, take care of myself and my family, but I was just not myself. I was able to do everything I needed to do, but really, really slowly. I never went back to the doctor and had no further treatment. I just rested for two weeks. I was scheduled for three victory-tour games several weeks later, but I didn't play in them.

Three months later I started working out again. I slowly got back into form to get ready for the US Women's National Team camp in December 2008.

To this day, I have no memory of the details from the 2007 World Cup. But I will always remember how ill that concussion made me feel.

From the NFL scandal and the CTE deaths to the famous athletes who claim they would never have played if they'd known then what they know now, concussion news has set the sporting world on fire. It is the most talked-about and media-driven sports story. Just over a decade removed from the 2007 World Cup, concussion research has exploded. Yet despite all the information we now have on concussions, the internet remains something of a Wild West when it comes to accurate and consistent data.

We dedicated a chapter of this book to concussions because they are both incredibly feared and incredibly misunderstood. Many parents and athletes will face a diagnosis of concussion at least once during a long sports career. Many parents remain confused about the injury itself, how to recover from it, and what, if any, lasting effects it can impart. Concussion is an injury like no other, because you can't see it. It's sneaky that way. When you break a body part, it's immobile. You limp. You need a cast or a brace. But if you sustain a concussion, you have nothing to show for it, not even a Band-Aid. You look...normal.

A concussion is defined as a mild traumatic brain injury caused by a direct or indirect blow to your head or body. It is characterized by immediate and transient changes in brain function, including an alteration of mental status and level of consciousness. In many cases, a person who sustained a concussion never loses consciousness, and there are rarely external signs of head trauma. Sometimes, people cannot remember what happened immediately before or after a concussion, and they may act or appear confused after impact.

It was thought that a concussion occurs only as a result of a blow to the face or the head. But a concussion can result from a blow anywhere on the body if said blow carries enough force to move the brain inside the skull. Our brains float around in cerebrospinal fluid, which protects us from everyday minor jolts and movements. In the case of concussion, the body is subjected to an excessive amount of force to the point that the brain moves inside the skull and neurometabolic changes occur inside the brain.[1] Picture the impact of a motor vehicle accident. When a car is hit from behind, the passengers jerk forward and backward with so much force that a concussion can occur even if they haven't hit their head on anything inside the car. If the brain moves in the opposite direction of the body with sufficient force, concussion can result.

A concussion restricts the flow of blood to the brain. When there is less blood flow to the brain, there is also a shortage of available glucose, or energy. The brain uses glucose to tackle everyday tasks like movement, exercise, reading, and processing noises. A person who has sustained a concussion has less glucose to spare. That is why immediate rest in the wake of concussion is so vital. If a person continues about their daily activities and using already depleted glucose, the more symptomatic that person who has sustained a concussion becomes. Headaches are the most commonly reported symptom of concussion, followed by dizziness, difficulty concentrating, confusion, light sensitivity, and nausea.

So, to repeat: if your child sustains a concussion, have them rest in response to this energy crisis.

Symptoms of Concussion[2]

- Physical: Headache, dizziness, nausea, fatigue, balance problems, problems falling asleep, sleeping less or more than usual, sensitivity to light, sensitivity to noise
- Cognitive: Short-term memory loss, reduced attention and concentration, mental fogginess, slowed processing speed
- Emotional: Sadness, nervousness, emotional lability, irritability

---

How a Concussion Is Diagnosed

Concussion is considered a medical diagnosis and should not be diagnosed by coaches or trainers unless they are medically trained. If a concussion is suspected during a game or practice, athletic trainers often perform sideline evaluations to record the player's symptoms and to assess the need for emergency care. Athletes are then referred to their pediatrician, primary care physician, or to a concussion specialist for diagnosis and concussion monitoring. However, athletic trainers and physicians are rarely available at youth, recreational, middle school, or travel games for sideline evaluation. Therefore, it is vital that parents and coaches understand the signs of concussion as well as how and when to intervene safely.

In young children, concussion diagnosis can be even more elusive because young children often lack the vocabulary to articulate symptoms or sensations. The American Academy of Pediatrics recommends that parents call their child's pediatrician for anything past a light bump on the head.

Signs that a Young Child May Have Sustained a Concussion

- Dazedness
- Listlessness or premature fatigue
- Irritability or crankiness
- Loss of balance
- Difficulty walking normally
- Excessive crying
- Change in sleep patterns
- Lack of interest in previously enjoyed activities

Sometimes an athlete seems fine, or denies having symptoms, or protests being examined even in the wake of intense impact. Sometimes no one even saw the hit. The golden rule here is, "When in doubt, sit them out." It can take up to twenty-four hours for symptoms to appear, so it is crucial that a kid sit out the remainder of the game if concussion is suspected. There is no game or second half worth an injury.

Danny had been playing football since he was eight years old. He loved the game. He came from a football family: his grandfather and father both played in the NFL, and two uncles played Division I ball. Football was in Danny's blood, and he had inherited the family gift. His family boasted that he might become the best of the whole bunch.

Danny sustained his first concussion in high school, during pre-season of his senior year. His parents knew of the concussion protocol, but the ER doctor had diagnosed Danny with a mild concussion. His parents expected Danny to be back in action within a couple of days. Meanwhile, Danny's high school athletic trainer referred his parents to Dr. Keane for concussion management.

I will never forget the daggers in Danny's mother's eyes when I told her that Danny was not cleared to play after his first visit to me. I explained that there is no such thing as a mild concussion. We don't loosely categorize concussions like that anymore. The previous concussion rating scales were devoid of science. Concussion recovery must play out for each athlete until they are fully recovered, and every concussion is unique. I have seen patients with severe initial concussion symptoms recover within weeks, and I have seen concussions that initially appear mild demand months of recovery. Plus, a concussion seems mild only if it didn't happen to you. It's a real head injury, and it's a serious one.

I explained the injury to Danny's mother as well as his symptoms: her son was having difficulty with his balance and cognitive functions, such as memory and processing speed. But Danny's mother wasn't having any of it.

"Do you realize that this is Danny's senior year?" she thundered. "He is getting looks from all the Big Ten schools. He is going to play DI, for God's sake! You can't keep him on the sideline for the beginning of the most important season of his life."

I told Danny's mother that if he was indeed Division I material, one concussion would not derail those plans. In fact, as a serious athlete, Danny knew better than most the importance of full and proper recovery. If he was to have a long career ahead of him, returning to the game with a concussion could only hinder his future, not help it.

So Danny missed the first three weeks of his season. He was asymptomatic during the second week and began a five-day return-to-play protocol

with his high school athletic trainer. He took off one game to increase his
fitness level prior to returning to a full-contact setting.

I ran into Danny's mother one year later. She told me that Danny had
received a full scholarship to play at a Division I university and was already
making connections with the NFL. She told me how grateful she was that
I insisted on keeping him off the field until he was ready. She said to me, "I
will never forget that day in your office. I didn't think concussion was that
big of a deal. I admit, I also thought at the time, 'How could this lady know
anything about football, let alone DI schools! She is going to destroy my
son's career!' But in the end, we realized it was the right thing for Danny.
And we are relieved now that we held him out and he got to recover the
right way."

You don't need to lose consciousness to be diagnosed with a concussion. You need only have some kind of alteration in consciousness
or symptoms such as blurred vision or balance problems after the
head impact. Medical professionals evaluate a concussion by assess-
ing the mechanism of injury and evaluating physical symptoms such
as balance and vision as well as cognitive functions. During an initial evaluation after a concussion, multiple objective tests specific to
concussion are vital to determine the presence or absence of concussion and related symptoms, especially when athletes deny they are
having symptoms.[3]

Gary, a sophomore at a local high school, came to the concussion
clinic referred by his athletic trainer. During football preseason training, he endured a head-to-head collision with an opponent, fell to the
ground, and then hit his head again. He said he had no symptoms
after the impact, not even a headache. But his athletic trainer thought
it was such a "bad hit" that Gary should be evaluated.

One week later, Gary adamantly denied having any symptoms
and was frustrated at being forced to undergo evaluation at a concussion clinic. His balance and vision tests were normal. However,

measures of processing speed and reaction time on cognitive tests were severely impaired. His father indicated that his son would never pass those tests—not due to any concussion but because Gary had an undiagnosed learning disability. Gary was new to the school and new to the football team, so his academic history and previous baseline testing were unavailable during his first visit.

Gary and his father were incensed that he was missing preseason scrimmages and games. They worried for his starting position on varsity. They were unwavering: Gary did not have a concussion. Gary was permitted to exercise and train with his team, but only in drills—no contact or scrimmaging allowed. He went on vacation with his family one week before the start of the season. He returned on week three of the protocol and was reevaluated.

On Gary's second round of postinjury tests, all his cognitive scores fell within the normal range. In fact, all his scores registered above average when compared to those of his same-aged peers. His balance, despite having appeared normal during his first evaluation, improved. All systems go. Here's the kicker: only after Gary had been cleared to play did he admit to having symptoms along the way. He just didn't think they were "that bad." Ultimately, Gary and his father were relieved that he'd sat out the preseason.

Athletes often deny being symptomatic or claim prematurely that they've recovered from a concussion. That's why athletes should be objectively tested after concussion. We cannot rely solely on their self-reporting. The neuropsychologist Michael McCrea investigated the frequency of unreported sports concussions and found that among 1,532 varsity football players, 66 percent did not report symptoms because they did not believe their injury was serious enough, 41 percent did not want to leave the game, 36 percent did not know they had a concussion, and 22 percent did not want to let their teammates down.[4]

Safe Kids Worldwide, a global research group, determined that a child is taken to the emergency room for a sports injury every twenty-five minutes. Their study, which surveyed three thousand athletes, coaches, and parents, further revealed that children tend to ignore sports injuries and feel pressure to play, even when they know they are hurt. Forty-two percent of athletes indicated that they play even when hurt. When kids continue to play with sports injuries, they needlessly put themselves at risk for more serious injuries. This deception goes up the ladder as well: 53 percent of the coaches indicated that they feel pressure to play athletes they know have been injured. Meanwhile, approximately one-third of the surveyed athletes stated that it is normal to play "rough" in a game in order to "send a message" to the other team. Safe Kids Worldwide researchers believe these numbers indicate the rise of a dangerous youth sports culture.

In Dr. Keane's practice, many athletes express regret at playing injured and not considering the consequences.

Many athletes tell me that their coaches and parents tell them to play through pain. And many of them express that they don't know when to stop or what the difference is between a game-stopping injury and something they should just play through. In terms of concussion, I instruct athletes to immediately take a knee if they've hit or jolted their head. Further, they must take time on the sideline to see if symptoms develop, as concussion symptoms sometimes develop over hours after the injury.

Typical concussion recovery times for young athletes range anywhere from two to six weeks. I often talk with athletes about the dangers of a second concussive blow—more serious injury and prolonged recovery time, sometimes resulting in the loss of an entire season. This goes for all sports injuries. Kids must be told that sports injuries are common and expected. They must also understand the consequences of playing injured and that they nor the team can afford to ignore or belittle an injury. Commonplace doesn't mean unimportant.

Young athletes need to understand that missing a game, a month, or a season does not necessarily make or break an entire athletic career. Many athletes reveal their fear of missing a specific game or tournament, with very little concern about possible reinjury. I find that young athletes benefit from shifting their oftentimes harried focus away from a return to play and toward the rest, recovery, and rehabilitation they need to get back on the field. If they don't, many young athletes may incur sports injuries that last well beyond a season.

Parents and coaches should talk to their kids about being honest and opening up about how they are feeling. Many sports injuries are the result of overexertion, and many of these injuries begin with minor pain that kids keep to themselves for fear of losing playing time. As they push through, athletes risk injuries that are otherwise avoidable with just a day or two of rest. Meanwhile, the injury might cause them to favor another muscle group, thus predisposing them to a different injury altogether.

The more coaches and parents talk about statistics, scores, and winning, the more youth athletes feel pressure to perform. Kids are more open to talking to parents and coaches whom they perceive as open to listening. They need to trust that you will listen, believe what they are telling you, and not think negatively of them because of an injury. The earlier our kids communicate injuries to us, the sooner they can be addressed, and the healthier they can be. Remember, when in doubt, sit them out!

As parents and coaches, it is our primary duty to protect our children, sometimes from themselves. Many kids do not realize the potential danger associated with head injury. Depending on their age, maturity, and level of development, they might not grasp the injury or even how to report the symptoms. Seek out specialists. Their ability to objectively assess injury is so vital for accurate diagnoses and for knowing when it is safe to return to playing.

Many schools and facilities offer baseline testing to athletes. Baseline testing usually comprises computerized cognitive tests that measure memory, processing and reaction time. Ideally, baseline testing also includes visual and balance tests. Baseline testing is given to athletes prior to beginning the sports season. After an injury occurs, the baseline tests are compared to the postinjury tests. Return-to-play decisions are never made solely from one test or measurement; however, when the results of postinjury tests are similar to those of baseline tests, the specialist has clear and objective data regarding the healing process. Returning to the discussion of concussion, there exists no one test that diagnoses concussions nor one that alerts us that an athlete has fully recovered. In fact, tests can only go so far. Ongoing research indicates that even after an athlete passes all objective clinical tests, their brain may still be recovering. Please, please be safe, and err on the side of caution when allowing an athlete to return to play.

Parents can talk to athletic directors, athletic trainers, school nurses, or school administrators to find out if their school offers baseline testing. Some schools restrict baseline testing and offer it only to athletes of contact sports such as football, hockey, soccer, and lacrosse. Parents can also contact local hospital systems or concussion clinics, as many provide baseline tests for a nominal fee. If your child plays on teams outside of school, contact league administration to find out if baseline testing is available.

After an athlete is diagnosed with a concussion, they are continually monitored for progress and recovery. The first thing an athlete should do after a concussion is rest.[5] The amount of rest, the type of rest, and the quality of rest remain debatable, but there is little debate that the first and best step in the wake of concussion is full cognitive and physical rest. That is, reduce all stimulation as much as possible for the first few days. This generally includes abstaining from video games, strenuous physical exercise, reading, using the computer, and using a cell phone.

That is not to suggest you lock your kid in a closet after a concussion. No science exists to support forcing a child to lie motionless all day with the shades drawn. Can you imagine locking yourself in your bedroom with no phone, no television, and no one to talk with? How long could you stay like that before you lost your mind? We think we could last about an hour.

The rule of thumb concerning rest after concussion is to minimize stimulation, not eliminate it. Most kids can tolerate watching television or at least listening to it after a concussion. If they want to, they should. After a concussion, the rest environment should mimic a "spa-like atmosphere," where the concussed athlete is calm and comfortable. Most kids get pretty anxious when alone for hours with the shades drawn and with nothing to do—especially if you take away their phone!

After a day or two of rest, parents can introduce activities like reading, walking, and even moderate phone use. If the athlete is able to partake with no increase in symptoms, then it's safe to proceed. Have them try reading for five minutes, then ten, then a half hour. Taper these activities by introducing regular breaks. Some parents are afraid that reintroducing cognitive activities will make things worse. If you read for an hour without a break, you will probably have a headache. But you will not have brain damage. There is no known research indicating that reading a book causes brain damage. Not even this book!

Years ago, athletes were told to rest for long periods of time after a concussion. If and when they returned with symptoms, they were told to rest for even longer. Eventually, science caught up: physicians realized that long periods of rest were causing athletes to become deconditioned from lack of physical activity. Ironically, the symptoms that appeared to be concussion-related were actually caused by too much rest! Light physical exercise as soon as it is tolerable is also recommended, especially for athletes used to working out regularly.[6] Of course, there is a fine line, and every athlete and concussion must be monitored and treated uniquely.

Christie's Second Concussion

My second concussion occurred on July 20, 2014. I was playing for Sky Blue FC in a game against Washington Spirit. I was in the middle of the field, inside the eighteen-yard line. The Spirit's Crystal Dunn took a shot on goal, and I cleared it with my head. I headed the ball using the same area affected by my 2007 concussion. I immediately saw white floaters but had no other symptoms. I finished the game and felt fine other than continued floaters in my right eye. My left eye was as clear as day—no blurriness.

After the game I thought I possibly had a concussion. I took photos with friends after the game. Then, without realizing it, I left my soccer bag in the parking lot and drove off—certainly unlike me. When I got home that night, my friends sent me the photos we'd taken hours prior. I had no recollection that we had taken the photos or even that the friends had attended the game. That's when I realized I had a concussion. I started to feel foggy again. I texted my trainer to let her know that I wasn't feeling great and that I had a concussion.

I was evaluated under our concussion program and I underwent cognitive testing, balance, and vision evaluations. Things had changed a lot since I'd been concussed in China seven years earlier. This time I had to take eye tests, balance tests, and cognitive tests. I had to be symptom-free and pass all the tests. It took me more than a week to recover. Once I passed all the tests, I began the concussion protocol with the athletic trainer, called the return-to-play protocol. It involved one week of gradually tapering back into physical activities under the supervisor of my athletic trainer. I was later cleared by our team physician. To this day, though, I still have issues with my eyes. If I am dehydrated or I bump my head, I get lingering floaters.

With both concussions I never got a headache. Both concussions were totally different. One hit I didn't see coming, and the other I did. When I got my second concussion, I felt strong, my neck was ready, and I was prepared to head the ball. I did everything right; I was set for it. And the ball just seemed to graze my head. But still, I sustained a concussion. I was told that one concussion makes you more prone to a second, even with much less of an impact.

You have to take concussions seriously and go through the right protocol. It's easy for an injured athlete to say, "I feel fine. I can play." But there is no getting around the testing; the facts are the facts. That is why I trust the test. It is an accurate reading. It helps us from returning to play too fast. It's like slowing down to speed up. Taking a week off helps you to play the rest of the season instead of coming back too early and getting injured again or playing poorly.

Physical therapists who specialize in concussion rehabilitation offer treatments specific to concussion such as balance therapy and vision therapy. They also treat neck pain and other physical injuries common after a blow to the head. Research shows that athletes who exercise soon after a concussion enjoy expedited recovery time.[7] In physical therapy, athletes can safely begin light physical activity as early as a few days after the concussion and can begin tapering back into their cardiovascular routine. As mentioned earlier, lying around after a concussion can cause athletes to not only decondition but also to become anxious or depressed. Exercise is well known to be emotionally enhancing, and its absence can trigger mood changes for athletes. In addition to worrying about returning to the game, athletes also report feeling nervous about regaining their previous position, playing as well as they were prior to the injury, or getting hurt again.

It is not recommended to keep athletes out of school for long durations or to wait until they're asymptomatic. On the contrary, concussion specialists return athletes to school as soon as it is tolerated, usually within a few days after the injury, if not the following day. Student athletes should be provided with academic accommodations upon their return to school to assist them in managing their symptoms.[8] Parents should work with their health-care providers to determine which academic accommodations are appropriate.

Classroom accommodations include test-taking assistance measures such as providing extra time, taking tests in a quiet place, or taking only one test or quiz per day. Homework and classwork may be completed as tolerated, and students may require additional time to make up work. If the student is having visual problems, lecture notes or presentations may be provided to them ahead of time. If they are sensitive to light, they may be able to wear sunglasses or a hat and to reduce the number of hours spent on the computer. If students show noise sensitivity, students may be permitted to leave classes five minutes early to avoid crowded hallways or eat lunch in a quiet place outside the cafeteria. For a full list of possible academic accommodations, please refer to the appendix.

While some athletes initially return for half days and taper to full, all student athletes should return with a set of accommodations specific to their symptoms.

If an athlete can sit home all day watching television or playing on their phone without symptoms, they can certainly attempt to sit in classes and observe their teachers. You want the athlete to get back into their regular routine as soon as possible. Lying around all day can interfere with a regular sleep cycle. Kids who stay home for long periods often sleep in, nap during the day, and later have trouble sleeping at night. Without proper sleep or a decent level of activity, athletes can develop symptoms related to sleep and exercise deprivation; though they might appear concussion related, these symptoms are separate.

Jenna, a high school sophomore soccer player, sustained a concussion when she collided heads with an opponent while attempting to head the ball. She fell to the ground but did not lose consciousness. She noticed immediately that her head hurt, and she was dizzy when she got to her feet. She was unable to identify the other team to her coach, and her teammates said she appeared confused when she made it to the sideline. Jenna left the game, and her mother brought her to the nearest emergency room for evaluation. A CT head scan was normal, so she was cleared of any threat of skull fracture or brain bleed. She was diagnosed with concussion and discharged the same day with orders to rest and stay out of school for two days.

Jenna's mother made an appointment to see her pediatrician, and Jenna returned to school two days later, as recommended. At school, her headaches worsened, and she couldn't concentrate on any classwork. With each visit to the nurse, her mother was called and Jenna left school early. After two days of leaving early, Jenna stayed home for fear of repeating the same routine. When it came time to see her pediatrician, she had already missed a week and a half of school and felt worse than she did in the immediate wake of the concussion.

Jenna was sent to a concussion specialist, who immediately instituted academic accommodations specific to her injury. She returned to school for half days and later for full days, with the recommendation that she take frequent breaks throughout the day as needed. She was also provided with class notes ahead of time to reduce her visual load, which proved to be the primary cause of her headaches. She was able to follow along and listen to the lectures in her classes without increased symptoms. The breaks during the day reduced the intensity of her headaches and helped Jenna feel less overwhelmed by the school day as she tapered back in. The concussion specialist asked that her teachers reduce her homework and makeup work by 50 to 75 percent.

Students who miss classes and academic work can have emotional difficulty upon returning to school. It can be very stressful to try to keep up with their current workload while making up missed work at home. This is especially true for cumulative subjects like mathematics and physics. Academic accommodations must be specific to the student's injury as well as considerate of the student's particular workload, academic style, and overall schedule. Accommodations must also consider the school's resources and level of understanding about concussion. While some schools offer designated personnel to assist students in the post-concussion return-to-learn protocol, many don't. In every case, the return-to-learn plan should include all stakeholders for the student, including parents, coaches, trainers, guidance counselors, the school nurse, and teachers.

Jenna fully returned to play after four weeks, which is common among younger students. While many internet sources cite a seven- to ten-day recovery from concussion, those numbers are typically gleaned from research conducted on college and professional athletes. Younger children can take longer to recover from concussion; given their vulnerability to the injury, we always treat them conservatively.

Why Are We So Worried About Returning a Child to Play Too Early?

Most parents don't debate the length of recovery time for a torn meniscus or fractured hip, but they often question the recovery time for concussion. Dr. Keane frequently sees this at her concussion program.

Many parents tell me their kids are fine while the child is telling me they still don't feel well. I have had more than one mother pull me aside and tell me

their husband was minimizing their child's symptoms so the child could be
cleared to play sooner. Many parents ask more questions about the recovery
time than about the injury itself or its effect on academics. Parents are usu-
ally up-to-date on the child's next tournament or their proficiency of play
and less aware of how their child is functioning.

That doesn't mean parents love their child less, as if they are more con-
cerned about their child's returning to sport than about their child's recov-
ery. Oftentimes, parents misunderstand the seriousness of the injury because
it's been overlooked, even untreated, in the past. No one wants their child
to miss practices or games, and many parents feel that their child will fall
behind if they do. They don't realize that returning too early could prolong
concussion symptoms and a second injury could end a career.

Although rare, there have been cases of athletes returning to play while still concussed and sustaining a second blow to the head, which resulted in prolonged concussive symptoms, serious stroke-like symptoms, and even death. It is not fully known how the brain deals with a second blow while it is still metabolically recovering from the first. It is also not fully understood why adolescent boys are more vulnerable to second-impact syndrome than are girls or adult males. What we do know, is that one concussion leaves an athlete more vulnerable to a second. Further, if they return to play too early and sustain a second impact, the results can be season changing, even life-changing.[9] Both authors have witnessed this among male and female athletes at every age and competition level. As a coach, Christie views a premature return to play as a negative for the entire team.

Ally, a player on my club team, was struck in the head while playing high
school soccer. She had symptoms, but she blew them off and didn't report
them to her coaches or the high school trainer. She was hoping they would

just go away. Since she didn't speak up, her high school coaches thought nothing of it and allowed her to keep playing.

The next day, Ally was playing for our club team and took a ball to the head. She had an immediate headache, felt sick, and could not focus on the field. When she came off the field, she told me she'd had an "incident" the day before and that she probably shouldn't have kept playing. She just didn't think the same thing would happen twice.

This is why I ask my athletes to alert the club coach if they've incurred any injury during school ball, be it middle school or high school, regardless of how minor they think it was. Ally's second injury could have been prevented. What could have meant a couple of weeks off from soccer turned into a few months. Our team lost one of its star players for most of the season. Ally also struggled in school and needed to take it easy for much longer than she would have had she sat it out the first time around.

As a coach, I felt helpless: I hadn't seen either incident happen on the field. As a first-time athlete on the high school varsity team, Ally didn't feel comfortable telling the coach what was going on with her. I wish I could have told her that a week off wasn't going to set her back. It is not worth your brain health. If you ask a majority of athletes, they'll say if they could go back in time, they would have rested properly. It's important to make sure that athletes of all ages and abilities know that sometimes you just have to take a deep breath and remove yourself from the game, even if you don't want to.

According to the Centers for Disease Control and Prevention (CDC), as many as 70 percent of young athletes with a possible concussion report playing with symptoms, and 40 percent of athletes' coaches are unaware of the possible concussion. Athletes are more likely to conceal symptoms from a coach or trainer during a championship game or other important sporting event because they're afraid they won't be allowed to play.[10]

Megan Rapinoe sat out one of her life's biggest games—the 2019

World Cup semifinal—because she'd tweaked her hamstring. It's hard to sit out, even for professionals well versed in injury. Everyone was well aware of the stakes—but they also understood the big picture. In Rapinoe's case, the decision to sit out was based not only on her injury but also that the United States was considered favorites to move past the semifinal. Her team would need her for the finals. Megan was most valuable to the team when she was completely fit, and the smartest thing she could do in that moment was get back to her best.

Even the best athletes performing at 50 percent capability due to injury are less valuable to the team than an uninjured player coming off the bench. Playing while injured makes an athlete more vulnerable to a second injury, regardless of the first injury. Megan's coaches wanted her to recover, to approach her top form. She took the time off and went on to score the winning goal in the World Cup championship; had she played in the semifinal, that goal might never have happened. So these caveats are not necessarily specific to concussion. No player recovering from injury should be rushed back. A return to play should be carefully and appropriately timed.

Concussion Prevention

According to the CDC, there are many ways to reduce the risk of concussion regardless of particular sport. Following are several recommendations.

- Helmets should be properly fitted and appropriate for the given sport.
- The team should create a safe-sport culture that models and expects safe play, positive reinforcement, and ease of symptom reporting.

- Athletes should support teammates who are sitting out of play for concussion or other injury.
- Coaches and referees should enforce the rules of the game to avoid unsafe actions such as striking another athlete in the head, using helmets to impact another player, or making illegal contact such as checking, tackling, or colliding with an unprotected opponent.
- Athletes should be free to talk about concussion without worrying about losing their position on the team, jeopardizing their future, looking weak, or letting their team down.
- Every team at every level of competition should have a coach trained for concussion and also a concussion action plan in place for the team.

Concussion prevention is about respecting the game, the rules, the other players, and the equipment. Athletes who show good sportsmanship and play by the rules may prevent injuries due to increased aggressiveness or purposeful fouls; the authors have seen their fair share of concussions that resulted from a hockey stick to the head—when the ball was on the other side of the field—or from spearing in football, though this tackling method has been eliminated from the rules of play.

Common sense can also help prevent concussions. Question things your children are practicing or doing on the field that seem dangerous or age inappropriate. Soccer heading is a great example of this and also a huge topic of debate. Some research indicates that soccer heading causes concussive symptoms, and other research deems it completely safe.[11] In recent years, despite ambiguous research, heading has been eliminated from youth soccer. But during Christie's formative years, she often practiced heading the ball. She still carries visual symptoms after a heading concussion sustained in her adult years. And, yes, she was doing it properly.

When I was training, I remember coaches punting the ball up and players having to clear the ball with their head in order to show their "toughness." I not only had to head the ball, but I had to improve the distance the ball traveled. As a team, we had to head the ball past a certain zone for points. We practiced this drill at least twice a week; it was part of our training environment. But, by the time the game rolled around, I wanted to avoid heading the ball altogether! My head was so sore from all that training, I dreaded the idea of it. In fact, my head still hurts from thinking about it!

As a coach, I handle heading by preaching confidence and making sure my athletes feel prepared. But I don't train them in it. I don't want them subjected to that kind of repetition. If we do work on heading, it is very limited—three or four attempts, just to get the concept. I teach where on the field to flick the ball when clearing it, and I teach how to protect yourself when jumping to reach the ball. Heading is all about attacking the ball and getting your timing down. We teach the girls how to protect themselves from those collisions. The game has changed so now you see keepers punting less and defenders not having to head the ball as often. Back when I played, I had to head the ball in practices every day. Now the game is played on the ground as much as possible, so players are not asked to head the ball as often.

A concussive injury often betrays the fierce, sometimes overpowering emotions that parents and coaches have about their children regardless of age or level of competition. There remains a tendency for parents to downplay the significance of concussion and an underlying fear of missing games, missing out on playing time, and losing one's position for sitting out. Then there are parents who fear the worst, like permanent brain damage. Many of these parents wake their children at night after a concussion to check their symptoms and may tyrannically limit screen time and socializing. Again, an hour of reading may give you a headache, but it will never injure your brain. Despite very different approaches, both sets of parents inadvertently hinder their child's recovery from concussion because of their fears about their child's health and their future in sports.

We have seen so many otherwise normal parents act crazily about sports. The parental behaviors we laughed about and were guilty of ourselves are born from the same place. We need to keep our children safe. We want to make sure our children succeed. Our goal is to make sure our kids grow up not only loved, respected, and healthy, but also having reached their full potential.

Injury can often leave parents feeling like we can't do both. But when lines of communication between kids, parents, coaches, doctors, and other players are kept open, the long-term impact of an injury doesn't have to be major. Young athletes need to know that the best thing for their playing time is to get any injury checked out right away and to be honest about how they feel. Parents need to know that their kids are resilient and that their athletic careers are evaluated as a whole, not on a game-by-game or even season-by-season basis. And coaches need to know that their best athletes are the ones who are able to play at full capacity, not the ones who are shaking off or hiding a potentially serious injury.

If there is one takeaway you glean from this chapter, we hope it is this: a concussion is in fact a brain injury and should be taken seriously. Concussions must always be carefully and conservatively managed so that our children can return to play safely.

CHAPTER 11

Slow Down to Speed Up

On the US Women's National Team, Coach Pia Sundhage taught players to remain poised and true to their style of play right up until the final moment of the game. Her philosophy was to teach players to use their skill-set and knowledge throughout the game, even in the last seconds. Many times, when a team has a lead, they try to run out the clock to keep their opponent from scoring as opposed to maintaining the same style of play that had earned them the lead. They are trying to ensure victory. But Coach Pia was not in favor of this tactic. When teams stall to secure a win, she said, they lose the quality of their game and are more prone to errors. Coach Pia believed that teams should maintain their quality of play and focus throughout.

Coach Pia, a Swede, competed against the United States for many years as both a player and coach. She saw that the difference between the US team and those of other countries had to do with mentality: the game was never over *until it was really over*. American players had a never-say-die mentality that she was unaccustomed to.

Since will was not in short supply, Coach Pia focused on bringing tactical awareness to the US team. She wanted the team to slow down and be more precise in hopes of aiding their efficiency. Prior to her tenure, Pia saw the US teams as moving fast and boldly throughout the game, in pursuit of the win. And the strategy had been

201

working, because the US women's team was one of the fittest teams in the world. But Coach Pia thought that by slowing down, the US women's team could be even better. And she was right. She brought a new mind-set that combined the US players' trademark never-say-die mentality with a tactical awareness, that is, a focus on productivity and efficiency every minute of the game. Other teams all over the world came to fear the US Women's National Team. Opponents knew that no lead was safe, and that a lead never ensured victory.

Before Pia, we knew how to compete and how to be the fittest and the strongest. But we didn't necessarily know how to problem solve when our best attributes were shut down by the opposing team. We couldn't problem solve at the very end of a tied or tense game. We just outworked other teams. Our fitness always carried us across the finish line. With Pia, we learned to slow down and use our minds. The US Women's National Team came to remain as focused in the game's final moments as they were during the first ten minutes.

During the 2011 FIFA World Cup, the United States was losing to Brazil in the last minute of the game. Had the United States lost, it would have been the earliest knockout in the history of the US Women's National Team. This scenario would have anyone panicking.

I can recall the last minute of that game vividly. Cristiane, a Brazilian attacker, dribbled the ball to the corner in an attempt to run the clock out. We were at the 121st minute, in extra time. The game should have been over at the 120th minute, but time was added to allow for a previous injury. The Brazilians were trying to waste time, knowing the game could end at any second. I ran Cristiane down and forced her to make a pass. Because of the pressure and contact that I applied to her, I forced her into a bad decision. Cristiane inadvertently played the ball to US defender Ali Krieger. Ali took one touch and passed it to Carli Lloyd in the midfield. Carli dribbled the ball from east to west, which strategically drew three Brazilian defenders to her.

She then passed to Megan Rapinoe, who was wide open. Megan took one look, made a quick touch, and served an amazing forty-yard ball to Abby Wambach. Megan's serve challenged the keeper into a decision. The keeper decided to come out of the goal, fearing that Megan had been shooting. Instead and without hesitation, Abby headed the ball into the goal!

It was literally four passes. It went from right to center to left and was crossed in. Carli could have tried to score. She didn't. We took it slow and made good decisions because we were not rushing. Instead of simply knocking the ball as far as we could up the field and trying to force a goal, we were thoughtful and trusted one another. We got the goal we needed by doing what we knew best.

The US team didn't let the ticking clock change the way they played; instead, the team relied on the instincts, judgment calls, and training inculcated in every previous moment to guide them down a path to success. They won the game because they knew how to speed up by slowing down.

Slowing down might seem a tough concept to swallow, but its benefits are worth the effort. Think about the iconic scene in *The Matrix*, when Neo, in a swirl of black trench coat, dodges bullets while in a slo-mo half backbend. Shown at normal speed, the encounter would be a blur of indistinct movement and just another fight scene. But the filmmakers purposely slowed down the filming to emphasize Neo's agility and speed, and the scene became transcendent. Neo was able to stay ahead of even the fastest-moving threat because of his newly discovered abilities to assess and evaluate the world around him.

Everyone, from parents and coaches to business leaders and corporations, is continuously searching for ways to perform better and improve productivity. Speeding up by slowing down is a cognitive and behavioral strategy that involves consciously deciding to slow down in order to produce desired outcomes. This strategic slowing down means stepping out of the moment, evaluating your goals, prioritizing what's most important, and then getting back into the moment with a more direct path toward those goals.

Speeding up by slowing down does not necessarily mean actually or physically slowing down, quitting teams, or reducing training (although it can, depending on your current schedule). It's about reframing the meanings of "slower" and "faster." Interestingly, increasing the pace of production leads to decreased value over time. In a study cited in the May 2010 edition of the *Harvard Business Review*, high-performing companies have begun the process of slowing down: being more open to discussions and new ideas, encouraging innovative thinking, and allowing time for reflection and learning.[1] Companies that focused too much on production and moving fast didn't allow for employee collaboration; these companies saw their employees' performance suffer.

In sports, we often see the same thing. In our attempt to get to the next level we miss opportunities to learn important values and skills. Sometimes, continuous focus on forward momentum can cause us to rush through the training, the learning, or the skill development we need for the long run. When we don't take time out to work toward our goals in a productive way, we end up getting in over our heads.

Losing Sight of the Goals because of Stress

The brains of the best and brightest athletes are wired quite differently from those of the average person in terms of their ability to handle stress while playing. Successful professional athletes are known for their calm in the midst of crisis, their tendency to slow down and see the entire play, and their ability to get into and remain in the zone.[2] When most people experience repeated stress, they find it difficult to see the whole picture or the entire court or field. Athletes with tunnel vision lose sight of the fact that the game is constantly changing; they keep doing the same things over and over again despite the game-time variables. The same holds true in life. Life is ultimately a series of changes, and repeated stress causes us to futilely repeat habits. We rally. We work hard. We keep bulldozing forward, getting all our familial, school, and occupational responsibilities finished every day, without taking the time to peek outside the tunnel.

Dr. Keane has found that many athletes who are not performing at their peak are actually struggling with tunnel vision, a vicious cycle. The more the athlete tries to improve performance in light of a certain problem, the more magnified the problem and the more acute the stress. Most athletes with tunnel vision focus solely on an end goal while skipping vital interim steps.

Kevin was a seventeen-year-old soccer forward who came to my private practice because his performance was declining. Kevin's parents were very concerned about his ability to play Division I soccer, and they were running themselves ragged to stem the tide: hiring additional trainers, driving ninety minutes each way so that Kevin could practice with a high-level academy team, traveling all over the United States to familiarize college coaches with Kevin. When Kevin stopped scoring goals, everyone panicked.

Kevin was under fire from a current coach, who threatened to cut his playing time unless he started scoring again. He really laid into Kevin. With reduced playing time, Kevin would have less exposure to college coaches. His anxiety soared. With each scoreless game, Kevin told himself he wasn't good enough, and if he wasn't good enough, he would never get to play in college.

Kevin developed tunnel vision. He became an individualistic player, focused only on his own ability to score rather than playing collaboratively and productively with his teammates. He had an uncanny ability to help his teammates during an attack, but he also lost his ability to defend. He became caught up in scoring goals and was hyperfocused on shooting: when to shoot, how to shoot, and whether his shot would make it into the back of the net.

Kevin had lost his confidence, and he wasn't playing with authenticity. So the first thing we worked on together was rebuilding his sense of self as a player. We started by listing all his attributes as a player. We forced him to slow his thinking and come up with a thorough and accurate list. He had both skill and talent, and when he focused on playing rather than scoring, the goals would come naturally. He did not need to force them.

Kevin learned to focus on his strengths as a player, such as his determination, perseverance, athleticism, soccer IQ, and playmaking ability. He realized that fear had been the culprit: he was so afraid of missing a shot that he would unknowingly avoid situations that would lead to his taking shots. He didn't need more practice or more pressure; he needed to slow down and to reconnect with the talent and ability that had gotten him where he was in the first place.

By taking the time to discuss his strengths, Kevin realized he was ignoring his natural gifts. Rather than thinking only about scoring, he created specific game-time goals for himself, such as making connections with teammates, beating defenders, taking on defenders, and utilizing his unique array of passes. These elements fueled his confidence and helped him to understand that he had much more to offer than just scoring goals.

Like Kevin, all kids have a lot more to offer than numbers on a board, winning games, or even playing sports. While some kids thrive on the rigor of multiple teams, trainings, and practices, most need a balance. It can be easy to get caught up in getting it all done and producing results and more arduous to take time for reflection, discussions, and new ideas—but that's where growth, development, and peak performance lie.

Performance Accelerators

Slowing down helps, but "slowing down" does not mean doing less. One of our favorite examples of speeding up by slowing down comes from Rasmus Hougaard's *One Second Ahead*.[3] He describes how a cheetah, the planet's fastest land animal, has been known to achieve speeds of seventy-five miles per hour. However, if the cheetah were to run at that pace constantly, it would be dead within hours: "For the cheetah to use its full speed while hunting most effectively, it starts very slowly. At first, it slowly stalks its prey, blood engorging its muscles and its brain maintaining a singular focus. This brief phase of calm actually enables the cheetah to explode into action when its prey is within range."

What does this mean for the sports parent who spends afternoons and evenings bouncing between multiple activities for multiple children? It means that pausing even five minutes between activities like dinner, homework, and getting into the car can help you act more efficiently. We call these pauses "performance accelerators" and their benefits are myriad. They create space for you to regain awareness of your intentions, your priorities, and your focus. They allow you to take a deep breath, reorient your energy, and reduce stress. A performance-accelerating pause gives you a chance to organize your thoughts so that you can communicate more clearly, collaborate with others more organically, and process information more easily—all values and skills you can teach your kids.

Reboot Your Brain

We know through experience that asking parents to "take a break," even for a brief moment, is something many feel is impossible. But we promise that no matter how busy you are, you can find little moments throughout your day to reboot your brain and accelerate your performance.

Adding performance accelerators to your child's daily routine teaches them to make a habit of self-awareness and self-monitoring both on and off the field. Many kids can kill two or three hours playing video games or FaceTiming with friends without a single break. Performance accelerators can help kids break these habits by teaching them the benefit of checking in with themselves and refocusing. For example, taking a moment for a sip of water could ward off a headache later in the day. A break in conversation with a friend could deter a needless argument or prevent them from posting something they might come to regret.

How Do I Use Performance Accelerators?

Start by taking a daily break, three to five minutes in duration. Focus on what you are doing while you are doing it. It's that simple. Be like the cheetah. Running on all cylinders all day long will just make you tired and irritable by the time you can't find those shin guards. As you begin to see the benefits of performance accelerators, find a few more break times during the day. Many parents already have calendars, phone apps, and multiple reminders built into their digital worlds that assist them in scheduling and prioritizing their day. Schedule in performance accelerators to supplement and enhance these aids.

Here are some ways to incorporate performance accelerators into your day:

- Before you get out of bed, place your feet on the floor and take three deep breaths. Think about what your body feels like. Visualize yourself walking through your morning. Bonus points if you throw in a positive affirmation. This is a great moment to set your intentions for the day. Take three more breaths before you move on. Get out of bed.

- While you are making dinner, take a moment to focus on your breathing. This is your time to regain your focus after a long

day. Smell the aroma of the food; listen to the sounds your
food makes while it's cooking; feel the textures of your food
as you eat it. Take three deep belly breaths.

- As you walk out the door and the kids pile into the car—yep,
you guessed it—it's time to breathe. Think, *I am leaving my
home and driving my kids to their practices. This is another transition in my day.* Identify any spots of tension in your body and
imagine them melting away. Before you pull out of the driveway, think about your breathing. These techniques help keep
us from feeling overwhelmed. Although we may have carefully created plans, something as simple as being asked to pick
up a teammate at the last minute or losing a practice shirt can
throw us way off course. When we take time to transition and
we maintain our self-awareness, we find that we have more
time and space for these unplanned curveballs because we are
meeting these challenges from a different emotional place.

Teach your child to practice performance accelerators too. During homework, have them open their book, close their eyes, and take
three deep breaths. Help your child notice their posture and any tension in their shoulders or face. Help them think about their transition
from play to sitting quietly.

How Can My Child Use Performance Accelerators When Playing Sports?

Young athletes are well aware of the tension built into the last few
minutes of a soccer match, the two-minute warning in football, or a
buzzer beater in basketball. These are the times during sports when
the fans get most excited, players panic, and parents turn downright

crazy. Under pressure, a team's original strategy is often scrapped and replaced with a desperate emergency plan aimed at settling the score. Christie knows well the chaos and coaches her players to recognize this common mistake.

If you watch the last ten minutes of a soccer game, you often see the losing team hitting long balls to their strikers in hopes of scoring. You will also see the opposing side respond by booting those balls right back just as quickly as they come in. The faster the losing team sends the ball up the field, the faster it comes back to them. It is very rare that a goal happens that way. Teams change their plan instead of sticking to the style of play that best suits them.

For the US Women's National Team, it was all about focusing and taking it slow during those last moments. When you stick to your method, you can be composed and confident. Shift only when you see a real opening to score. The other team can't expose you when you are in that state.

When an athlete uses an on-field moment to check in with their physical and mental state, they are more likely to play energetically and creatively. Taking time to self-monitor makes identifying stressors easier and helps everyone control their reactions to them.

The Physical Benefits of Speeding Up by Slowing Down

Consider the case of Stefanie, a triathlete, avid runner, retired professional soccer player, and licensed counselor at Dr. Keane's private practice. Stefanie participated in a course of biofeedback in order to reduce muscle tension that she believed had been contributing to her headaches. Biofeedback training is a method of therapy that measures the body's heart rate to determine a person's physical response to stimuli. The subject is taught to use the readings to control bodily functions that the body regulates automatically, such as heart rate, skin temperature, muscle tension, and blood pressure. After five sessions, Stefanie learned how to reduce her heart rate and achieve a state of relaxation, which in turn reduced the muscle tension in her neck. She practiced multiple breathing techniques coupled with body awareness and progressive muscle relaxation to regularly reduce her heart rate.

Since beginning biofeedback training, Stefanie realized that she could lower her heart rate by at least ten beats while in the middle of a race—important to keeping her heart rate in optimal range. While running, she focuses on her breathing and takes deeper rhythmic breaths. When she takes deep breaths, she increases oxygen and lung capacity, and with more oxygenated blood in your brain, your muscles relax. She noticed that by slowing her heart rate, she increased her stamina and has since been able to shorten her running times, often finishing a given race in the top five.

She is slowing down to speed up. You and your kids can too.

Key Points to Remember

- Taking three- to five-minute breaks throughout the day helps you to refocus, become more efficient, and have more energy. During each break, breathe, think, and refocus.
- Taking time to transition between activities assists in maintaining composure and ultimately leads to confidence in handling unexpected stressors.
- Think about how much time you spend *doing* versus how much time you spend purposefully *being in the moment*. Help your child to self-monitor as well.
- Create a monthly calendar and refer to it every day, as well as a daily schedule that organizes and structures your day, especially if it is a busy one. Make this monthly calendar and daily

schedule visible to your children as well. This is the foundation for your performance accelerators. Look for opportunities
to introduce those very accelerators.

- Get your priorities straight. Instead of trying to do everything,
  set a list of tasks, ranking them from most to least important.
  Minimize distractions and time wasters. Turn your phone off
  when you need to. You don't have to answer every call, text, or
  email immediately.

- Pay attention to your overall health. This can be as simple as
  staying hydrated, having adequate nutrition, and exercising
  consistently. Many times, however, these basic necessities are
  among the first sacrifices when we tangle with busy schedules, work, and other commitments.

- Sleep is the foundation of slowing down to speed up because
  sleep governs the efficient use of any cognitive skill! Despite
  understanding the value of sleep, we often neglect it. Even
  mild sleep deprivation can increase stress.

- Learn to relax! We talk with loads of parents who are overwhelmed by their schedules: their kids are on the school team,
  the local team, and the travel team. Don't forget the private
  lessons, camps, and other training opportunities—sometimes
  for more than one sport. Slowing down fosters growth and
  a budding athletic career. Rather than saying yes to every
  coach, parents should first make sure their kids are happy and
  excited about the commitment they're making to their sport,
  that they're not feeling burnt out or trapped in one activity,
  and that they're still getting a lot out of the experience as a
  whole. Taking a step back to look at the big picture is as rel-
  evant to an athlete's career as it is to their ability to make the
  best game-time decisions.

CHAPTER 12

The Reality of Early Specialization in Sports

Every family has a different relationship with athletics. For some, a certain sport is in the blood: generations have played soccer, had season tickets for the local baseball team, or gathered to watch certain golf tournaments. For some athletes, sports scholarships mean entrance to a college that otherwise would be out of reach. For still other athletes, sports are simply for fun.

Lately, we have witnessed a disconcerting trend sweeping the athletic community—sports specialization. That is, in order to "succeed," kids must commit to one sport as early as ages seven or eight. Early specialization in youth sports is defined as the participation by a prepubertal athlete, typically younger than twelve years old, in one sport to the exclusion of any other sports and training for eight months or more within a year.[1]

Back in the day, when a sport's season lasted only a few months, most kids played multiple sports, sampling some and committing more time and effort to another. Kids were encouraged to enjoy a variety of sports to see which ones they liked, to have fun and play with their friends, or just to run around and get out of the house for a few hours. Organized youth sports were initially put together as an outlet for kids to develop social skills, self-esteem, sportsmanship, and fitness.[2]

Over the last decade, youth sports have seen the explosive growth of highly selective and competitive leagues and organizations: so-called elite, academy, club, and even Olympic development teams. Athletic scholarships to high schools and colleges alike add even more pressure to perform. Thus, the trend of early specialization: playing a single sport, all year round, to the exclusion of all other sports.

There is a pervasive, pernicious myth that for an athlete to be competitive, more games, more practices, more competition, and more intensity are required. Sadly, many parents feel no choice but to acquiesce. They believe that if their child does not specialize early, they may never catch up to the kids who did.

Some superstars were raised seemingly from birth to become an expert in a given sport, like Tiger Woods and Gabby Douglas. Then there are those who played multiple sports and are deemed late bloomers, like Alex Morgan and NFLer Clay Matthews. There are still others who ascended to the rank of superstar while in the midst of an already blooming professional career, like Tom Brady or Stephen Curry. There are films, documentaries, and an ever-growing pool of research that caution against playing only one sport during childhood, but the trend toward early specialization continues. The common belief is that if you don't specialize early, you don't become a superstar.

Christie was a multiple-sport athlete.

Whenever I tell my story, people are stunned to learn that I was a walk-on to my university soccer team. When I was a kid, coaches would steer me to basketball year-round, but I wanted to play more than one sport. Back then, it was easy to do. Now I watch my kids struggle to balance multiple sports because of time commitments, strict schedules, and sports seasons that never really end. I think most parents and coaches have the right intentions, but they get caught up in the winning and the FOMO and miss the big picture about sports and what they bring to your life.

I may have lacked the skill of peers who played soccer 24/7, but I had the competitiveness and drive to make up for it. Remember: I attended college on a basketball scholarship but ended up playing professional soccer. I loved playing both. I didn't specialize, and as a result, I was a well-rounded athlete. I was coached by so many different voices and learned to cope with so many different personalities. Over the years, playing multiple sports taught me to adjust to many different teammates, trainers, and dynamics.

When the US Women's National Team coaches moved me from forward to defense, I believe I transitioned easier than others might have because of the adaptability I'd learned from playing multiple sports. Further, I was relatively injury-free for most of my career, consistent with the research on kids who play multiple sports in their youth. I never had overuse injuries like most kids have today; I remember fewer injuries, period, than I see today. I don't remember asking to come off the field because something on my body hurt and I don't ever remember a bench full of injured players. Every three months I played a new sport, so I always wanted to train and practice and improve for each new season. I remember always feeling fit, having time to interact with my friends when I wanted to, and playing games on the streets of my neighborhood every chance I got.

That said, we should acknowledge the benefits of early specialization:

- Sought-after coaches want to work with higher-level players, so kids who specialize early enjoy better coaching and skill instruction.
- Specialization provides hours of practice, which leads to increased skill and competence.
- Due to the time commitment, kids learn not to waste their discretionary time. They use free time wisely because they don't have much of it.

- Kids enjoy achieving and developing their unique talents.
- Specialization reduces parents' fears that their kids are missing out or losing a competitive edge relative to same-aged peers.

Even still, the drawbacks to early specialization outweigh the benefits:[3]

- Stress and burnout are more likely, related to perfectionistic or excessive coaching, overtraining, and even lack of sleep.
- Kids who specialize early have problems with social identity because they are isolated from peers throughout their childhood.
- Some experts believe early specialization may create a lost childhood, which interferes with normal identity development and a child's sense of who they are.
- Early specialization is associated with decreased intrinsic motivation, or a lack of internal enjoyment in playing sports.
- Kids who specialize early are more likely to sustain sports injuries than those who play multiple sports.[4]
- Early specialization demands time and financial requirements that do not necessarily justify the end results, since only a small percentage of kids become elite athletes.

Many kids who specialize early experience burnout, overtraining, and even lack of sleep due to perfectionism, excessive coaching, or parental pressures to perform. A common problem for youth athletes who specialize early is the potential for the loss of a sense of self outside of their sport. An emotional consequence of highly intense, single-sport focus is the possibility that the child sees themselves exclusively as an athlete and thus loses sight of themselves outside of the sport. Many kids develop the erroneous belief that they are without value outside of sports. This ultimately causes kids to lose enjoyment in other areas of their childhood, which are vital to their emotional development. Dr. Keane has treated many athletes for depressive symptoms that follow a sports injury, a consequence of loss of self. The kids wonder, *Who am I if I am not playing?*

Emily was referred to my office by her athletic trainer. She had injured her ankle and, while in recovery, had begun showing signs of depression. She had played for the previous three weeks, and the trainer was concerned that her inactivity was taking a toll on her, emotionally and socially. She was listless at practice, talked less, and overreacted to ostensibly mild pain during physical therapy sessions. Her usual demeanor—smiling, laughing, and expressing concern for her teammates—diminished. Symptoms of depression after a sports injury are common and expected; however, Emily admitted to her trainer that with each injury, even minor, she found it harder and harder to pull out of her emotional slump.

Emily had played soccer since the age of five, beginning in recreational leagues and quickly moving up the ranks of her town club teams. She had both speed and innate knowledge of the game. Her father took notice of her talent and enrolled her on an academy team by the time she was ten years old.

Emily practiced three times per week with her team and with a personal trainer one other day per week. She maintained this schedule from age ten all the way to her high school graduation. She played in high-level leagues and elite tournaments at least twice a month. She started on the high school varsity and served as team captain during her junior and senior years. She was well known locally for both her offensive and defensive prowess. Emily was accomplished.

When Emily set foot in my office for the very first time, she burst into tears—immediately followed by a barrage of apologies for crying. She'd never felt so bad in her life, she said, and wasn't sure what to make of it. Her mood had become worse and worse with each day following the injury. She was no longer socializing with her teammates. Practice, which for her meant physical therapy at the field, had become intolerable. It was hard to watch her teammates play, she said, while she was stuck on the sideline. Things had gotten so bad that she wouldn't even leave her bedroom unless she had to.

During our first hour together, we discovered that Emily felt lost without soccer. She was paranoid about what her coaches were thinking, and she worried for her spot on the field. She believed that her injury would cost her playing time and, possibly, her place on the team. When I asked her how I could be of help to her, she responded, "Help me get back out on the field. If you can do that, I can feel better."

Emily had no sense of herself beyond her identity as a player. Once injured, and out of the game for longer than she'd ever been, she had no idea what to do with herself. She had not developed a sense of who she was outside the game. She didn't ask me to help her cope with the mental rigors of her injury or help her feel happy and whole again. She asked how I could get her back to play, as that was the only conceivable solution to her unhappiness.

Unfortunately, Emily's scenario is not uncommon. Sports specialization from a young age can result in an insular lifestyle. Emily didn't grow up interacting with peers outside of soccer, and she rarely attended meetings and events held by clubs she'd joined in high school. She had no idea who she was or what she enjoyed outside soccer. Without a strong sense of who she was, Emily was easily overwhelmed by her injuries.

The initial work with Emily centered on her understanding her values. She realized that from a young age, she'd said yes to everything to do with soccer at the expense of everything else in her life. As Emily acquiesced to things that made her unhappy out of an obligation to soccer, she had gradually lost sight of what actually made her happy. Always eager to please, Emily learned that her inner compass was centered on pleasing her coaches and her parents, rather than doing or saying things in line with her *own preferences. Ultimately, Emily couldn't break these patterns until she learned to ask herself,* What would I choose to do if I didn't have to please anyone?

Emily finished her college career and went on to play soccer professionally. She continues to develop her interests outside soccer, without the feelings of guilt, doubt, and fear that had accompanied them. Now, Emily works on loving herself with the same grit and determination that she has poured into soccer. She learned that a sense of self crystallizes over the course of life's journey. Moving forward, her wins and her championships will come from within.

Did early specialization cause Emily's recurrent bouts of adult depression? Perhaps. Certainly, her unilateral focus on soccer impeded her ability to cope with her athletic injuries. Her story reminds us that we need to rethink the insanity of youth sports.

Where Did the Pressure for Early Specialization Come From?

One theory that helps to explain early specialization comes from the oft-cited work by K. Anders Ericsson, a psychologist who studies top performers in fields ranging from music to business to medicine to sports. The best, he says, follow a learning model he deemed the gold standard. He called their pursuits "deliberate practice."

Ericsson states that it takes deliberate practice to become an expert in anything, including sports. He is widely known for his claim that ten thousand hours marks the threshold to expertise. Ten thousand hours translates to twenty hours per week for fifty weeks a year for ten years.[5] His work shed light on the importance of the *development* of expertise, rather than the notion that athletes are born with talent unattainable through training. If you credit Ericsson's approach, the math dictates that our kids need to get cracking pretty early on if they want to be successful.

Is deliberate practice indeed necessary during childhood? Does it ensure elite performance come adulthood? Many believe Ericsson's research to be imperfect and open to critique. It begs the question of at what age must a child begin to develop expertise, and, more important, at what cost to their overall development. We wrote this chapter because we see early specialization affecting kids and families not only personally but also professionally, mentally, socially, and physically. As parents of young athletes, we have both felt the pressure toward early specialization and to buy into higher-intensity or so-called elite teams for our kids.

Here's the simple truth: most medical professionals, orthopedists, physical therapists, surgeons, rehab professionals, and sports coaches argue against early sports specialization.[6] And their message is clear: if your child intends on a long athletic career, do not encourage them to specialize early, no matter what well-intentioned coaches, trainers, and sports-business owners tell you.

Given Christie's own experience, we can reassure parents that early specialization is not necessary; she played multiple sports, even getting a full scholarship to play basketball before walking onto the university soccer team. Dr. Keane regularly treats athletes and families who are suffering because early specialization led to overuse sports injuries, burnout, or disinterest. Both Christie and Dr. Keane see more high school and college-age athletes dropping out of sports altogether because the process of early specialization has become too much.

Further, there is growing evidence that early specialization is not just a bad idea fundamentally; it can also impair an athlete's long-term performance when compared to peers who played multiple sports. With this in mind, let's review the existing science on early specialization and why you should just say no to elite teams, higher-intensity teams, and playing one sport year-round with minimal breaks.

What the Experts Say

The International Olympic Committee (IOC) created a consensus statement on youth athletic development and identified several physical and mental health concerns associated with early specialization, including insufficient sleep, increased overuse injury rates, overtraining, burnout, and eating disorders.[7]

The IOC recommends that children participate in different sporting activities and acquire a wide range of skills until they reach puberty. They also recommend the integration of strength and neuromuscular fitness in conjunction with whole-athlete development as regards competence, confidence, connection, and character. (Gymnastics and figure skating stand as exceptions to the early specialization recommendation, as performance peaks in the midteens.)

On October 2, 2015, the American Orthopaedic Society for Sports Medicine (AOSSM) put forth the "AOSSM Early Sport Specialization Consensus Statement," in which they defined early specialization according to the following three criteria.[8]

1. Participation in intensive training and competition in organized sports eight months out of the year
2. Participation in the sport at the exclusion of others (limited free play overall)
3. Involvement by prepubertal children (seventh grade or roughly twelve years old)

The statement concluded that childhood diversification of sports—rather than early specialization—leads to increased long-term sports participation, increased personal development, and increased adult performance. The statement discusses the importance of playing sports freely, without consistent intervention from coaches, as free play is necessary for developing a good skill level prior to age thirteen. Free play is integral to child development because it fosters life skills that cannot be learned within structured settings like team sports or practices. When kids are engaged in free play, they are able to try new things, use their imagination, problem solve, and take control of situations that would be out of their hands were a coach or parent running the show. Free play helps kids develop confidence, relationships, creativity, and motor skills. Most important, free play is an integral part of childhood just because it is fun.

The AOSSM consensus statement debunks the myth that early specialization distinguishes between athletes who become experts and those who do not. The statement indicates that early sport specialization is no guarantee of high-caliber athletic performance at the national, Olympic, and professional levels, and may, in fact, be detrimental. Instead, the AOSSM recommends a balance between intensive sports participation and other childhood commitments such as time for friends, school, and extracurricular activities. Factors such as these determine kids' overall health and wellness.

The AOSSM indicates that kids who specialize early may not develop the same sports-specific skills as those of same-aged peers who diversified, especially when they do not participate in youth-led activities (deliberate play) with their peers. When kids have daily team practices and games every weekend, they miss out on free play with their peers.

When kids engage in increased organized play over free play, the risk of injury is increased by greater than two-to-one. Further, athletes who specialize before age twelve have an increased risk of injury. Kids who participate in more than sixteen hours of intense training, or who specialize in sport activities, should be closely monitored for burnout, overuse injury, and potential decrements in performance due to overtraining.

The AOSSM indicates that specializing may prevent kids from fully developing certain neuromuscular patterns that protect them from sports-related injuries. Growing kids should be provided a range of outlets for development of fine motor skills, combined with neuromuscular training to help optimize potential for success and reduced injury risk.

Parents should remember: youth sports is a large, ever-growing, and lucrative industry. Athletes who utilize private facilities are often encouraged to participate year-round because those facilities are businesses reliant on income.

The American Academy of Pediatrics (AAP) also put forth a statement from its Council on Sports Medicine and Fitness called "Sports Specialization and Intensive Training in Young Athletes."[9] The AAP agrees that children should be involved in multiple activities and develop a range of skills; the statement confirms that kids who specialize early are not only denied the benefits of learning multiple life and physical skills, they also face additional demands from intense training, such as overuse injury, poor nutrition, and missed educational and social opportunities.

The AAP also notes that early specialization can interfere with normal psychosocial development, resulting in physical and emotional stress, hindered growth, disruption of family life, unrealistic parental expectations, and possibly the exploitation of children's desires for financial gain. The AAP acknowledges that many kids enjoy the life of travel and club teams, but it cautions about the impact of travel on family life as a whole. What pressure does a child feel when they feel like their performance impacts the family's well-being? How many children in a family can realistically be involved in year-round, single-sport, intensive training? What of the lives and interests of the siblings who do not play?

The American Academy of Pediatrics makes the following recommendations.

1. Children should participate in activities that are consistent with their abilities and interests. Early specialization is discouraged as it pushes young kids beyond their limits before adolescence.

2. Pediatricians should work with parents to make sure they favor or employ coaches who understand proper equipment, training, and the unique emotional and physical attributes of young athletes.

3. Physicians and coaches should strive for early recognition of overuse injuries and also early prevention. Athletes should never be encouraged to "work through" the injury. Athletes are likely to ignore treatment recommendations for rest or for a temporary hiatus; further, these recommendations do nothing to prevent additional injury.

4. Children undergoing intensive training should be routinely monitored by their pediatricians for weight, cardiovascular health, growth and maturation, emotional stress, and signs and symptoms of overtraining.

5. Intensely trained and specialized children should have routine nutrition checks.

6. Physicians, coaches, and families should be educated about the prevention of heat injury.

Sports psychologists find that multisport children enjoy a wider array of experiences with coaches and other athletes, which in turn offers greater opportunities for positive development and finding their talents. By the age of thirteen, say sports psychologists, kids have only the cognitive ability to determine if they want to specialize. However, by age sixteen, they have developed enough psychologically, socially, cognitively, motorically, and physically to informedly make the decision to specialize.[10] Remember, only a small percentage of high school athletes will play Division I sports, and only an infinitesimal percentage go on to play professionally. Keep these stats in mind as you guide your children, and look for the balance.

How to Find and Maintain Balance

- Consider what activities offer different or complementary skills.
- Involve your child in multiple sports and also activities outside sports.
- Plan things for your child and family just for the fun.
- Teach and model the value of self-care and relaxation.
- De-emphasize outcomes! It's the process, not the destination, that matters.
- Protect and prioritize your family and personal private time.

The current youth sports culture demands that kids commit at the expense of the whole self. Athletes are considered distracted when they enjoy other interests or engage in activities outside their single sport. But to truly prepare a young athlete for success, parents must create a well-rounded and fully developed environment for their children. If your child favors a particular team sport, complement that with something that teaches individual performance—perhaps not even a sport at all. Rather than shuttle between three or more teams, prioritize one team—prioritize, not specialize—and create opportunities for your child to cultivate other interests. As kids get older, they'll be able to decide whether the time commitment for a certain sport is worth it. But for kids generally younger than the ages of thirteen to fifteen, parents should watch carefully for the pressures associated with early specialization. If a child is going to earn playing time only by practicing twelve hours per week, is that the best team for them? If a child isn't starting homework until 8:00 p.m. because of sports commitments, what message does that send about priorities?

Before you sign up your kid for that additional team, register them for that next clinic, or write that next tournament on the calendar, take a step back and look for balance in your family's lives and those of your kids. Are your values in balance with your schedule? And when you do take that minute to step back and assess, remember the essence of this chapter. While early specialization is touted as the preferred route to expertise, to a high level of mastery, and to long-term success in sports, the experts and research say otherwise. Diversification—rather than early specialization—leads to increased long-term sports participation, increased personal development, and increased adult performance.

CHAPTER 13

Little Sky Blue

Several years ago, my daughter Rylie played for a U8 youth soccer team in Neptune, New Jersey. Her participation marked a unique transition in our lives. I was watching Rylie play and not the other way around; for years, Rylie and her little sister had watched me from the sidelines. I was excited to be a sports mom, but it was a daunting process to pick the best team for Rylie. I settled on a team thinking it would be a good fit. Its coaches understood the game, and I wanted Rylie have fun while also learning proper fundamentals.

One day, Rylie's team faced another local team called Sky Blue. Obviously, this was not the professional New Jersey team Sky Blue FC, for which I was playing at the time. The little Sky Blue was known for being very successful in their local division, league championships, and even some regional and state tournaments. They were considered one of New Jersey's top teams for their age group. Collectively, the girls were bigger, faster, and stronger than most teams their age. They looked the part too. But the reality was, despite their success, they were all just nine years old!

When Rylie's game against little Sky Blue started, it wasn't the players I took notice of—it was their parents. It was hard not to. Some of the parents were loud, boisterous, and hanging on everything that happened on the field. They were excitable, and they called out to the referees as much as they did to their players. Many of the parents coached from the sidelines. Any goal scored, either for or against their team, brought out the worst in these parents. Little Sky Blue's players seemed accustomed to the rowdiness and mimicked their parents by using an aggressive style of play known as "kick and run." In kick and run, a team will kick the ball as far as they can up the field and use their athleticism to run the ball down. This strategy is also known as "boot it." Obviously, it favors bigger and stronger athletes who can outrun and outmuscle smaller ones. Unfortunately, kick and run doesn't teach the game or develop technical skills. It involves very little thinking, adjusting, or problem solving. Winning was clearly the priority at little Sky Blue.

A few days after the game, the parent coach for little Sky Blue asked me to help coach their team. He was impressed with Rylie's play and thought she would be a great addition to the team. He told me he was bringing in a trainer I knew personally as well as some new players. His current players were skilled and naturally gifted, he said, but he wanted them to enjoy better training and stronger competition. He hoped Rylie and I would consider changing teams: Rylie would benefit from a new environment, and little Sky Blue would benefit from my experience.

My immediate answer was no. Not a chance! In my view, little Sky Blue was clearly compromising player development in order to win games. I couldn't be a part of that. To me, focusing solely on winning games is developmentally inappropriate for nine-year-olds. Those parents could only see the here and now. They didn't understand that things would look very different in a few years, when the competition had caught up. Many kids who excel on athleticism alone are eventually left behind technically. They lose confidence, fall back, or even drop out. When the focus is on winning and championships, development takes a back seat. This kind of focus sets up all the kids for long-term failure while also offering very little experientially along the way.

I communicated my concerns to the coach. He was shocked. He thought he was doing what was best for the girls on the team. That had always been his intention. The girls were having fun and winning; let's face it, winning feels great. Little Sky Blue was practicing twice a week, so the coach believed he was developing the athletes as well as winning games. However, to his credit, he listened.

I took a moment to reevaluate, too. I saw good intentions, well-meaning parents, and true potential in little Sky Blue. I explained to the coach that if I were to join them, the girls would need to shift from goal oriented to process oriented. I would need to educate the parents about my philosophy and they would have to embrace the changes too. I told him that while winning would no longer be the focus, it would become a by-product of development. I really respected the coach's openness to a new mind-set. He was all in.

Accountability

My first order of business was to hold a team meeting with the parents. We needed to communicate our expectations for the families on the team; they would need to agree to these expectations and then be held accountable to them. We told the parents that coaching from the sidelines was no longer permissible. The only acceptable shouts from the sidelines would be words of encouragement and support. I asked the parents to provide positive reinforcement such as "Good work" and "Keep it up," and not actual directives such as "Pass the ball," "Shoot," and the like. There would be no more yelling out plays or schemes, protesting calls, or anything related to their child's decision-making.

We explained why we didn't want parental coaching from the sidelines. We intended to change the players' approach to the game, which we couldn't do in an atmosphere of conflicting messages from parents. Our point had to be heard. We warned the parents that our new style would look unfamiliar, perhaps even uncomfortably so. In fact, our new approach would guarantee growing pains. But we asked the parents to expect and encourage this part of the process.

We wanted to turn little Sky Blue into a training ground for lifelong competitors by teaching them to think strategically, to learn from failure and disappointment, and to develop a lot of useful tools rather than relying on just one. While kick and run works like magic when you are nine years old, it wears thin against skilled older players. We explained that when kids get older, their bodies change. They cannot always be the fastest kid on the field. Instead, players should develop skills that complement their athleticism and not simply exploit a lucky bit of physiology. We wanted the girls to get comfortable learning and developing, which would require risk taking and vulnerability. The girls would need to accept playing outside their comfort zone. We asked the parents to buy in and trust the process. We needed them to support and encourage their daughters. The parents would anchor this change. We needed them to reinforce our message at home if the program was going to work.

With the parents on board, our first practices were used to instill our long-term philosophies in the girls. In addition to teaching goal-scoring tactics (which they were quite familiar with already), we would be teaching sportsmanship, our philosophy on skill development, and what it meant to be well-rounded. We wanted the girls to get closer to the ball, literally. They needed to feel it at their feet rather than kicking it forward as soon as they could. That took technique and trust. We introduced some tactical skills, such as how to interpret or read a game. We introduced new technical skills that reinforced the bigger picture and spoke to our out-of-the-box messaging. The girls were eager to learn and, slowly but surely, their understanding of the game improved. They no longer ran with their heads down, solely focused on a goal that would please their parents, coaches, and teammates. They had their heads up, and they were looking to connect with teammates. They were trying things they never had before.

Mental Game

As the girls started learning, they started losing. We were okay with losses—as long as we felt the team was growing through the process. Dr. Keane's daughter Cameryn joined the team just as it nosedived into a string of losses.

Cameryn's strengths were her speed and goal scoring. But the coaches knew that would have to change. Being quick and scoring goals are certain crowd pleasers but were immaterial to Cameryn's overall development. In youth soccer, when goalkeepers are quite small in stature, most shots on target are likely to result in goals. This changes over time, as goalies grow taller and more skilled. A strike in the general direction of the net is no guarantee of success. Most important, we wanted Cameryn and her teammates to see themselves as more than just goal scorers. We wanted them to learn to contribute to their teammates in different ways. It was vital to us as coaches that Cameryn learn some of the roles and responsibilities of the other positions on the field.

Growing up, I had only ever been a fast forward. I struggled when I was asked to change positions—not so much playing them but rather learning to appreciate them. I was as used to the thrill of a goal as much as anyone. I wanted to avoid that same scenario for our players; the modern game requires flexible players with a deeper understanding of the game. As Cameryn fell into step with our team and adapted to our style, she stopped scoring so many goals. But she was learning to play the game on a new level. That isn't always to see on the surface, however.

The following spring was brutal. We lost many of our league games. With each loss, the parents became increasingly uncomfortable with the new style of play. Some of the parents thought we were asking too much of the girls and that they simply couldn't perform to our level of coaching or expectation. We as coaches heard constant grumbling about letting the team return to playing kick and run.

One family came to us and specifically asked that we let their daughter play the way she used to. Their daughter was one of the fastest players on the team. We listened and politely countered. We wanted her to develop her technical skills. We would be doing this young player a disservice by allowing her to coast on a single skill. She needed to supplement her speed with a greater technical and tactical understanding of the game. That would be her best chance for long-term success.

We knew their daughter was struggling, but we asked them to keep the big picture in mind. What might be hurting her confidence in the short term was making her stronger and more resilient in the long term. They decided to stay with the program.

There had been another component to this discussion. The parents made it clear that they were unopposed to removing their daughter from the team if we didn't bend our philosophy to theirs. Instead of getting our backs up, we used this as a teachable moment about staying true to team mission and honoring commitments. We would have hated to lose their daughter, but if her parents could not trust our process, then losing that player would've actually benefitted the team. Her staying begrudgingly would have let to bitterness and negativity. During this back-and-forth, we realized that educating parents is often more of a challenge than educating our players. But we all needed to be all in. That was certain.

We also knew to expect some level of performance anxiety. The girls were not only being asked to change philosophies, they were being directed away from their strengths. We forced them to address their weaknesses, take risks, and problem solve, even when they didn't want to. We encouraged mistakes and failures and asked them to be brave on the ball. We asked them to challenge themselves and not to fear failure. Yes, learning new things can be uncomfortable, but so too is an environment solely focused on winning games. That kind of anxiety is actually more common in sports today and more harmful long term. Attacking players agonize over their stats while defenders stress about holding a shutout or letting a forward get past them. We were relentless in our philosophy with the girls. Our focus on learning obviated the need for

immediate success, which in the long run would reduce their fleeting perfor-
mance anxiety.

Authenticity

Our losing streak continued. My daughter Rylie, also one of our fastest and
most powerful players, struggled with performance anxiety the most. When
she joined the team, she felt the added pressure of having me as her coach.
People would ask, "Which one is your daughter?" so that they could com-
pare her playing style to my own. I felt a certain déjà vu, flashing back to all
the times my siblings had been compared to me growing up. Tougher yet, I
was asking Rylie to learn a new position. She could no longer take solace in
any offensive statistics.

When Rylie joined this team, to my surprise and chagrin, she seemed to
lose confidence. Our challenge was to teach her to find and meet internal
goals rather than externally imposed goals that were outside her control, like
winning and scoring. By her second year on little Sky Blue, Rylie began to
shift. She had gotten more comfortable with making mistakes and under-
stood that failing was an important step in the learning process. Things
started to click. Her willingness to compete and trust herself was blooming.
The same was true of many of her teammates.

The girls were getting it. They were connecting with one another, taking
risks, and enjoying some success on the field as a result of their hard work
and changes. Then came the state cup final. We knew our opponent well,
a team known for their direct and aggressive style of play. They were not
technical, but they were athletic and relentless in their pursuit. While their
playing was focused on physical assets, we were determined to remain true
to our good habits. Plus, we had accrued confidence: little Sky Blue had fared
well against this team in the past.

Oops. That team beat us five–nil. The game was horrible, and many
of the girls cried. They were disappointed in themselves and also in their

new style of play. It had failed them. In truth, it wasn't so much the system but typical grade-school jitters. The girls had tried to follow the coaches' instructions, but their nerves got in the way. Breakdowns gave the opposition opportunities. The girls nearly abandoned ship. Many wanted to revert to a head-down, kick-and-run style of play. But, despite the loss, we knew we were moving in the right direction. We didn't allow the girls to revert to focusing on their own individual strengths, the "me" stuff. You can put your head down, take a bad shot, and overdribble, and you might still score, but you didn't play the game with your teammates. You didn't connect to your teammates. We kept our messaging as coaches consistent: we were proud of their hard work, their growth, and their commitment. We let them know that they were so very close to triumphing.

We kept encouraging and reinforcing comfort with the ball. We didn't want players hiding from the ball at that age. For example, we didn't allow the keeper to punt the ball long, the easy way out. When the ball is farther up the field, it's less stressful for the defenders. It simply makes a goal less likely. When the keeper has to throw the ball or make the play from her feet, players and parents get uncomfortable. It's riskier. But no risk, no reward. We were okay giving goals up in pursuit of our new style and strategy. The girls were learning new techniques and resiliency during stressful situations. We saw signs that our girls were playing collectively, taking risks, and showing teamwork. There was more movement off the ball, and they understood why and when they should've been moving.

Car Ride Home

One of the parents told me that when she and her daughter left the field that day, they congratulated her former teammates and parents on their win. One of the parents said to them, "Are you happy you changed teams? I bet you're not so happy now."

The mother was shocked. Did the woman really think they switched teams just to win games? Just to beat one team? The comment hurt her daughter, who was already stung by the loss. On the car ride home, the parent stayed true to her intentions, and ours. Instead of bad-mouthing the other team, she explained to her daughter that she didn't join little Sky Blue just to win. Winning would come with time. She joined the team to learn and to develop her true potential. No one game was going to make an impact on anyone's future. They are all steps on a very long path. The car ride home was that of encouragement and support when it might have been spent dwelling on an ugly game.

Confidence

Near the end of our second year as coaches, we placed the girls in a tournament that was far below their playing level. We wanted to rebuild the girls' confidence and let them use their newfound skills for success. Though many had improved skill-wise, they weren't yet sold on the results. We thought that an easy tournament and several wins would be a great place to gain some confidence.

To our utter disbelief, our team lost every game that weekend despite objectively inferior opposition. After the final game, we asked the girls for a written commitment to the team. Given the poor effort they'd shown during that tournament, we were no longer going to coach them unless they each committed to giving their best effort at all times from that day forward. Each and every one of them had to be all in. Not just to come and play, but to live the mission: accountability, commitment, resilience, communication, and connection. By the end of that week, every girl on the team committed. And it showed.

From that moment on, there was something different about little Sky Blue. The following year, little Sky Blue faced a team they had previously lost to, 4–0, a team that had dismissed them as "terrible." They remembered the game very clearly and, from the very first moments, were intent on reclaiming that field. The girls remained focused on who they were and what they were about from start to finish. It was as if the girls built confidence with each passing minute of that game. You could see their trust in themselves, in one another, and in the game plan. I think the other team noticed the difference too. The parents of both teams were shocked, in fact. In the end, the game wasn't even close. We had a higher percentage of possession and had purpose to our possessions, which made it look very easy. We won the game in lopsided fashion. The win was an aha moment for the entire team. We had slowed down to speed up.

By the end of that third year, little Sky Blue finally earned their way back to the state finals. We were facing a high-level academy team, one that parents had paid thousands of dollars to so that their kids could belong. Their team was a full commitment with a high price tag, but it wasn't unmerited. They were well known for their skill and their athleticism. The game was tight. Little Sky Blue fought, stayed true to their form and themselves, and, if there were any nerves out on that field, they didn't show. They worked together as a team and applied the tactics that we asked of them. We couldn't be any prouder of them.

We lost the championship game 1–0. Going into the game, the girls had been full of confidence and positivity. They left the field that day with tears and grimaces, their heads bowed. Once in the huddle, though, they were stunned to find the other coaches and me beaming at them. We asked the girls, "Did you do everything you could to positively influence the game?" We got a resounding "Yes." We told them that was all we could ask for. "Looks to us like you stayed true to your playing style and you didn't let another team rattle you," we said. We told them that we had never been more proud of how they played. In our eyes, they played brilliant soccer, the kind of soccer we were proud to teach them. And they were the kind of team we were proud to coach: authentic, connecting, communicating, smart, and resilient.

The very next year, little Sky Blue, full of confidence in themselves and their teammates, not only won their league again but also went on to reach another state cup final and won. We felt that the girls were now in control of what they wanted from soccer, had become very aware of the process, and continued to show signs of learning and growth.

Little Sky Blue is a team of well-trained, enthusiastic athletes that have learned new ways to solve problems, approach challenges, and ask questions. Through the years, they learned to be comfortable with the uncomfortable, and they learned to value perseverance. Some of the girls will take what they have learned and continue to play in college. However, all the girls will apply elsewhere what they have learned on the field: grit, determination, confidence, and willingness to learn and to take risks.

The coaches relish the differences between their girls. They encourage diversity, playing multiple sports, and participating in numerous outside-the-game activities. The coaches teach the girls to look for one another's strengths and highlight them, and when they see a weakness, to cover for them. They simply ask the girls to stay committed to their purpose, their own truth, and their teammates.

The little Sky Blue story is not going to end with a great championship win or an amazing Cinderella run to an imaginary finish line. No Miracle on Ice or Hail Mary here. They haven't climbed their way to the number one spot in New Jersey soccer. They have no championship story because you really can't teach winning, and, if you try, too much is lost. Focusing on winning games over developing skills and mind-set is like trying to succeed on the SATs before you have taken algebra! When you focus on the process, the learning, and the development, the win is in the rich sediment.

By the time they'd reached high school, the players on little Sky Blue knew how to apply the physical and mental skills they'd learned, regardless of their athletic ability or personal gifts. They all became fluent in the system they'd learned, they established good habits, communicated with one another, connected, remained accountable, and stayed true to themselves. These are the gifts the little Sky Blue coaches had hoped to instill in each player on their life journeys away from the soccer field.

When Christie met this team, she was worried about how little Sky Blue would represent the professional team. Now she is confident about her team, a little braggy, and a little sports-mom-teary-eyed proud. Who among us wouldn't want to be that? What better lesson is there? That, my friends, is the win at the end of this story.

Please see Appendix A for additional and rare insights into
Christie's explicit tutoring and coaching philosophies.

Appendices

Appendix A
My Coaching Philosophy

As one of the coaches, my mission was to help guide the girls to be complete and well-rounded soccer players on both sides of the ball. We had a responsibility to develop the technical and tactical understanding of the game while also ensuring that we were positively impacting their mental and physical growth. To implement our philosophy, we needed to have all the players and parents on board and convinced of our way of thinking. At the beginning of the season, we arranged a team meeting involving all the parents and players. We felt it was vital for us to communicate our vision, explain to everyone what it was we wanted to do, why we felt this was the best thing for their child's soccer development, and how we intended to do it. We spoke about our long-term vision for the team collectively and their respective children individually. We also expressed our expectations for the parents and players and what they should expect from us in return.

Without communicating a clear set of expectations, we could never move forward in a productive manner. If we did not outline these standards at the outset, it would be impossible for us to hold one another accountable for our behaviors. We discussed practice attendance, punctuality, attitude, work ethic, and parents' sideline demeanor, among many other topics. We continually preached simple guidelines, such as the need for players to arrive at the field with a growth mind-set and with the willingness to want to learn. This was a message for both the player and the parent; we appreciated that so much information can be pushed on the kids during their rides to practice or to games. We worried that misguided conversations in the car could skew the bigger message of learning and improving. Rather than encouraging their child to score a goal to make sure the team wins, we encouraged parents to share our message of long-term growth and continual learning. By all accounts, these car rides became incredibly important moments for many players.

The early tactical focus was on ball movement: how the team moved the ball from one end of the field to the other through a purposeful, possession-oriented style of play. We wanted to establish our identity, both to the players and to the parents. There are many ways to play the game of soccer, but we chose a style we believed would be conducive to long-term development and success for each player. Beyond that, we wanted to ensure that the players had a framework to rely on, something to stay true to when games got difficult. Soccer, like many other sports, is a complex game with many variables; at times, it can be tempting to compromise your beliefs for short-term success. We wanted to avoid such temptation, so we always encouraged the girls to stay true to who they were and what they knew. We encouraged them to trust in themselves and their own abilities rather than be swayed by the lure of winning a single, meaningless game. This authenticity proved key.

Additionally, we coached them on the importance of transitional moments within the game—moments between losing and regaining possession of the ball. We felt it was important that the players understand how to recognize these transitions and the decisions available to them in those moments. This was about taking a deep breath, trusting the process, and believing that in the long-term benefits. We never sought immediate results. We asked that the girls slow down to develop their skill sets; only then would they understand what the beautiful game gives back to us. As we've reiterated, it can be very easy to agonize over results. Everyone wants to win. However, in focusing solely on wins, we skip the learning of fundamental skills that accompany players throughout their whole careers. Establishing a process behind youth development and then trusting that process is key to a young athlete's journey. We must all remain patient and allow athletes to experience growing pains. Bypassing this critical stage just to win some games is ultimately a disservice to every young player. We as coaches preach that constantly, for we too must speed up by slowing down.

Learning

Unsurprisingly, learning is an enormous part of the equation. How do they move the ball from one end of the field to the other? They must arrange many pieces in the jigsaw puzzle to make this happen. We encourage awareness of their teammates, the opposition, the space, the ball, and the goals. We coach them about their body shape—how and where to position themselves and their bodies to see as much of the field as possible. From there: How do they control the ball? What surface of the body do they wish to use?

It's a coach's job to put the players in the best possible scenario to be successful. We must create an environment that rewards experimentation while also minimizing fear of failure. We want to empower them to take full ownership of their growth as young soccer players. My approach with young athletes regardless of the sport is to ensure they understand the why. Rather than simply arm them with skills, I prefer to provide more depth to their understanding. This way, they comprehend why they are learning certain skills and how and when to actually employ them. Understanding the why enhances their on-field decision-making, particularly amid a competitive game.

We put children in game-realistic scenarios and encourage them to train at game speed. We understand that the transition from a practice environment to a competitive game environment can be very daunting. Understanding how to remain calm, confident, and composed in a game will not happen overnight. This is a learned behavior acquired through both practice and game play. Mental mastery is acquired over a lifetime of purposeful practice and is just as important as any technical skill, perhaps more so. We hear all the game-day jargon about mental toughness and how the parents want their children to be tougher. But this does not simply appear game day; it's inculcated over time. By creating the correct practice settings, we can build our athletes' confidence and self-awareness so that, regardless of the situation, they are able to lean on what they have learned. To us, that's mental toughness.

Training

Technical skills are taught at each training session. When teaching a new skill, we typically start the players unopposed and then progressively add to the difficulty. We preach repetition and establishing good habits. We teach the girls to be comfortable using all body surfaces and both feet. Executing a pass to the correct foot with the correct pace at the correct time sounds simple. It's not. It doesn't sound that exciting to a young player, either, but it is crucial to their long-term development. The best players consistently execute fundamental skills with a high level of competency. With this in mind, we ask our players to hold themselves accountable to standards and to not accept or allow laziness to sneak into their game. Standards are a controllable—and vital—component. Inconsistency is prevalent in youth development as athletes learn new skills; however, they should never compromise their standards in pursuit of a new skill or goal.

Soccer is a complex sport. The introduction of key game phrases, such as "spacing," "timing," "weight of pass," "speed of play," "change of speed," "change of point," "breaking lines," "angles of approach," and "numerical overloads," can confuse a young athlete. These concepts are not easy for kids to grasp, and the ability to understand and implement them varies from child to child. As we approach the team with a progressive mind-set, one intent on constantly adding layers to each child's growth, it is vital that we establish an open feedback loop between coaches and players. We as coaches must maintain a clear, compassionate understanding of each player's pace and position on their own development pathway. As mentioned, innumerable variables can affect an athlete's growth at any age. However, maintaining awareness and an open feedback loop allows us as coaches to make the most informed and beneficial decisions for each child when establishing their roles and responsibilities on the field.

We stress these points during contact time with the girls, but we never deviate from the overarching message of practice, practice, and then practice some more when they are not with the team. They must learn to use their own time in a nonstructured environment to experiment with the new skills they have learned with the aim of mastering them.

How to Determine Positions

Determining what position best suits a child is an ongoing process that starts at practice. A child's best position can change over time based on many factors. Coaches must assiduously avoid pigeonholing a player into one position prematurely. I grew up as a forward, but when I reached the national team, I was told I was a defender. At the age of twenty-one, I had to learn how to defend—from scratch. Tougher yet, I was tasked with defending against some of the best players to ever play the game, such as Mia Hamm, Michelle Akers, Tiffeny Milbrett, and Shannon MacMillan.

I ensure that every child in the early stages of their development be allowed to sample all the positions and learn the game from a range of perspectives. In youth soccer, the fastest players are typically forwards or defenders; this is a tried-and-true approach to maximizing scoring chances and minimizing those of opponents. We feel this is a disservice to any player; you force them to rely on their speed, which will inevitably fade, rather than on learning new skills that can better ensure future success. Further, the best players are coaxed to the front line to enhance a team's scoring potential. But a coach should determine the best position for a given player by evaluating them in training and game situations. Are they a central or outside player? Are they better when they can see the field in front of them? Do they have a good awareness of their surroundings? How is their skill on the ball in tight spaces? Do they have a bigger influence or create more havoc in wide areas of the field during training? Do they know how to create space for themselves and others? How do they handle pressure? Do they communicate with those around them? How is their fitness? Can they run all day, or would they be better suited to a position that requires less running?

Countless factors go into identifying the right position for a player, which is why coaches must be open-minded to a player's changing positions based on evolving attributes. From age six to age eighteen, players' skills and attributes mature. Coaches should encourage players to sample various positions in the hopes of developing a more complete player. That said, very few players can play multiple positions effectively—Crystal Dunn comes to mind as an exception—without compromising their impact on the game. I try to be flexible with players in both practices and games so that I might help create more tactically and positionally versatile players.

Appendix B

Concussion in the Classroom

Academic / Sports / Physical Activities Guidelines

Student Name _____ Age _____ Grade _____ Date of Injury _____

Concussion: LOC / No LOC   In Effect: _____ To: _____

Based on today's evaluation, this student was diagnosed with a concussion, and the following academic accommodations may help in reducing the cognitive (thinking) load, thereby minimizing post-concussion symptoms and allowing the student to better participate in the academic process during the injury period. These academic accommodations are recommended as part of medical care and treatment for this medical condition.

CURRENT SYMPTOMS

- ☐ Headaches
- ☐ Sleep difficulties
- ☐ Cognitive difficulties
- ☐ Nausea
- ☐ Sensitivity to light
- ☐ Sensitivity to noise
- ☐ Dizziness
- ☐ Visual dysfunction
- ☐ Fatigue
- ☐ Nervousness / irritability
- ☐ Emotional lability

ATTENDANCE RESTRICTIONS

- ☐ Full/partial days missed due to concussion symptoms should be medically excused
- ☐ Full days
- ☐ Modified days: _____
- ☐ Initiate or continue homebound education (5 hours/week)
- ☐ No school until: _____
- ☐ Return to school: _____

PHYSICAL ACTIVITY

- ☐ No Physical Education class
- ☐ No sports participation

TESTING

- ☐ Extra time
- ☐ Test in a quiet environment
- ☐ Allow testing across multiple sessions
- ☐ One test or quiz per day
- ☐ No standardized tests
- ☐ No tests or quizzes
- ☐ Open note / open book / take home tests
- ☐ Reformat from free response to multiple choice or provide cueing (e.g., a notecard for formulas)
- ☐ **Note taking:** Allow student to obtain class notes or outlines ahead of time to aid organization and reduce multi-tasking demands.

- ☐ **Breaks:** Allow student to go to nurse's office or home if symptoms increase.
- ☐ **Extra Time:** Allow students extra time to complete and turn in assignments.

WORKLOAD REDUCTION

- ☐ Reduce overall amount of make-up work, classwork, and homework (recommended: 50–75%)
- ☐ Homework and classwork as tolerated
- ☐ No homework
- ☐ Limit homework to _____ minutes a night
- ☐ Limit computer work

OTHER ACCOMMODATIONS

- ☐ Allow for snacks and drinks
- ☐ Allow student to wear hat and/or sunglasses
- ☐ Change setting (brightness/contrast) on computer screen
- ☐ Avoid busy environments (e.g., leave class early to avoid hallways, cafeteria, and assemblies)
- ☐ _____

Notes

Chapter 1. Giving the Sports Back to the Kids

1. Emilie Le Beau Lucchesi, "Why Sports Parents Sometimes Behave So Badly," *The New York Times*, November 1, 2018, https://www.nytimes.com/2018/11/01/well/family/why-sports-parents-sometimes-behave-so-badly.html.
2. Travis E. Dorsch, Alan L. Smith, Steven R. Wilson, and Meghan H. McDonough, "Parent Goals and Verbal Sideline Behavior in Organized Youth Sport," *Sport, Exercise, and Performance Psychology* 4, no. 1 (2015): 19–35, https://doi.org/10.1037/spy0000025.
3. Abby Wambach, *Wolfpack* (New York: Celadon Books, 2019).
4. Brooke de Lench, "Mission Statements: Important in Youth Sports Programs," *Moms Team: The Trusted Source for Sports Parents*, May 21, 2008, https://www.momsteam.com/print/705.

Additional References

Camilla J. Knight, Steffan R. Berrow, and Chris G. Harwood, "Parenting in Sport," *Current Opinion in Psychology* 16 (2017): 93–97, doi:10.1016/j.copsyc.2017.03.011.

Jennifer A. McMahon and Dawn Penney, "Sporting Parents on the Pool Deck: Living out a Sporting Culture?," *Qualitative Research in Sport, Exercise and Health* 7, no. 2 (2015): 153–69, doi:10.1080/2159676X.2014.901985.

Basejester, "Message to the Managers," *Umpire-Empire*, January 22, 2013, https://umpire-empire.com/topic/51794-message-to-the-managers.

Thomas Søbirk Peterson, "What Makes a Good Sports Parent? Ethics, the Parent-Child Relationship, and Sport," *Nordic Journal of Applied Ethics* 4, no. 1 (2010): 23–37.

Jay Coakley, "The Good Father: Parental Expectations and Youth Sports," *Leisure Studies* 25, no. 2 (2006): 153–63, doi:10.1080/02614360500467735.

Chapter 2. Communication

1. Albert Mehrabian, *Silent Messages* (Belmont, CA: Wadsworth, 1979).
2. "6 Tips for Coaches When Communicating with Athlete's Parents," Ohio University blog, https://onlinemasters.ohio.edu/blog/6-tips-for-coaches-when-communicating-with-athletes-parents.
3. J. N. Giedd et al., "Brain Development during Childhood and Adolescence: A Longitudinal MRI Study," *Nature Neuroscience* 2, no. 10 (1999): 861–63.

Additional References

Nikolaus Jackob, Thomas Roessing, and Thomas Petersen, "Effects of Verbal and Non-Verbal Elements in Communication," in Andrea Rocci and Louis de Saussure, eds., *Verbal Communication* (Berlin: De Gruyter Mouton, 2016): 39–53.

Nicholas L. Holt et al., "Parental Involvement in Competitive Youth Sport Settings," *Psychology of Sport and Exercise* 9, no. 5 (2008): 663–85.

John P. Caughlin, Ascan F. Koerner, Paul Schrodt, and Mary Anne Fitzpatrick, "Interpersonal Communication in Family Relationships," in Mark L. Knapp and John A. Daly, eds., *The Handbook of Interpersonal Communication*, 4th ed. (Thousand Oaks, CA: Sage, 2001): 679–714.

D. Gould et al., "Examining Expert Coaches' Views of Parent Roles in 10-and-Under Tennis," *Sport, Exercise, and Performance Psychology* 5, no. 2 (2016): 89–106.

Chapter 3. Get Your Head in the Game

1. Abraham Maslow, "A Theory of Human Motivation," *Psychological Review* 50, no. 4 (1943): 370–96.

2. "Napping," Sleepfoundation.org, https://www.sleepfoundation.org /articles/napping.

3. Ursula Debarnot, Emeline Clerget, and Etienne Olivier, "Role of the Primary Motor Cortex in the Early Boost in Performance Following Mental Imagery Training," *PloS One* 6, no. 10 (2011): e26717, doi:10.1371 /journal.pone.0026717; K. M. O'Craven and N. Kanwisher, "Mental Imagery of Faces and Places Activates Corresponding Stimulus-Specific Brain Regions," *Journal of Cognitive Neuroscience* 12, no. 6 (2000): 1013–23.

4. R. Lindsay, M. Spittle, and P. Larkin, "The Effect of Mental Imagery on Skill Performance in Sport: A Systematic Review," *Journal of Science and Medicine in Sport* 22, supplement 2 (2019): S92; Bianca A. Simonsmeier and Susanne Buecker, "Interrelations of Imagery Use, Imagery Ability, and Performance in Young Athletes," *Journal of Applied Sport Psychology* 17, no. 1 (2017): 32–43.

5. Costas I. Karageorghis, "The Scientific Application of Music in Exercise and Sport: Towards a New Theoretical Model," in Andrew M. Lane, ed., *Sport and Exercise Psychology* (New York: Routledge, 2016), 276–322.

Chapter 4. Accountability

1. Stephen Covey, *The 7 Habits of Highly Effective Families* (New York: St. Martin's Griffin, 1997).

2. Jack Zenger and Joseph Folkman, "Your Employees Want the Negative Feedback You Hate to Give," *Harvard Business Review*, January 15, 2014, https://hbr.org/2014/01/your-employees-want-the-negative-feedback -you-hate-to-give.

Additional Reference

Brett and Kate McKay, "Creating a Positive Family Culture: How and Why to Create a Family Mission Statement," *The Art of Manliness*, August 21, 2013, last updated May 27, 2018, https://www.artofmanliness.com /articles/creating-a-family-culture-how-and-why-to-create-a-family -mission-statement.

Chapter 5. Mental Toughness

1. Angela Duckworth, *Grit: The Power of Passion and Perseverance* (New York: Scribner, 2016).

2. Antonis Hatzigeorgiadis, Nikos Zourbanos, Sofia Mpoumpaki, and Yannis Theodorakis, "Mechanisms Underlying the Self-Talk–Performance Relationship: The Effects of Motivational Self-Talk on Self-Confidence and Anxiety," *Psychology of Sport and Exercise* 10, no. 1 (2019): 186–92.

3. Albert Bandura, *Self-Efficacy: The Exercise of Control* (New York: Freeman, 1997).

4. SickKids Staff, "Self-Efficacy: How to Foster in Children," last updated August 30, 2012, https://www.aboutkidshealth.ca/Article?contentid=196 4&language=English.

5. Sara W. Lazar et al., "Meditation Experience Is Associated with Increased Cortical Thickness," *Neuroreport* 16, no. 17 (2005): 1893–97.

6. Saskia van der Oord, Susan M. Bögels, and Dorreke Peijnenburg, "The Effectiveness of Mindfulness Training for Children with ADHD and Mindful Parenting for their Parents," *Journal of Child and Family Studies* 21, no. 1 (2012): 139–47; Alice G. Walton, "Science Shows Meditation Benefits Children's Brains and Behavior," *Forbes*, October 18, 2016, https://www.forbes.com/sites/alicegwalton/2016/10/18/the-many-benefits-of-meditation-for-children/#31aaad4edbe3.

Additional References

D. R. Vago, R. S. Gupta, and S. W. Laza, "Measuring Cognitive Outcomes in Mindfulness-based Intervention Research: A Reflection on Confounding Factors and Methodological Limitations," *Current Opinion in Psychology* 28 (2019): 143–50.

"Our Potential Is One Thing," *Better Life Coaching Blog*, December 7, 2017, https://betterlifecoachingblog.com/2017/12/07/our-potential-is-one-thing.

Darrin Donnelly, Darrin. *Old School Grit: Times May Change, But the Rules of Success Never Do* (Kansas City, MO: Shamrock New Media, Inc., 2016).

Darrin Donnelly, *Think Like a Warrior: The Five Inner Beliefs That Make You Unstoppable* (Kansas City, MO: Shamrock New Media, Inc., 2016).

Daniel F. Gucciardi et al., "Implicit Theories of Mental Toughness: Relations with Cognitive, Motivational, and Behavioral Correlates Sport," *Sport, Exercise, and Performance Psychology* 4, no. 2 (2015): 100–12.

Chapter 6. Authenticity

1. Brené Brown, *The Gifts of Imperfection* (Center City, MN: Hazelden Publishing, 2010).
2. Carl R. Rogers, "The Necessary and Sufficient Conditions of Therapeutic Personality Change," *Journal of Consulting Psychology* 21, no. 2 (1957): 95–103, doi:10.1037/h0045357. PMID 13416422.

Additional Reference

Maureen Healy, "Authentic Parenting: Are You Doing It Differently?," *Psychology Today*, December 19, 2008, https://www.psychologytoday.com/us/blog/creative-development/200812/authentic-parenting.

Chapter 7. The Car Ride Home

1. D. S. Goldstien, "Adrenal Responses to Stress," *Cellular and Molecular Neurobiology* 30, no. 8 (2010): 1433–440; Walter B. Cannon, *The Wisdom of the Body* (New York: W. W. Norton, 1939).
2. Katherine A. Tamminen, Zoe Poucher, and Victoria Povilaitis, "The Car Ride Home: An Interpretive Examination of Parent-Athlete Sports Conversations," *Sport, Exercise, and Performance Psychology* 6, no. 4 (2017): 325–39.
3. Hans Kirschner et al., "Soothing Your Heart and Feeling Connected: A New Experimental Paradigm to Study the Benefits of Self-Compassion," *Clinical Psychological Science* 7, no. 3 (2019): 545–65, doi: 10.1177/2167702618812438.

Additional References

"What Is the Fight or Flight Response?," November 11, 2015, https://www .slideshare.net/Godschild24/what-is-the-fight-or-flight-response-final.

"Managing Stress and Anxiety," *Daily Press*, February 12, 2015, https:// www.dailypress.com/news/vg-ugc-article-managing-stress-and-anxiety -2015-02-17-story.html.

John O'Sullivan, "The Ride Home," *Changing the Game Project*, May 1, 2014, https://www.changingthegameproject.com/the-ride-home-after -the-game.

Carston H. Larsen, Dorothee Alfermann, Kristoffer Henriksen, and Mette K. Christensen, "Successful Talent Development in Soccer: The Character-istics of the Environment," *Sport, Exercise, and Performance Psychology* 2, no. 3 (2013): 190–206.

Chapter 8. Confidence

1. Leon Festinger, "A Theory of Social Comparison Processes," *Human Relations* 7, no. 2 (1954): 117–40.

2. Noelle Nelson, Selin A. Malkoc, and Baba Shiv, "Emotions Know Best: The Advantage of Emotional versus Cognitive Responses to Failure," *Journal of Behavioral Decision Making* 31, no. 1 (2017): 40–51, https://doi.org/10.1002 /bdm.2042.

3. Moe Machida, Rose Marie Ward, and Robin S. Vearly, "Predictors of Sources of Self-Confidence in Collegiate Athletes," *International Journal of Sport and Exercise Psychology* 10, no. 3 (2012): 172–85.

Additional References

Alex Dalenberg, "The Value of Failure," *Time: The Science of Success*, 2019.

Kirsten Schuder, "How to Help Your Child Develop a Positive Inner Voice," *A Fine Parent*, 2018, https://afineparent.com/positive-parenting -faq/positive-inner-voice.html.

Chapter 9. Beating Performance Anxiety

1. Julia Asbrand, Jennifer Hudson, Julian Schmitz, and Brunna Tuschen-Caffier, "Maternal Parenting and Child Behaviour: An Observational Study of Childhood Social Anxiety Disorder," *Cognitive Therapy and Research* 41, no. 4 (2017): 562–75, https://doi .org/10.1007/s10608-016-9828-3.
2. "Three Breathing Exercises and Techniques," WEIL: Andrew Weil, MD, https://www.drweil.com/health-wellness/body-mind-spirit/stress -anxiety/breathing-three-exercises.
3. "How to Master Rhythmic Breathing When Running," *Runner's Blueprint*, https://www.runnersblueprint.com/rhythmic-breawthing-when -running.
4. Alison Wood Brooks, "Get Excited: Reappraising Pre-Performance Anxiety as Excitement," *Journal of Experimental Psychology: General* 143, no. 3 (2014): 1144–58.

Additional References

Reed Maltbie, "It's Time to End the Sideline Sportsanity," *Changing the Game Project*, April 10, 2017, https://www.changingthegameproject .com/time-end-sideline-sportsanity.

Jessica Ford, Kenneth Ildefonso, Megan L Jones, and Monna Arvinen-Barrow, "Sport-Related Anxiety: Current Insights," *Open Access Journal of Sports Medicine* 8 (2017): 205–12.

Fadel Zeidan et al., "Mindfulness Meditation Improves Cognition: Evidence of Brief Mental Training," *Consciousness and Cognition* 19, no. 2 (2010): 597–605.

Chapter 10. Concussion and Sports Injury

1. Christopher C. Giza and David A. Hovda, "The New Neurometabolic Cascade of Concussion," *Neurosurgery* 75, supplement 4 (2014): S24–S33.

2. "HEADS UP to Youth Sports," Centers for Disease Control and Prevention, last updated March 5, 2019, https://www.cdc.gov/headsup/youthsports/index.html.

3. Paul McCrory et al., "Consensus Statement on Concussion in Sport—The 5th International Conference on Concussion in Sport Held in Berlin, October 2016," *British Journal of Sports Medicine* (2017): 1–10.

4. Michael McCrea et al., "Unreported Concussion in High School Football Players: Implications for Prevention," *Clinical Journal of Sport Medicine* 14, no. 1 (2004): 13–17.

5. Rosemarie Scolaro Moser, Colette Glatts, and Philip Schatz, "Efficacy of Immediate and Delayed Cognitive and Physical Rest for Treatment of Sports-Related Concussion," *The Journal of Pediatrics* 161, no. 5 (2012): 922–26; Kathryn Schneider et al., "The Effects of Rest and Treatment Following Sport-Related Concussion: A Systematic Review of the Literature, *British Journal of Sports Medicine* 47, no. 5 (2013): 304–07.

6. McCrory et al., "Consensus Statement on Concussion in Sport."

7. McCrory et al., "Consensus Statement on Concussion in Sport."

8. Mark E. Halstead et al., "Returning to Learning Following a Concussion," *Pediatrics* 132, no. 5 (2013): 948–57, doi:10.1542/peds.2013-2867.

9. Michael W. Kirkwood, Christopher Randolph, and Keith Owen Yeates, "Sport-Related Concussion: A Call for Evidence and Perspective Amidst the Alarms," *Clincial Journal of Sports Medicine* 22, no. 5 (2012): 383–84; Paul McCrory, Gavin A. Davis, and Michael Makdissi, "Second Impact Syndrome or Cerebral Swelling after Sporting Head Injury," *Current Sports Medicine Reports*11, no. 1 (2012): 21–23.

10. Centers for Disease Control and Prevention, *Concussion at Play: Opportunities to Reshape the Culture Around Concussion* (Atlanta: US Department of Health and Human Services, 2015).

11. R. Dawn Comstock et al., "An Evidence-Based Discussion of Heading the Ball and Concussions in High School Soccer," *JAMA Pediatrics* 169, no. 9 (2015): 830–37; Adrienne D. Witol and Frank M. Webbe, "Soccer Heading Frequency Predicts Neuropsychological Deficits," *Archives of Clinical Neuropsychology* 18, no. 4 (2003): 397–417; Monica E. Maher et al., "Concussions and Heading in Soccer: A Review of the Evidence of

Incidence, Mechanisms, Biomarkers and Neurocognitive Outcomes," *Journal of Brain Injury* 28, no. 3 (2014): 271–85.

Additional References

Peter A. Arnett, ed., *Neuropsychology of Sports-Related Concussion* (Washington, DC: American Psychological Association, 2019).

Michael W. Kirkwood and Keith Owen Yeates, ed., *Mild Traumatic Brian Injury in Children and Adolescents: From Basic Science to Clinical Management* (New York: The Guilford Press, 2012).

Jennifer Niskala Apps and Kevin D. Walter, ed., *Pediatric and Adolescent Concussion: Diagnosis, Management and Outcomes* (New York: Springer, 2012).

Frank Webbe, ed., *The Handbook of Sport Neuropsychology* (New York: Springer, 2011).

Chapter 11. Slow Down to Speed Up

1. Jocelyn R. Davis and Tom Atkinson, "Need Speed? Slow Down," *Harvard Business Review*, May 2010, https://www.hbr.org/2010/05/need-speed-slow-down.
2. Harald S. Harung and Frederick Travis, *Excellence through Mind-Brain Development: The Secrets of World-Class Performers* (New York: Routledge, 2016).
3. Rasmus Hougaard, *One Second Ahead: Enhance Your Performance at Work with Mindfulness* (New York: Palgrave Macmillan, 2016).

Chapter 12. The Reality of Early Specialization in Sports

1. Gregory D. Meyer et al., "Does Early Sport Specialization Increase Negative Outcomes and Reduce Opportunity for Success in Youth Athletes?," *Sports Health* 7, no. 5 (2015): 437–42.
2. Greg Schiable, "Early Sport Specialization is Killing the Health of Our Kids," *Dr. John Rusin*, https://drjohnrusin.com/early-sport-specialization-is-killing-the-health-of-our-kids.

3. Daniel Gould, "Early Sport Specialization: A Psychological Perspective," *Journal of Physical Education, Recreation, and Dance* 81, no. 8 (2013): 33–37; Angela D. Smith et al., "Early Sports Specialization: An International Perspective," *Current Sports Medicine Reports* 16, no. 6 (2017): 439–42.

4. John P. DiFiori et al., "Overuse Injuries and Burnout in Youth Sports: A Position Statement from the American Medical Society for Sports Medicine," *British Journal of Sports Medicine* 48, no. 4 (2014): 287–88.

5. K. Anders Ericsson, Ralf T. Krampe, and Clemens Tesch-Roemer, "The Role of Deliberate Practice in the Acquisition of Expert Performance," *Psychological Review* 100, no. 3 (1993): 363–406.

6. Robert F. LaPrade et al., "AOSSM Early Sport Specialization Consensus Statement," *The Orthopaedic Journal of Sports Medicine* 4, no. 4 (2016): 1–8; Michael F. Bergeron et al., "International Olympic Committee Consensus Statement on Youth Athletic Development," *British Journal of Sports Medicine* 49, no. 13 (2015): 843–51; American Academy of Pediatrics Committee on Sports Medicine and Fitness, "Intense Training and Sports Specialization in Young Athletes," *Pediatrics* 106, part 1 (2000): 154–57; DiFiori et al., "Overuse Injuries and Burnout in Youth Sports."

7. Bergeron et al., "International Olympic Committee Consensus Statement on Youth Athletic Development."

8. LaPrade et al., "AOSSM Early Sport Specialization Consensus Statement."

9. American Academy of Pediatrics, "Sports Specialization and Advanced Training in Young Athletes."

10. Gould, "Early Sports Specialization"; Robert J. Schinke, Natalia B. Stambulova, Gangyan Si, and Zella Moore, "International Society of Sport Psychology Position Stand: Athletes' Mental Health, Performance, and Development," *International Journal of Sport and Exercise Psychology* 16, no. 6 (2018): 622–39, doi:10.1080/1612197X.2017.1295557.

Additional References

Brook de Lench, "Early Sport Specialization: Some Benefits, but Many Drawbacks," *MomsTeam*, March 22, 2014, https://www.momsteam.com /print/7249.

Ken Reed, "Youth Sports Specialization Defies Logic," *HuffPost*, October 31, 2014, last updated December 31, 2014, https://www.huffpost.com /entry/youth-sports-specializati_b_6084732.

N. Jayanthi et al., "Sports Specializations in Youth Athletes: Evidence-Based Recommendations," *Sports Health* 5, no. 3 (2013): 251–57.

Acknowledgments

We would like to thank Carie Goldberg, Christie's amazing manager, for believing in our project from the outset and for her continued support of our message to sports parents and athletes.

We are so grateful for our outstanding literary agent, Lisa Leshne, whose excitement and dedication to this project was evident from the moment we first met and has never wavered. Thank you for being the agent and the sports mom who exemplifies our Be All In message, with your authenticity, mental toughness, and grace. And special thanks to Samantha Morrice of the Leshne Agency, for your tireless work in making this book come to life.

Thank you to the original Be All In team at Hachette Book Group. We're grateful to Leah Miller, who chose to work with us on this important message. Your passion for our project was inspiring, and we appreciate your outstanding guidance. Thank you also to Haley Weaver and Karen Kosztolnyik for your professionalism, reliability, and attentiveness throughout this work. We are delighted to have Gretchen Young's wisdom and insight, even late in the game. We are also so grateful to our outstanding Hachette Team: Staci Burt, Tiffany Porcelli, Kallie Shimek, Tree Abraham, Kristen Lemire, Xian Lee, Albert Tang, and Ben Sevier, for your devotion to this project. We could not have asked for a better team.

To Daniel Sozomenu, one of our amazing editors, who made our words shine. We appreciate your willingness to burn the midnight oil until the final whistle blew. Your presence on this project was unparalleled.

Thank you to John Archibald, whose technical expertise and endless positivity was invaluable to us. Special thanks as well to Jonathon Harris, Phil Costa, and the folks at AthLife for their endless support and exceptional work with athletes at all levels.

From Christie Pearce Rampone

Special thanks to the little Sky Blue Team and their families, who continue to amaze and inspire our soccer journey with their talent, dedication, loyalty, and friendship.

Words wouldn't do justice to the level of thanks and respect I have towards each of my teammates over the years. I am so fortunate to have been surrounded by so many strong, powerful, and inspirational women. Each one of you contributed to the fabric of these valuable stories I am so fortunate to write about. Special thanks to Shannon Boxx, Sydney Leroux, Natasha Kai, and Siri Mullinix.

Abby, you are my forever friend and the ultimate teammate. I am so thankful for your honesty and for always showing up when I need you! I love your authenticity and how you have always accepted me for me. My life wouldn't be the same without our friendship.

Thank you to all my coaches, for believing in me, being incredible role models, and allowing me to learn from you! I am also thankful to my longtime trainer, Mike Lyons, for giving up his time with family to help pursue my dreams. No task was ever too big for you! I appreciate your vision and compassion for the game.

Special thank-you to Dr. Keane for opening my eyes and giving me a positive perspective while I was playing the beautiful game, and afterward while we were writing this book! The sports world benefits greatly from your experiences. Dr. Frankenstein, thank you for seeing something in me that I couldn't.

I am forever grateful to my parents for their guidance throughout my childhood. Thank you for allowing me and my siblings to explore and figure out our why. Your strong morals, expectations, consistency, and reliability made it easy to just be a kid and to later know how to navigate the real world. I am also thankful to my siblings, Wendi and Jeff, for their continued support, when nobody else believed in me.

I could have never completed this book without the support of my Rincon crew: MaryBeth Stehle, Heather Garrett-Muly, Sue Coble. So thankful for our friendship and your understanding, even when I never reply to any group texts. Love you girls! A special thank-you to Tracy Ramire, who I have unbelievable respect for. I am grateful for your knowledge and willingness to help during the final push to complete this book. You are a rock star!

Thank you to my little Sky Blue girls: Abby B., Abby A., Amanda, Ava, Cameryn, Emily, Grace, Jamie, Katie, Kieran, Makenzie, Quinny, Peyton, Rylie, and Sam. You girls have breathed new life into the game for me. Love every day I get to spend on the field with you.

Grateful for my soulmate, Christy Holly, who showed me what true love is on and off the field. Thank you for brightening my future! You have a special gift of making those around you better, and your passion for life is contagious. Your continued positivity, patience, and support are the reasons why I was able to see this project through. Forever grateful our paths crossed over our love for soccer and continue on in our love for each other and our family.

Thank you to my beautiful daughters. I love seeing the game through your eyes, Rylie. You inspire me every day. Reece, I love the challenge you bring. Thank you for reminding me to think outside the box.

From Dr. Kristine Keane

I am deeply grateful to the guy who can fix anything and who never looks at me like I need fixing. This work would not be possible without my husband, Ray, who does all the heavy lifting while I write and pursue my dreams. Thank you for being my inspiration, respecting my work, loving me selflessly, and encouraging me every day, for all our days.

Thank you to my children, who unwittingly contributed to this book with their grit, determination, and passion for sports. Christian, you are the Buddhist face of relentlessness and determination! Cameryn, you are the light, laughter, and the spirit of our world. Sebastian, you embody the love, kindness, and character of the game.

This book would not have been possible without my mentor, Dr. Frank Webbe, who first introduced me to working with athletes when he invited me to be a part of his pioneer team researching soccer heading and concussion. Thank you, Dr. Webbe, for encouraging me to pursue a career path in sports neuropsychology, even when it was in its infancy.

I also would like to thank Dr. Alan Colicchio for his support and his unwavering belief in me, and in our outstanding concussion program. I am so grateful for the mentorship of Dr. Joe Albanese and Dr. Michael Rothberg, whose hearts of gold never go unnoticed. It is a true privilege to work with such wise and exceptional leaders in healthcare.

Special thank-you to the Christies! I am so fortunate to work with both of you. Christie, I am so grateful to have traveled this life-changing rookie journey with you. Your power, graciousness, and *myriad* talents are awe inspiring. Christy Holly, thank you for your thoughtful and enlightening contributions to this book and for your passion and dedication to all the youth athletes you serve, on the field and in the office.

I also want to recognize my staff and colleagues at Shore Neuropsychology. I am eternally indebted to April Knauer, my office manager, my "Gayle," and my forever friend. Thank you to Kelly Stephensen, for your work ethic and true understanding of what it means to say "I am a sports mom." It is impossible for me to think about writing without thinking about Jenny Glieden. You were the original edit and my first reader. I am ever so grateful for you.

Grateful to a group of amazing women who have touched my life: Sue Perry, Christina Bauer, Christy Woodrow, and Liz Talley. Special thanks to my beloved sports moms, Christina Geddes, Jen Pupa, and Fran Cohen, who taught me that despite the competition, the sideline can be a very comical place!

Lastly, I want to thank my mom and dad for their endless love, support, and encouragement. Weather, distance, or timing, you never miss a game. Thank you to my siblings, John and Adrienne, for the football games in the front yard, so I could know firsthand how important free play is. Special thanks to Aunt Jo, the hugest creative force I have ever known, who always believed. Everyone needs an Aunt Jo in their corner.

About the Authors

CHRISTIE PEARCE RAMPONE is the most decorated female American professional soccer player of all time. She is currently an active speaker, coach, and sports broadcaster. Pearce Rampone played in five FIFA Women's World Cups and four Olympics women's soccer tournaments. She is a 1999 and 2015 FIFA Women's World Cup champion and a three-time Olympic gold medalist, winning championship titles at the 2004 Athens Olympics, 2008 Beijing Olympics, and 2012 London Olympics. Pearce Rampone is the oldest player to have appeared in a FIFA Women's World Cup game, and she is the second-most "capped" player in US and world history, having played in 311 international games for the United States.

Pearce Rampone played in the W-League from 1997 through 1998. She was a founding player for all three iterations of women's professional leagues in the United States. Starting in 2001 through 2003, she played in the Women's United Soccer Association (WUSA). From 2009 through 2011, she played in Women's Professional Soccer (WPS). In a unique turn of events during the WPS's 2009 inaugural season, Pearce Rampone took over as Sky Blue FC player/head coach for the final stretch of the season and was named WPS Sportswoman of the Year. From 2013 through 2017, Pearce Rampone played in the National Women's Soccer League (NWSL) and continued to captain Sky Blue FC in her home state of New Jersey.

Pearce Rampone has a BA in Special Education from Monmouth University, as well as an honorary doctoral degree in public service. She coaches high school and club soccer and basketball teams. Pearce

Rampone is a devoted sports mom of two daughters, Rylie and Reece, who play soccer, basketball, and softball; and swim; and dance. She lives on the Jersey Shore with her fiancé, Christy Holly, her two daughters, and her very energetic Brittany German shorthaired pointer mix, Lucky.

KRISTINE KEANE, PsyD, is a clinical and sports neuropsychologist who has been working with professional athletes, physicians, and mental health clinicians for the past twenty years. She is a brain health expert with experience treating a wide range of neurological disorders, learning disabilities, and brain injuries, as well as helping athletes and professionals reach peak performance.

Dr. Keane earned a doctoral degree in psychology with a specialization in neuropsychology from Florida Tech and served as an intern at the University of Rochester School of Medicine and Dentistry. Dr. Keane earned two bachelor's degrees from Rutgers University in English and in psychology. She is the owner, developer, and clinical director of two multispecialty neuropsychological private practices in New Jersey.

Dr. Keane is a clinical director at Hackensack Meridian Health System's Neuroscience Concussion Program, which serves children and adult athletes. She is also an assistant professor in the department of Psychiatry and Behavioral Health at Hackensack Meridian School of Medicine, at Seton Hall University.

Dr. Keane is a dedicated sports mom of three children who play soccer and basketball and run track. She lives on the Jersey Shore with her husband and children and their three-pound Scottish warrior Maltese, Murray MacTavish.